THE
WAY
NORTH

THE
WAY
NORTH

Collected Upper Peninsula New Works

EDITED BY RON RIEKKI

WAYNE STATE UNIVERSITY PRESS
DETROIT

Library of Congress Cataloging-in-Publication Data

The way north : collected Upper Peninsula new works / edited by Ron Riekki.

pages cm. — (Made in Michigan Writers Series)

Includes bibliographical references.

ISBN 978-0-8143-3865-0 (pbk. : alk. paper) — ISBN 978-0-8143-3866-7 (ebook) (print)

1. American literature—Michigan—Upper Peninsula. 2. Upper Peninsula (Mich.)—Literary collections. I. Riekki, R. A.

PS548.M5W39 2013

810.8'097749—dc23

2012047997

∞

Publication of this book was made possible by a generous gift from The Meijer Foundation

Designed by Judith Banham / Middlecott
Typeset by Maya Whelan
Composed in Adobe Garamond

CONTENTS

CONTENTS

STORIES

PREFACE

EVEN IN THE TWENTY-FIRST CENTURY, THE UPPER PENINSULA of Michigan is a mysterious, mythic place to those of us who live here. I first set foot there in the Fifties after riding a ferry from Mackinac City with my parents in a new '56 Chevy Station. Before the trip I fell asleep at night looking at a map thumbtacked next to my wall and traced the places I wanted to see: Grand Marais, the Keewenaw Copper Country, and most of all Lake Superior. I suppose there is an argument to make that no place is really much different than any other, except for all its particulars. I know every state has its urban places and its wild ones. And Michigan is no exception, but the U.P. harbors some wild places, lost swamps and bogs, whole rivers almost untraveled, deep copper mines, and the haunted shores of the big lake. And it has the ghosts of writers like Hemingway and Robert Traver slumping through dark cedar swamps. This wild country, jutting out from Wisconsin and resting between two of the greatest lakes in the world, is home to a wondrous tension. Here, you can walk ancient Indian ground, or you can stand on some of the oldest rocks on earth. The tension: far below are Michigan's great cities, especially Detroit, home of the auto industry, the mechanized world and the internal combustion engine, themselves forces that helped to shape and change this incredible Michigan landscape. In this anthology you will find a collection of writers who have given us stories and poems shaped and colored by this sprawling, wild U.P. landscape. There is much in this anthology to remind us that the heart of fiction and poetry is the nature of story itself. Once we were hunter-gatherers and we lived as close to the land as you can get in places like the U.P. Around ancient fires we heard stories and we knew that paying attention to them would help keep us alive, physically and spiritually. Nothing has changed over the eons. Pick this book up and take it inside; use what's here to pack in close to your heart to remind you that you came from wild places.

Michael Delp

INTRODUCTION

Jonathan Johnson

THE U.P. IS THE MOST INTIMATE LANDSCAPE I KNOW. THE WOODS are dense and close, the mountains low and old, the rivers narrow and mostly quiet. Most of the lakes are small and dusky and dark. The tavern ceilings are low and the cabins tight around their woodstoves. All but a few of the cemeteries and neighborhoods have aged back into their leafy habitats, and shabby and gentrified storefronts collect closed-shouldered into outposts and a few little downtowns, each no more than a handful of lights glimpsed from the crest of a highway at night.

Even the U.P. coasts—where the forest ends at rock and cliff and dune and cove and long, long beach against vast inland sea—even these wind- and aurora-exposed coasts are intimate. You can sink back from awe if you need to, into the brush and wind-shaped pine. Sooner or later the waves will settle and the water still so flat the spring goslings will trace silver wakes across its surface. Sooner or later the ice will flow in and harden and speak its strange language, its cold, thousand-foot syllables to only your ears.

And sooner *and* later it's going to snow. The most intimate weather of this intimate place, snow will transform what you thought was the endlessness around you into a space that just fits your longing. Your loss. Your solitude.

Like the region from which they come, the stories, poems, and essays editor Ron Riekki has gathered in *The Way North* are intimate. The aesthetics represented here are vibrantly diverse—Marty Achatz, Catie Rosemurgy, and Emily Van Kley are about as different as it gets in all but the most experimental of current American poetry, for example—yet in the main the writing in *The Way North* is more attentive than attention seeking, more sincere than hip. That pretense should be generally absent from an anthology of U.P. literature comes as no surprise, but it's refreshing just the same. Many of these pieces are reticent or beautifully understated, most are contemplative, and the anthology as a whole is deeply companionable. These are not vistas and narratives of sweeping, terrible sublimity, but quieter studies of the close range, the delicate and intricate, the small and the beautiful, from a part of the world often (and thankfully) unconsidered.

The great majority of *The Way North*'s readers will already know something of the U.P., of course, and that's as it should be, for what these writers do is renew the U.P. for our eyes and imaginations and deepen our experiences of its graceful and difficult truths. And they teach us about ourselves who are so drawn to this place. "The ice grows more enormous. The final verdict is snow," Rosemurgy reminds us before asking, "So what are you and for how long?"

Chad Faries says, "We all have lake in our eyes up here." People inhabit neighborhoods Janice Repka calls "make-the-best-of-it places." Our old friends live like Barbara Henning's Susan, on four hundred dollars a month in uninsulated cabins, "in the winter when there is a three-foot snow cover for months on end   solitude   stillness   distance." Linda Johnson describes a cabin "moved in the early twentieth century from Canada [. . .] pulled with a sled and team of horses across the frozen bay. / It is a remnant of better days, busy lumbering days." But the impoverished children inside now are "exiles on this icy shore."

Vincent Reusch inhabits other disconsolate children of the U.P., in an old farmhouse along another stretch of Lake Superior, where they sit before the open, cast-iron doors of the woodstove, the weak flames "reflecting dully off our cheeks and throwing hollow shadows over our eyes." Sometimes, as Austin Hummell writes, ice "takes our children / when they drive home from college for clean clothes / and stuffing." Heartbreak and fear find us, like Jennifer A. Howard's Clara, "scraping the ice off the windshield alone."

And yet, "winter is the old pal of this place," as Julie Brooks Barbour reminds us. Even in the desolate awareness of violence Manda Frederick evokes, even in the "mid-December chill, a hundred degrees colder than the core / temperature of your body," solace comes. Frederick writes, "you love / to watch the plows, blades and teeth, their disregard for the deference / expected of the night." With the people of Ellen Airgood's Grand Marais, we wait for the fishing boat on the horizon of Superior that means "the water is open and the ice out, that summer is hovering so close it might as well already be here." Beverly Matherne asks, "Who would want to leave the Upper Peninsula of Michigan? Lake Superior—so blue, so huge—you see no end of it?"

We endure because here we might know something of April Lindala's "Grand entry goose bumps" at the Baraga powwow. We endure so that here we might contemplate with Randall R. Freisinger, "Why is it a place for dreams, this bar and grill / so far out on the Boatjack Road it's better reached / by boat?" And we endure because here (if we're lucky) we remember a Wetmore Landing of beach fires and lovemaking much like Seth S. Marlin describes—"how the pine knots snap / in a fire" and a "length of hair falls, / shrouding [. . .] the shape and press / of a mouth."

The writers of *The Way North* know that much of who we are is what this place has made us. The long-planned weekends Van Kley gives us from in a U.P. minister's datebook are full of "canoes [. . .] & forest / service cabins" and "cranberry bogs," which must somehow sustain him against the "church members dying / from sorrow & icebreak & chainsaw error, from age, / from age." Ronald Johnson's couple edges toward peace and renewal as they eat their dinner and look out their dining room window at an ore boat, "downward bound, a pencil line of smoke dissipating into the rose tinted sky." And even as far away as Italy, John Smolens's poetry professor is identified by her subjects, "ice and snow, and long winter nights," to which she will inevitably return. L.E. Kimball shows us that we are of a place with nights full of "the black humped bodies of fallen trees, another kind of deadfall," and the "small creatures, the vast wildlife huddled under them and under the cedar sweepers." "For Sale signs tattoo the shops" in Janeen Rastall's Negaunee, and "owls return before dawn to the ore dock" of her Marquette. Outlast winter and once again, as Ron Riekki himself says, you have, "your room, this summer, / the slumber of days." But once again, loneliness finds you, where "the cold / at night gets so cold / without her."

"So what are you and for how long?" Rosemurgy asks.

The U.P.'s answers are as intimate as its rivers and thickets and close neighborhood snowfalls at night. As intimate as the voices in these pages.

POEMS

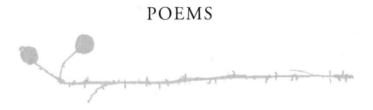

Marty Achatz

THE UGLIEST FISH IN NORTH AMERICA

For Lydia

The mother worries about DNA, how helix
Can twist, like shadows on bedroom walls,
Into something terrifying, tree into banshee,
Chair into dragon, son into a person
She'd avoid on street corners, thin
As a blade of grass, arms full of purple
Canals, a universe of scabby stars.
She wonders how the collision of egg
With sperm inside her belly created
This creature so drawn to the smell
Of carbon monoxide, the taste of razor.
From where in the evolution of family
Did this vestigial finger or toe of insanity
Come? Was it grandpa from Buffalo,
Who got drunk at Niagara Falls, walked
The railing like a Wallenda, one arm
Stretched toward his new bride,
The other toward thunder, mist, oblivion?
Was it great grandma from Russia,
Who buried two daughters in wheat
Fields before they could suckle because
They were daughters, couldn't work the earth
From rock and frost into mud, into yam,
Corn, cabbage? Or was it someone she
Didn't know, someone further than memory,
Who planted this seed in her tree,
This son flower who now fills her pillows
With the wail of loon over moon and lake?
One day when she was a girl, she stood
In the shallows of Superior, her body just

A promise of woman, mother. She felt
A monster slide by her in the water,
Larger than her father, a freight, all
Cartilage and fin, scute and armor,
A live fossil against her skin. She reached out,
Touched its flank, her fingers connected
To a thing ancient: carnosaurus, tarbosaurus,
Pteranodon. It moved slower than glacier,
Gave her time to know its prehistoric form,
Shape unchanged by seventy million years
Of spawn and weed, the skim for minnow,
Mayfly, mosquito. As a girl, the mother
Didn't fear this car of a fish, instead accepted
Its presence as blessing, Paraclete, spirit
To pass on to her mother, father, mate, child.
Beside her son's hospital bed today, she watches
Him, counts his breaths, wants to press
Her thumb to the flutter in his wrist.
She thinks of Longfellow's hero, swallowed
By the sturgeon, crawling down its throat,
Through rib, toward the drumming darkness.
She closes her eyes, wraps her arms around
Nahma's great heart, lets it throb, convulse
Against her face and breasts, hears blood
Roaring in and out, to gill, brain, nose, tail.
She holds on the way she wants to now hold
Her son. To save him, reverse Darwin, genetics.
Force Him backwards to the time when his life
Was still cretaceous, a mystery. A shining,
Black egg in the vast water of her womb.

AS THE DEER: A PSALM

As the deer lopes through dark woods
So my soul chases the Lord, over
Birch, fallen and mossy, victim
Of June storms, wind, rain
Shaking its white trunk and limbs
Like God's voice on the mountain
With Charlton Heston, deep as flood
Water. Before dawn, the deer leaps
In fog, sure hoofs lifting, reaching
For the true path from tree to tree
To pool to boulder to gully,
Panting, thirsty for running water,
Life-changing water that saves,
Washes leather tongue with the taste
Of God, the wild and sweet raspberry of it.
The black river rises from forest,
Divides pine and maple in two,
As the heavens from earth, night from day,
Seas from land, beast from human
At the beginning of creation.
The deer bounds into the black river,
Into twin beams, the eyes of Yahweh.
Praise God for car insurance.

Robert Alexander

WHATEVER DANCE

Whatever dance she was doing, it wasn't one I was familiar with. I kept stumbling over my own feet, or perhaps it was her feet, I was never too sure about that. Picture this: the river stretching out before you, lights of the city glittering off its surface—or maybe you're deep in the woods and the river is there before you, a presence in the night. Japanese lanterns on the black wrought-iron fence, the dance floor smooth beneath your feet (bare feet, no doubt, it being summer).

And the music? I couldn't tell you, after all this time. A waltz or two, a few sad sentimental tunes. You know the story, boy and girl, he off to the war and she along to college. A walk to the water's edge—and, bare feet, a splash in the current. As though it were yesterday, the smell of shampooed hair. Perhaps, for a moment or two, we got it right, the dance, our feet together, sliding on the sawdust floor. It's hard to say.

Julie Brooks Barbour

AUBADES FOR THE NORTH

1

A half hour after sunrise, crows call to each other
across the tops of my dying trees, trunks blackened,
infested by birch bores. The birds perch in the bare branches,
voices louder than their dark bodies. When they leave,
they mark the sky as they cross over tree and house and street.
They blank my thoughts, my mind an open slate for birdcalls,
for my daughter woken by their racket, staggering out of her room,
legs shaking, complaining of the noise.

2

The freighters bellow on the river, making their way back
and forth between the borders. Not like the train whining
in the night, announcing arrivals and departures, announcing
solitary travel beyond the fields of home. The freighters call
to one another, call to the men waiting at the locks, announcing
arrival, announcing greetings. Hello to the lakeshore where
no children wait or wave, hello to the observation decks where
no one watches, hello to the city where men and women
greet the morning for work.

3

On this chill morning, the sun rises over
the church's rooftop, shining out of the dark.
From my study window I watch the world wake,
wait for the trees to come into view, the roof
to slant itself, the window to erase my reflection.

4

Snow coats the power lines, sugars the tree trunks.
The city is silent except for the roar and scrape
of snowplows. The air shone blue and bright when I woke,

snowflakes spinning. Winter is the old pal of this place,
freezing the lakes, lining the roads, muting the echo of life.
But this, too, is life swirling outside, exiling birds.
The land renews itself, cold and shivering.

5
Stunned awake by winter knocking at my window,
I rise, unable to settle down, and search each side
of the upstairs for silence. At the west, the house might
come crashing down. At the south, the rushing sound
of water. At the north and east, a persistent roar.
Snow pelts the storm windows with the wind's fierceness,
shaking the glass. I return to bed, expecting
some terrible crash to spring me from rest. I lie awake
waiting for it, listening to every creak and crack,
hoping for sleep, a release from this vigil.

READING

Afternoons at my grandparents' house, waiting for the end
of my father's workday, I'd spend the hours reading to my aunt
who rarely left the front bedroom except to warm her hands
over the kitchen's wood stove or eat small bites of food.
Afternoons I'd collect pamphlets or old magazines
from cluttered tables around the house, then crack
my aunt's bedroom door and ask to enter. She always
let me in, her faint voice coming from a top corner of the bed,
head lifted slightly from her pillow to greet me. Once I started,
the sense of the words didn't matter. I loved their sounds.
They rolled off my tongue, igniting the air, putting every dresser,
every chair, every book in the glass cabinet at attention.
My aunt listened intently, even on the afternoon
I read from a pamphlet bordered with roses, even though
the words spoke through me like advice, even when I stalled
at one I'd never seen before: *depression*, even when I kept going,
like all good readers. When I finished, I waited for her
to praise me, like usual. I waited in that hushed room,
light struggling through the heavy curtains. I waited,
but no sound came from the bed, not a rustle or sigh.

Sally Brunk

LAC VIEUX DESERT

This road fills my dreams
Mother says it is nine miles long
Full of twists and turns
I can close my eyes and remember every curve
Grandfather Frank Brunk Sr. walked this road every day
Father Al walked it with his siblings to get to school
This road connects Watersmeet to the old village
When I visit this place, I offer tobacco to the ancestors and
My relations who have passed on
This sacred place where Father was born and raised
Where my relations are buried and now rest
I dream of it when I miss Dad the most
I wonder what the village was like when he was young
This place is where the eagles dance and connect with the Anishinabe
This place is held close to our hearts
Generations have connected
Through the dances of old and
The powwows now held there
If you close your eyes and listen close,
You can hear the old songs mingle with the new
The dancers of the new powwows
Share these ancient grounds with the old ones
Whose dances now inspire them today
My Grandparents brought their children up in the old village
The foundation of their home is all that is left
I took a brick home, one of the last times I was there
It has a place of honor on my bookcase
When I see it as I rise for another day,
I am pulled back to Lac Vieux Desert
To the eagles, the voices held on the wind
The dreams of my Grandparents so long ago
That our blood would continue on

I think they would be proud to know
We as a family are still here.

THE RITUAL OF FRY BREAD

Her hands move rhythmically
As she molds the pieces of dough that will soon become fry bread
They move left, then right as she stretches the dough
We talk of the coming day, of the poems I just read to her
. . . I am most nervous when I read aloud to her
We talk of stories she has recently told me,
I do my best to remember, I hang on her every word
I absorb every movement, hypnotized by her hands as she cooks
As she gestures when she speaks
Her movements are automatic, yet measured
The hissing of the grease as the dough hits the fryer
The hum of the television in the background
I smile because these times, these sounds are so special to me
So different, yet so familiar each time they are played out
These moments with her, cooking fry bread as she speaks, is its own
    ritual
The fry bread itself at the end is its own reward

She smiles shyly as I tell her I want to record her stories
We tried once, and she froze as soon as she looked at the recorder
We laugh as I tell her, "Next time, you'll never even know if I have
    one."
Conversations with her are so easy and comforting
Momma has knowledge, stories and memories
I want to record every one.
The chance for that with my Father was taken from me
Cancer took him from us eleven years ago
I will not lose this chance with my Mother

So recorder or not, I listen
Sometimes we laugh, sometimes tears are involved
All conversations are healing
I will close my eyes and embrace what she has to give me

I will be thankful for what we share.

Chii-megwetch, nii-mama.

Jennifer Burd

Vacation over—
Lake Superior sailboats
lean into the race

Lisa Fay Coutley

POST-STORM

I'm sure by now the oregano's gone
  to seed, & the ants have found
    the shortest road from their nest

in the old oak stump to the cupboards
  & counters of our cabin, skirting
    the burners while I cook. Funny,

how I slip so easily into that last summer,
  as if your cigarettes & whiskey cling to me
    still. I should have known

when I told you I trust my nose the most—
  that I would never be able to tell you
    how happiness felt, but I could

tell you how it smelled. That I know
  when a child's getting a cold or a woman
    is soon to bleed. The death

on my mother, not yellow but gray. Maybe
  the year she died was the year we should've
    quit trying, but I never know

when to quit. I swore to you that summer
  I smelled more than rain, more than the metal
    that called the clothes from our backs

& our bodies to the street to dance. Once
  it came, there was nothing we could do
    from behind the bay window but watch

hailstones the size of plums pummeling the car
        we'd left in the gravel drive, the pond
                churning to a full boil, the mallards

we'd named after each other both diving
        from the floating dock into that second,
                angry sky, & us—not touching

but close enough to feel the hair between us—waiting
        for them to rise. To lumber up the bank
                to the long grasses of their nest,

to the ducklings we were still naming.
        Post-storm, we never touched again.
                Never chose another name.

Never bothered to walk out to that bank
        where neither hen nor drake surfaced.
                Even as we both drove away

in separate cars, to separate places, that fall
        we knew it was for the best to never speak
                of what was left alone, waiting.

Amber Edmondson

BELLY, CARRY YOU

In the morning, we will spill down stairs,
liquid like fish to say our salutations,
bubble-mouth kisses on our lips.
Scent of silt on our skin like scales,
and we fold ourselves inward,
rub our bodies on the clay banks
until we are painted like warriors.

At midday, we will fish in the footprints
of great and ancient beasts. Our toes will dig
into the wet clay like hooks, and we'll watch
the slippery bodies weave themselves through
the ripples like silver thread. We'll lurk
in the caverns, in the deepest bellies
of migration.

And in the night, you will swim back to me,
sheets damp and tangled as streams,
a silver prayer on your lips like a hook.
And you will stick to me like scales,
reel to my mouth like a nighttime tributary.
I will swallow you, the rust and cool and stones,
and in my belly, carry you to water.

LENT

I

Her sister dies in early February, too soon to see the fleeting glimpse
    of spring to come, the melted

snow streaming down the street, slick silver strands of it, her hair thin
    and spilling over the flat pillow

on her sick bed. Pastries untouched on the counter for days. Her
    sister never gave up food for Lent.

Instead, one year, music, spent days in her own head, slipped rosary
    beads through her fingers like

children's hair.

II

We are Polish, she says, and we must eat.

III

Thick fingers in the kitchen, grease and flour and prunes. Dough
    rolled thin on the same dulled round

of counter, women—the precision of machines, food enough for a
    ship of immigrants. Forty days of

scarcity rising cold and clear, and first they will prepare golabki,
    krupnik, kielbasa, if the boys come, if

the boys come and eat, and the boys, they always eat so well.

IV

The liturgy, sacraments, and rites. Hail Mary, glory be.

HOTEL STAMBAUGH: MICHIGAN 1977

Oh basket, when my heart beats
my eyes canter, sudden jolts
like when I stuck the knife
in the toaster, mother napping
at 2 p.m. The room filled with smoke
from burning grains, my bones shaking,
eyes locked on you, breadbasket.

In the basement of that house, bags of grain were busted
open all over the concrete and dusted the air. A music staff
of sun shined through a Plexiglas window.

> *Try some*, my buddy, Jessie, said with a handful,
> sifting the dirt out through the spaces between his fingers.
> > *Why the hell is it here?*
> *To feed the horses.*
> > *What horses? We live in a neighborhood.*
> *I don't know. Wild ones.*
> > *Do you hear that music upstairs? I got shocked earlier.*
> *Really?*
> > *Yeah. Hey, my mom said I'm staying at your house tonight.*
> > *Your sister Tami's babysitting. She's a mustang.*

The first time I saw Tami she was whinnying
on the couch under the weight of a naked man.
She looked sort of uncomfortable. Behind
her a translucent mane of curtain hung over an open
window. The night was reserved. Out front,
a parked Ford Pinto. Across the street
book pages in the abandoned school flipped,
turning into pigeon wings and flying
out of the belfry. The sound no different

than clothes being thrown onto the floor.
No different than a pony blow.

Three numbers changed on a digital clock.
One of the naked man's hands hung off the couch.
The hand was trembling, trying to grasp on to a reign,
or let it go free.

WATERWAYS

What is there in your body, unflinching,
still as a rafter of wild turkey stuck

to a tree at 10 below midnight? Maudlin
notes in the dark on a staff of birch branch.

With each gust across a paper meadow,
the moon-shadows change the tune.

We all have lake in our eyes up here
and secrets in our beds. And in this

snow-dark, there is no good and bad,
there are only milky kisses and green

waves of northern light that steal
our tractors as we sleep. And we awake

not knowing where to plow, so tread in our own
great slushy waters.

Manda Frederick

EVACUATIONS

1.
In rape defense training, they make you practice screaming; it is un-
    natural
to your kind, so you must learn to vocalize fear, open the throat

and do it. It must not rise before you as a squeal or a song; it must
    advance
full-mouthed, stronger than any sound you've ever made. It must

strip oxygen from cells, darken your skin blue as you shape your voice
into an obstruction between you and the last sound you will ever
    make.

2.
This mid-December chill, a hundred degrees colder than the core
temperature of your body—labored air to strengthen your breathing.

Gather outside with the others despite the storm to practice:
wend your elbows backward into banks, drive knuckles into drifts,

feign escaping on the ice—white scramble falling, chests under pres-
    sure.
You must practice fear—the crucial sensation that tempers lungs
    feral, strips

control, conscious choice to hold the breath that would trap
your voices quiet; you must breathe because fear requires air.

Fear asks the heart to urge the limbs toward motion, to circulate
a bone-deep need toward flight; without breath: air hunger, lungs
    cannot

offer sound, cannot compel muscles strong—they will soften, made tender
   with contraction, that familiar sensation of shivering or falling asleep.

3.
Later, the dark soft sizzle of propane, space heater at your feet,
an occasional flash of light from outside, a low crunch of sound

spreading through Marquette, a dense noisy fog. Get out of bed
and push aside the gauze that lazes over your window—you love

to watch the plows, blades and teeth, their disregard for the deference
expected of the night, their symmetry of sound carving exits

in the streets. Imagine tomorrow, all the buried people will use their
   shoulders
against their doors, force away the snow that traps them in their
   homes.

Some of you will climb out your windows, cut down the drifts
with ice picks and brooms. Greet your neighbors as you walk to
   school

but keep your scarf-strangled mouth down, do not stop to tell them
what occupies your mind: Blake's *Visions of the Daughter's Albion*—

you obsess over Othoon, a woman who is raped by Bromion
who Blake tells us overcomes her like a great storm as she flies

across a cold expanse to greet her Lover; her Lover, self-sick
with envy that she has shared a bed with someone else, he curses her,

binds Othoon and Bromion back to back forever—though she cries
to him, he does not listen because he will not hear her.

4.
Having rape on the mind is like having fever in the limbs,
its ache reckless through the skin. Leave your window and draw a
    bath

to clear your mind. Strip down, stand naked in the steam,
drag your palms up your legs and wonder where they were that
    night—

wedged between the floorboards of this house so old the radiators
double as soup can phones; this is where you learned to keep

your voice low. You must forget this, now. You must wipe the wet
from the mirror, study the vocal reflection of your neck, confront

the superstitions that soak this room, acknowledge the deaf weight
that is your body: make it listen to you as you say your name three
    times.

Randall R. Freisinger

BOATING TO THE DREAMLAND BAR AND GRILL

"Surely, surely, slumber is more sweet than toil . . ."
—Tennyson, *The Lotos-Eaters*

You steer for land, just as Ulysses did
in that other myth right before his men, grown tired,
found themselves seduced by dreams of escape.
No one needs to remind you of the many points
at which your story and his diverge.
Ulysses refused, and the only lotos blossoms here
will be a few beers and a plate of fried fish.
Nor is your estranged wife devoted and waiting
at home, weaving shrouds to buy you time.
If there are suitors in her life, you would be the last
to know, and even if you did, you can't remember
the last time you strung an arrow in your bow.
Why is it a place for dreams, this bar and grill
so far out on the Bootjack Road it's better reached
by boat? Rumor has it during the days of boom
copper it was a hotel with a fleet of prostitutes.
On paydays one could rise up from his labors
deep in the earth to buy himself a cheap binge
and a quickie or two—about as far as dreams went
for the Finns and other immigrant moles
who made their mine bosses rich enough to leave
them all behind in toxic piles of tailings
and chemical spills. Bent over your meal, you dream,
but not from the food or the slow-motion waitress.
And the locals at the bar—loggers, odd-jobbers—
are certainly not speaking in languid whispers.

At the Dreamland dock you sit in your boat
sipping another beer, waiting for the festering sun,
blind and bloody as the Cyclops's eye,
to disappear. The homeward journey
will take minutes rather than years. You need
no assistance from a blind prophet.
That aureole of light in the distance
is not the beckoning fires of Ithaca,
but Houghton's bare, denotative glare.
You know perfectly well these Portage waters,
so placid tonight, can swiftly rise to a torn bag
of ill winds and blow you far off course.
You've been there before, and had more than your fill
of enchanted women. For years you felt fear
a siren's song at midnight could instill,
but you no longer think very hard about death.
As the gods will, a boat becomes a raft,
a raft a spar, and there's nothing left but to swim,
putting one hand in front of the other, digging
deep into that element in which your life began.

AT THE BISHOP BARAGA SHRINE
Keweenaw Bay, Baraga, Michigan

In the fall, for the sake of sheer movement
and time alone, she had come this far north from Florida,
land of Ponce de León, tracing U.S. 41
on her way to its source up in Copper Harbor.
Now this sculpted jut of chin, eyes of a raptor, staring
far out to where the bay meets Superior.
At the rest stop she had seen the flier's imperative:
See the Shrine of the Snowshoe Priest!
Something in her had been piqued, if not curiosity
then perhaps needs which she had left unattended
for years. *Deus absconditus, deus ex machina*—
Since college she hadn't thought it really mattered.
Catholic but long since lapsed, she thought
this bronze cassock seemed no different
from the lampblack gowns of the grade school priests,
a wrap barely containing its messianic rut, useless,
she had always thought, a matter of sheer waste
around which the sisters constantly clucked
and fussed, flirtatious brides of Christ engaged
in a chaste estrous dance. True, in her own way
she was something like a pilgrim, her motive
more modern, more profane—to save what might
yet be redeemed, though most of her heart had refused
to leave the galvanic thrum of Miami
for this lonely peninsula pointing across
this plumb-less expanse of lake like an arthritic finger.
She drops a few coins from her purse
into the box for donations, but as she begins to drift
absently back to the parking lot, some buried reflex
makes her turn back and kneel in the rustic grotto
before radiant rows of votive candles left by hosts
of summer visitors already gone before her.

Touching the wick to one of the transfixing eyes
of flame, she thinks suddenly of Pascal's wager,
and, like an agate picked up quite by chance
on a beach, her mind retrieves a melodious bit
of song, a TV ad from her childhood: *If everyone lit
just one little candle, what a bright world
this would be.* And because she does still believe
in the saving power of gesture, irony's inner
voice is little more than an insect's faint gossip
in her ear, a black fly's perhaps, which, she's heard,
no longer bites this late in the year.

Eric Gadzinski

WAWASHKESHGIWIS

Wawashkesh
these apples are
for you,
red on the white
snow,
their cider tang
will find you
in the gray woods.
There is a story
how a snake
offered an apple,
so sweet, so cold,
whose bite was
sorrow.
I will lie
on my belly
in the bush,
waiting for
your hunger,
and if my aim
is true
you'll never
know.

ETIENNE BRULÉE

I know what the first white men found here—
not the priests with their minds made up—
but such as Etienne Brulée,
Burnt Steven, soldier of fortune,
seeking furs and sa gloire—
du Roi, bien sûr—
a hard land, a weather a man
must lean into to walk, home
of a handsome, dangerous people,
and for me, as Etienne maybe
a welcome absence of history,
not the age-old village, though
certainement, c'est vrai
de l'Ojibwe, mais pour moi,
poured here by water,
and duty, and my own
willful paddle, the plume
of my breath in the frost
of the forest.

Joseph Daniel Haske

TAHQUAMENON

In the thrilling torrent

        ice thrusts
        chill toward amity

pallid froth

        mingling in russet streams
        under the stilted cedar

glistening

        far-off bay
        around the fog.

Austin Hummell

LOOK AT THE PRETTY CLOUDS

The most important thing about ice
is that it has no pattern. It takes our children
when they drive home from college for clean clothes
and stuffing, not yet awake to the mythology
of gathering and the beauty of food.
The most important thing about logging trucks
is the whoosh that diverts their attention from the ice
they think is asphalt. After the first whiff
of cedar they hang on, and when they look up
it seems like god for a second
has parted the snow with a piece of night.
And that's when they die. The most important thing
about Thanksgiving is that we're always looking
the other way.

Otherwise we blame the Ice Age
for the Great Lakes and the lakes for letting go
of their water. Otherwise snow is a type of ice
and crystalline a word too fragile for children
to pronounce. It seems cruel to implicate vapor
or the clouds we tested their genius with.
It seems mean that black ice is not black
but transparent, like rime ice, which forms from fog
by trapping the most ephemeral of all things. Children
never last the way we want them to.
The most important thing about the sky
is that it is always there.

IN CANNABIS VERITAS

It's midnight and fishflies are praying
against the screen door. They're barely born
and bored already. Or pious. If you were here,
you'd see their arms folded across their chests
like yours last Saturday when you said no
and forked your corn into rows. God knows
you are happiest without the world.

For wanting such a pretty thing as kudzu
to line the ditches I drove back home
I owe my throat and nose. It's my heart.
You can't stop me from loving the way it strangles
daisies. You can't make me love lavender.

I gave up the gibberish Scotch makes of my mouth
for you. I let go of the female flowering tops of hemp. There's a guy
    in King Lear
who pushes his eyes out with his thumbs.
I thought of that. When I thumb another screen
into a pipe all I remember are movies,
are the days I wanted to rhyme your panties
with trash. The bruised parts of my life
stink like orchid. You are one of these.

CINDER GIRL

She flicks ashes from a filtered Winston
onto her stepmother's porch while explaining how
the girl she's moving in with is like a real
sister. Pretty. And what a voice.

Been a year since she's sewn the dress
she drops shyly while explaining with her hands
behind her how she loves the smell. How her tongue
tending gum never once felt this
competent. It's not about the clock
on her beauty. Not how at 27 it feels
like a stopwatch. Take off your fur
and marry your father. Or someone like him.

It's about how she wakes on Tuesday with blue jays
and the sarcasm of arms across her mouth.
How when she looks up from a diamond
she sees her boss nodding. Like she's
got the job. Odd that it's her father
that dies that day. That same day, on the same floor
he used to dizzy her with dancing. Floor where she falls
and pulls hard at the ashes, hard at the lavender.

Jonathan Johnson

FOR AMY

The photograph of the body
of water on the gallery wall
does not change. The wave
never arrives on the rocks.
The rocks have lost
not even the thinnest
layer of skin. Grown
not one molecule more lichen.
The tide pool of reflected sky
retains the precise angles
of clouds and a blue,
in exact hue and saturation,
that existed only once.
Yet everything comprising this,
even the moment, isn't here.
It has perished into the far,
unseen ocean of the present.
The photographer, too,
has taken her existence
and her eye elsewhere.
What remains, at the axis
of lights, framed
against fresh paint,
is nothing, not one thing,
but the seeing.

Raymond Luczak

ONTONAGON

Deep in the moss of Ontonagon River
are majestic trees felled and bones of bears
hunted, skinned, and roasted with their fat
dripping into the fingers of fire hungry for more
as these hunters, long before the white man,
glanced up at the crisp constellations,
reminding them of yet another tale
about the Great Spirits who roamed the land.
Mornings they left behind shards of bowls
that voluminous snow and silt of spring
would bury, cradling the maws of moose
and lining these magnificent bones
in unmade beds of minuscule copper ore.
One day everything will be refitted whole.

TO MYSELF AT FIVE YEARS OLD

In response to seeing a newspaper photograph of myself with other
deaf classmates titled "Doelle Oral Deaf Class," published on
Thursday, April 29, 1971, in the *Daily Mining Gazette*

You are the boy who traveled the farthest of all
away from home. You are the boy who wondered
why you had to stay with a family not yours
from Sunday night to Friday afternoon,
then carted from Tapiola to Ironwood
in a college student's car. You are the boy
who always dreamed of climbing the stars
like a ladder to the roof above your bunk bed
overlooking the valley below, seeing far
in the 110 miles the singular lamp your mother left on
just for you in case you arrived late at night.
You are the boy whose parents shed tears
when they first dropped you off at Calverley Avenue,
a small house filled with nasty little secrets.
There wasn't a special program for deaf kids
in the town where you were supposed to grow up.

You are the boy who hadn't understood how
those damn ears of yours would exile you
in that strip of land between them and that other world
of oral failures and militant signers
you didn't know existed. You are the boy
who hadn't understood how you could never come home
again, not ever once your parents sent you away
to learn how to speak and behave like them.
Your brothers and sisters were already living
separate lives from you. You knew them only
on weekends. You are the boy who gestured
in secret with his deaf classmates among the tall pines

next to the playground at Doelle School
what kind of family you would have
if you'd lost everything but your classmates.
You are the boy who swung back and forth
between that negligent foster family and your own,
never feeling rooted enough to stop dreaming
of a time when you'd stop taking the U.S. 26
every weekend. You are the boy who hadn't yet
learned the cruelty of hearing kids your age. You
are the boy who did his homework so diligently
in hopes of never having to go back to that awful house,
a place where home didn't belong. My boy,
you managed to survive. I'm so proud of you.

23 SKIDOO

n. ~ a bar, restaurant, or other establishment that is a regular hangout in the winter for snowmobilers. Such places, usually located next to a popular snowmobile trail, often double as "biker" bars in warmer months where motorcycle enthusiasts gather, but this is not always the case.

Etymology ~ This Canadian idiom refers to the tendency for such establishments to have half of their parking lot filled with snowmobiles, of which Ski-Doo is a popular brand. Thus, one looking at the bar might see a line of 23 Ski-Doos. This idiom has since come into popular use in the U.S. Upper Midwest and Northern New England.

v. ~ Less common as a verb, this idiom can refer to the patrons of the aforementioned establishment leaving all at once, such as at closing time. Thus, they will get up, pay their tabs, and "23 skidoo."

TRACKLESS LAW

A black
swan or woman
playing

a kantele
(into the) river

water
(into the) mouth
sound box

voice box
only five (vocal) chords

a simple song
a mountain
I've been carrying (all day)

in my shoulder
 bag

going down the street
under it
filling with water

Seth S. Marlin

WETMORE LANDING

fireflies. talk laugh drink. if you
let your eyes
follow the lines of light
all the way curving up

into the dark

you'll realize how cedar smells
like a heartbeat
and thus is transcendent

because later

on some other night
you'll remember just enough
of that promise to smile.
of what was. what will be again.

you have to love

how the woodchips, mushrooms,
the evergreen,
the wine tobacco indigo

draw themselves out

on ten-year-old parchment,
doodles giving way
to the quill-pen scratch
of windblown grass.

paper gripping

like your tongue to the inside
of your upper lip,
so you know the sturgeons feel this

all. unspoken.

you have to remember
how the pine knots snap
in a fire, like fingers
cologned in wood smoke,

how that length of hair falls,
shrouding everything
save the holding of a breath,

the shape and press
of a mouth.

Mary McMyne

ROTKÄPPCHEN

The beauty of being eaten by the wolf is that you do not remember. You do not live to regret the path that you took, or the flowers that you stopped to smell in the woods. There is only the moment of realization that he's eaten your grandmother, that the body in the bed is not hers, but the one who's consumed her and will soon consume you. There is only the flash of great long teeth, white as ivory in the moonlight. Eyes like holes, gaping wide, as he reaches for you—

The better to eat you with. These are the last six words you hear, before those teeth rip into your white skin. *The better to eat you with*, as the red hood slips from your shoulders to the floor. There is only a moment of the pressure of hipbone to hipbone, a moment before the tearing of flesh and the crunching of bone. And then nothing. Sweet nothing. Instead of the infinite maze of regret and remembrance, instead of the eternal image of his body pressing yours to the floor—

Oh, the beauty, the kindness, of being eaten. Huntsman, leave us dead as stones in the wolf's belly, without memory, without regret, once the deed is done.

Jane Piirto

BEHIND

"Know I well the source of metals / Know the origin of iron."
—Runo 9, Kalevala

Here we are, Michael and I
reading Wendell Berry nature poems
from *A Timbered Choir*
on Jasper Bluff in Ishpeming
on a Sunday morning in August.
Isn't it peaceful?
Seeing woods stretching to the horizon,
an old iron-mining town nestled below,
we sit among striated jaspillite outcrops
with sun and blue sky.

Behind us lies
the biggest manmade footprint
ever made in the state of Michigan,
bigger than the Great Wall of China,
bigger than the pyramids,
the open pit iron mine, Tilden,
its flat skyline above the green forests.

Over Lake Angeline trucks clank,
prehensile giant silhouettes
on the anomalous horizon.
The monsters dump offal from conveyer belts,
ore magnetized into pellets
to make the autos to make America what it is,
earth turned inside out to yield
a garden of iron for bridges and girders.

Behind our backs rises a barren red mountain,
a landfill without odor or gulls,
pebbled, bouldered cliffs so steep
mountain goats or llamas could not get foot.

Beyond that skyline in back of us
the gouged pit is miles across
a crater that goes deeper than Lake Superior
with ore-boat sustenance for Pittsburgh's steel mills,
far down there, slanted roads and ribbons
of magenta and stark gray.

They will go down another half a mile
in the next twenty years,
the Cleveland Cliffs Iron Company says
on official tours. No photos permitted.

The full time digging casts dull yellow light
on cloud bottoms all night long.
Daily blasting shakes the woods—
the lakes, rivers, trees, deer,
bear, squirrels, fish—
every noon at 12:15 p.m.,
(an old mining tradition—
blasting during lunch break)
even today.
This quiet Sunday.

God, how can the sun shine
without regard and innocent
on this green pastoral foreground,
while in the background all devastation
proclaims the necessary victory of mines?

THE ONLY THING TO
DO THIS FALL DAY

"She knew, my mother knew, how to get an apple."
—Runo 20, Kalevala

The only thing to do this fall day on Jasper Street,
what with this fierce tumble of leaves
bright as young children's sweet cereal
as auguring as a battle cry
or a prophet's ram's horn,
a visible press of invisible chaos
summoned by gray banks of fog,
blind clouds, waves of leaves,
spray of sticks,
sleek tides of shingles blown from roofs,
is to make applesauce.

Split beams like spars litter these inland strands.
Melodic bass bellows caterwaul.
Clanging thuds of sinister surge
indicate the season's sure change.
Down there a sturdy old maple lost her waist,
slashed as if with a sharp ax.
Speckled yellow leaves spackle
heedless the wet street
now blocked off with barricades.
The only thing to do today
is to make applesauce.

Put on music.
Hildegarde Von Bingen's nun visions,
Des Hommes et Des Deux chants, Finnish flutes.
Quarter September's apples to soften in slow heat
until, translucent and panting with steam,

they release holy cider.
Find the old food mill with its rusted screw.
Spoon the hot brew into the mill
over a blue Fiesta bowl.
Turn the wheel
until skins and seeds yield meat and juice.
Fill an orange bowl
with sienna sauce.
Sprinkle with brown cinnamon.
Grind dark nutmeg.
Sniff autumn's bouquet
while you stand safe inside the rattling window
snug in your old green sweat suit.
Now. Fueled with all sweetness, eat the warm fruit.

Saara Myrene Raappana

STUCK

Cousin, all I know of geography
is what Uncle Seppo, on Air Force leave,
carved in the sauna wall about Thai girls

so now, as we shoulder-boost your pickup
by its fender, I imagine headlands
to the east, ridges fading like thighs.

Tell me which road reaches under those
redwood skirts. Tell me I can gun this engine
and get something more than mud. What I know

of migration is a tune flying circles
in my brain. Seppo says, by the Mekong,
he saw a wasp with humming wings. It ate

cow flesh. It chewed through lumber. Our sky
is sandpaper teaseling through the birches.
We're slivers in the thumb of this off-ramp.

Your ex-wife ignores your calls, pulls wood
from her finger-quicks with baking soda salve.
We have no choice, cousin; we lift and lift.

Maybe, between sobs, you say, *I don't
have anywhere to go.* Maybe there's no
answer for that, except to push you home.

Beneath the sauna bench, a wasp is caught
in a spider's web. There's thrashing.
That's disbelief, legs ripping themselves out

to get free. It's hopeless. Still, I can't but
root for him to rev up and make a go,
with all the force of his life, out, out and away.

Janeen Rastall

UNIMPROVED

He likes roads without a center line:
belly soft,
all the gravel pushed to the edges.
He wants to see how deep his tires will take him.

YELLOW DOG YEAR

There is a cool channel
that runs along this bed of rock
so calm
when turtles shift their feet
skimmers ride the wake,
a stream, pouring past the pine stands
carrying coaster trout
down the Yellow Dog
down to Superior's hungry mouth.

I. First Arrest
I will show you fear in a handful of dust. — T. S. Elliot

The ground was gouged,
dirt brandished in a backhoe's hand.
Cynthia thought through every walk:
   the deer tracks pointing to the brush,
   a pine-fringed face of slip rock,
   the stream stuttering and blurting from the hill
   to a field of berries below,
the birds waited for her cue.

As if sitting
   could shift the balance
   and hold the earth in place,
Cynthia Pryor sat down at Eagle Rock.

II. Lansing's Math
No matter how long they looked at the problem, the solution was the
      same:
         the number of unemployed voters was > the entire Ojibway
      population.

III. Encampment at Eagle Rock
Soon the others would arrive:
ATVers and activists,
Kennecott with paper promises of jobs.
Charlotte Loonsfoot pitched her tent,
back flap facing the earth mover.
She would cut a plot for potatoes,
plant flowers by the cyclone fence,
pray where her ancestors sought their vision quests.
For now, *Migi zii wa sin* was silent.

IV. Here there is no rock
Perched on top of miles of mines,
Negaunee's sidewalks lead to caved in lawns.
Snow Street crumbles into Merry.
For Sale signs tattoo the shops.
At the Iron Inn
they still talk about when Ropes was running
and their fathers' fat Friday checks,
how they pile job on job these days,
while their women work the Walmart in Marquette.
Drink up tho' Kennicott'll be calling those guys not afraid to sweat
once them greeners are gone and the reporters forget.

V. The Ruling
"Michigan mining law references buildings that are places of worship.
   Eagle Rock doesn't fit into that" — DEQ spokesman Bob McCann

If there were walls among the birches
or only walls and no birches.
If there were pews instead of rocks.
If there were spires that rose as high
as the smoke from the sacred fire . . .

VI. Riverwalker
Moran walks the river in hip waders.
His eyes run over its familiar form.
Plump with snow melt
its banks are pliant,
ice saucers jiggle and bump to its edges.
He pulls the tube from his pack
leans low over the lip of a rock ledge
and catches the stream mid fall.
He holds the vial gently
dates the label on the glass
—his river caught in time.

VII. The Queen City
Snow covers the mine portal, paints the digger white,
lightens the wooded hills all the way to Marquette.
After a clear cut, the jack comes back first
followed by some white and red pine,
thick enough for wolves without collars to stalk.
In the city, owls return before dawn to the ore dock.
Its metal arm thrusts a claw deep into the harbor's sand
holding fast Marquette's claim to both the water and the land.

Ron Riekki

AFTER THEY LEAVE

You still have your arms,
your fingers, your lips,
your own, not hers,
not her wrist or her stories
or her stomach that you placed
your hand on and
pretended there
was a baby
inside. You have none
of that now. You have
your room, this summer,
the slumber of days,
the mosquito
by your ear, and the cold
at night gets so cold
without her. But you have
your life; enjoy it
the way you enjoy
the music on your head-
set during the long air-
plane flight, the way
that you enjoyed holding
her when you could hold
her at the sink, but you have
all of this air now, to breathe,
so breathe it, enjoy it,
deeply, the love of knowing
it keeps you alive
until the next little death.

Catie Rosemurgy

FOUNDED 1903

Should I blame the birds, the way their feathers are stuck into them?

What about the pine trees pushed into the dull sand hills,
brush brush brushing away any face that tries to form?

You see what I'm driving at.
Shapes. Designs.

By limiting our numbers we were supposed to be removed
from the problem of being stacked like kindling and shoveled into
    the ground.

But it backfired and made us less than human.
We stuck our hands into traps we'd rigged hours earlier.
We could recognize whether or not we were stabbing one another
but not whether or not we were dreaming. Once you believe

you are the quaking fertile pistil, the notion is hard to shake,
but why did we ever believe it? All morning we dried out and bent
    together
in a field. In the afternoon, four or five of us waded out

and watched our dresses flower around us in the lake.
Our babies were gone or blurred under the water so it must have
    been a dream.
You can feel how natural it is for your body to come apart
as the waves lift your hair away. So in that sense it was a relief
when the fire turned out to be real.

GHOST DOG

A good day to be black and white, Ghost Dog.
Only the faint colors, the dim emotions, are left.
We can come out from our hiding places.
The wanting-to-live and all its houses
have disappeared. We can be honest now.
I never liked shapes.

The ice grows more enormous. The final verdict is snow.
So what are you and for how long?

An animal flickering in the arctic.
Across the lake, in the murk, coming toward me, you were like a man.
Except for your unhurried trot. You went right past me
on your patrol. A furred planet orbiting
around and around the lake.

What do you eat, Ghost Dog?
The swirling smoke of the new thing is caught
under miles of ice.

In the stopped water, something that isn't there
hits against something that is. With your circling,
do you keep it in or let it out?

FIGURE FOUR DEADFALL

The ground is covered with the makings of traps.
Just change the angles. The mentality of rigging

is hard to let go of when he walks into a living room, all those
    wooden, leggy objects.
The positions he assumes with women seem potentially fatal

to the small life scurrying between them.

———

To prove he's strange, that's why hair kept growing out of his face.
Organisms right with the world are furred or unfurred, not a little of
    each.

———

He always gets angry when the wind tastes of little carved wooden
    boxes
and European women,
which is a redundancy. The good news is
he'll turn something language-based onto its stomach in less than a
    week's time.

———

He's decided several times to move back to town
and turn his attention toward arranging himself advantageously
toward his own kind. But he doesn't know how the action works,
what the closing means. He isn't sure how to predetermine the out-
    come,

whereas in the forest all he does is wait. He disappears into the
    waiting,
whereas in town he is magnified.

———

He doesn't know what to do for these lost people so he decides again
    to feed them,
dress them, and watch what they do.

———

A young aspen is the whistle of the forest, a slender girl's more slender
    flute.

———

His arms and legs are unconvincing. He's a sack and he's been dropped.
It's bad enough something has been carrying him,
but now, before he can size it up, it's gone.

———

The city has too many tongues to speak.
The cultures mew together in a basket and their eyes cloud with each
    other's milk.
The New World is a notion held up with sticks and loaded with
    stone.
Often at night all that keeps the motion from closing are the bones of
    his face.

Andrea Scarpino

LOVE AS TACONITE

Dark globes of iron ore,
pockmarked, heavy for their size,
spread along the highway,
train tracks, river banks.
Left by tankers, freight cars,
seagull beaks, deer hooves,
heavy boots. Like that, my love
for you. Quiet, steadfast.
Scattered around town,
lake bottom, sidewalks, grass,
poisoning your lungs, brain cells.
Calling out, reminding you.

PICNIC ROCKS

Because of days like this—
clear sky, rolling waves,

children playing in sand—
because the name invites

wading, lunch carried
on shoulders, back—

a fearlessness. And then
an undertow, longshore

current, a couple caught
in the pull until their lungs

lake-fill. Love like this.
A sun-filled day. And then

a turn. Gasping-for-air.

Keith Taylor

DRUMMOND ISLAND FOSSILS

Take the ferry east out of Detour
then drive up across the alvar plains
to a path that leads you to the shore.
There, rock ledges step down to the lake.
Kneel. Look closely. You'll see shadows, then
limestone honeycombed with delicate
coral branches that waved from the floor
of an ocean we can't imagine.

Emily Van Kley

WAYS TO HUNT DEER

rifle & hooftrack (stretch your eyesight so long it sores, comes back
                recollection. rubbed bark, snapped alder. you,
                again, the purist, allowing only what you can carry,
                knees creaking like old trees in the fall-froze woods)

rifle & saltlick (low-tone radio in Kmart plastic shack. fidget. piss.
                check your phone for time & no messages. endure
                grouse out of season; two does at noon. when the
                buck finally comes, stepping light as snowfall, hate
                & love the surge, his trust, your need. the noise that
                breaks the waiting, confuses gift with death)

dodge 4x4 & halfrack (Sunday morning—sober, sorry—hammer
                out dents & replace hood panel with gray from the
                junkyard. soap away hide & blood)

MY FATHER'S DATEBOOK

is red & worn, smaller than a travel Testament,
corners pressed like a child's crayon rubbing
into the back pocket of his jeans. Each day minutely
ruled & apportioned its several square centimeters,
as if order could be made of the drop-stitch script,

letters sharp & steep as the lines of a heartbeat
monitor, of the sermon notes, the lunch
& breakfast calorie measures, Colombian phone
numbers, mileage logs between Negaunee
& Watersmeet. For a quarter-century of Octobers

the same volume has arrived by post just as snow
is starting, its vinyl cover & little clutch of coming days
stamped with the rose seal of his denomination.
He knows the envelope, waits for it, breaks
the little book's spine & splays its pages

like a fish gill at the kitchen table. Now,
before the blank begins to fill, it is possible
he will be sufficient to answer the demands
of so many promised hours. He takes up the pen.
First in are the few, long-planned weeks away,

days of canoes & cranberry bogs & forest
service cabins—by which he means to endure
the crumbling steeples & Fourth of July hymnsings
of the path he's chosen, the church members dying
from sorrow & icebreak & chainsaw error, from age,

from age. Sometimes killing each other on purpose,
like the grade-school teacher who will shoot his friend
over rights to the living room sofa, both of them lost

on booze & something stronger, the town's third-graders
unhelmed, the subsequent warring families

for whom no separation of pews will suffice.
Such a loss can be neither inked nor even voweled.
For now he continues with the congregational
meetings and first communions, pencils in days off,
lone flags half-raised on one weekend or the next.

When I visit, my father lends me his datebook
at a lake between compass bearings. I write;
the others fish. In the back section labeled "notes,"
I take down the bell of my lover's hips curving
into thigh-deep water, my brother looking

another sort of brotherly in a rain poncho belted
with a piece of cord. *Sight the line, self,* I write,
not a one goes unencumbered. It is the weight
of days, the evidence of a good heart
pressed between obligations; it is time,

a made thing which bends at certain speeds
& yet is built up sturdy as a warehouse
through which we must forklift our best
intentions that brings me to wonder

by what measure we will be
what we mean in this life.

Cameron Witbeck

ISLAND POEM NO. 23

I was alone with the loons who couldn't be alone with me.
They sang the night full of ghosts, and blood-moons fell
in the coldest water. I whispered *venison come home*
to my tongue. I prayed for rain to lie with me.

On pale mornings, I picked greenstones from the shore.
Buried in my lip, I loved their grit—forgot how to starve,
watched a snake die. Like a heart unfolded. In the sun, alone
by huge water, I wanted to drink all the beautiful venison I saw.

PREDATOR AND PREY

"Eyes in front, born to hunt.
Eyes on the side, run and hide."

For my brother

In my dream, you're dead
the night I wake as a wolf
howls across the basin.

This is where they keep the old gods.
Pray the lake will never freeze.
You must live with a knife.

At first light, I go into the woods, singing
about skulls, tracing the socket
you once fractured. A scar of bone

beneath my skin.
So much below—the air
tastes like blood, the sweet marrow

of broken ribs. My fingers rim
a paw-print in the mud.
Brother, run.

A moose carries enough blood to bless us all.
You can starve till your teeth fall out.
I'm warning you of me.

We must run from each other.
The bones of wolves are cracked
like lines on a map,

but they won't unlock their jaws.
This is how we'll live.

Jim Zukowski

THINGS MAMA SAYS

That whiskey ain't fit for a dog.
My eyes hurt from all this cryin.
The sky has eyes, and it's lookin down on us.
The air is shiny with Daddy's soul.

THE BOOKS WE FOUND IN
THE ATTIC TELL US

our ideas are right, what we thirst for,
and we still have water in the ground, near the orchard.
But the smart of being right about ideas in books
feels different next to the shame of purple,
the scar on your hip where Daddy pushed you
into the trees outside the kitchen window.
It was around the time Mama thought her bed was spinning.
She said it was ghosts from the revival ground in the next county,
the ones that live in that big clearing.

MIDWEST

Sun, farewell.
Clock, goodbye!

Hello, small sorrows
that will not die.

STORIES

Ellen Airgood

SYSTEMATIC BOTANY

My girlfriend Lorene has taken the baby for the day. She made me cash in one of the babysitting coupons she gave me at the shower. This is the first one I've used since Annie was born, eight pounds, three ounces, and three months ago.

It's so hot today, and muggy, I'm thankful I didn't have a summer pregnancy. Even un-pregnant, moving through the house is like swimming, and it's almost too much trouble to do it. I haven't had the energy I did before Annie came along. It seems like I can't get my gumption back, regardless of the fact that Annie is the best thing that's ever happened to me, including marrying Harlan, which I wouldn't say to him flat-out like that, of course. When I told Lorene I felt about as lively as a cardboard box, she said, "You need a day off."

"Oh, no," I said, making a gaga face down at Annie where she was snoozing in the crook of my arm. Lorene had come over to see her, but I could hardly stand to let her out my hands for even a minute.

"She's the cutest thing since sliced bread, Bev, but that doesn't mean you can't take a break now and then. I'll tell you what. I'll take her one day this week, and you can do whatever you want."

I laughed. "I can't think what that would be."

"You'll figure something out. I have confidence in you. Pick a day."

She nagged until I said, "Wednesday, then," and at eight a.m., here she came. I just barely had time to pack up Annie's blanket and bottles and diapers and all before Lorene was hoisting up her basinet, slinging the diaper bag over her shoulder and striding out the door. And there I was, high and dry as a trout cast up on a riverbank, all alone with the clock ticking choppy seconds by and the refrigerator humming.

I made myself some coffee and sat down, I admit at a loss. Not for the first time, Lorene had given me a gift I wasn't quite sure I wanted. At Christmas she gave me a pair of long, dangly silver and turquoise earrings that must've cost at least fifty dollars, which was more than I'd spent on Harlan or him on me. I have a habit of losing earrings, and if you lost one of these, it'd be a real shame instead of just a nuisance, which is more responsibility than I generally like to shoulder with my jewelry. I'd never say a thing like that, of course. When I opened the box and saw them reclining there on their velvet bed, I thanked her like it was not only a real surprise but also one of the nicest gifts I'd ever received, which it was.

Lorene looked at me real intent the way she does sometimes and said, "Bev, I want you to *wear* them, not put them away. It's not the end of the world if you lose one. They're just things."

"Expensive things," I couldn't keep myself from saying.

"Never you mind how expensive," she said, sounding just like her mother, or mine, which made me laugh. But I still didn't hook the earrings on the way I knew she wanted me to. Instead I sat holding the box in my hands like a schoolbook or a Bible.

You know I hadn't gotten her anything but a poinsettia from the Ben Franklin, and I felt like a nickel waiting for change. But when I gave it to her, her face lit up like I'd just handed her the keys to a greenhouse. Plants are what she studied at college—systematic botany is what she calls it. She's going to get a doctor's degree in it, which seems maybe not too useful, but I guess she knows what she's doing. She told me once that there are patterns to almost everything and that it makes her feel better about life in general when she can see them.

"Patterns to plants?" I'd said, maybe just a little bit skeptically.

"Yep."

"And that makes you feel better."

She grinned at my doubtful tone and said, "Yep."

"Do you know the red isn't really a flower?" she said when I gave her the poinsettia. "The flower is this tiny thing you hardly even see. The red is *leaves*. Well, bracts, really, which are just modified leaves that set off a flower. It's from Mexico, and it's an evergreen. Down there it's a shrub and up here it's a Christmas decoration. Isn't that funny?"

"It is, kind of." I took another look at that poinsettia, so far from home and so misunderstood.

"Yep, and you can keep them alive year-round, if you try. I've always wanted to see if I could. That's what I'm going to do with this one."

I saw that I had better plan on wearing those earrings right away, maybe even just to do the dishes in, if I was going to keep up with Lorene at all, and I opened up the box and slipped the posts in.

She always tugs at something in me. When she comes over I pull words out of my vocabulary that I haven't thought of since before I was married, at least. The other day I said to her, "That trip Harlan and I are planning up north this summer is going to be a real endeavor with the baby." *Endeavor.* Now where did I come up with that?

I knew she'd be disappointed if I didn't do something with this day of mine, something I couldn't do if Annie was here. I sat there for the longest time with my coffee, getting used to how quiet the house was, realizing I could hear the wind rustling the leaves of the trees outside, a sound I hadn't heard in a while, between winter and having a baby.

What I finally came up with was, I made a tablecloth.

I made it from a piece of fabric I bought back before my mama died the spring before this one just past. We were uptown together one Saturday while Daddy and Harlan were rototilling the garden. It was actually Harlan who was rototilling while Daddy supervised, and Harlan was sweating up a storm, I remember. The back of his shirt was wet down the middle, and he was frowning, with his bottom lip caught between his teeth. Daddy is very particular about his garden and has more to say about rototilling than you might think. Anyway, Mama and I took the car and went into town to run some errands, which was really just an excuse to get away from the men, and look around in the Ben Franklin, and maybe get a sundae at the Dairy Freeze. Daddy is skinny as a rail and doesn't have a taste for sweets, and always pestered Mama like crazy for eating desserts, so she liked to go out with me once in a while and enjoy a Fudge Whirligig in peace.

Mama found a piece of fabric in the remnants bin at Ben Franklin, a stiff white piece of cotton with sky-blue and lavender stripes running both ways through it. You could just see how cool and crisp it would stay looking even on a hot August afternoon. She said it was just the size of the dinette in my breakfast nook, and why not get it for a table-cloth? So I did, and I put it away until I could get to finishing it—I just had to hem the two edges. But Mama passed away about a month after that, and I never touched that cloth again until today.

You never think that what happens to everybody else is going to happen to you. You don't stop in the aisle of the Ben Franklin and see that it's the last time your mama will lift a square of fabric out of the bin and say, "This is pretty," or the last time you'll debate sharing one Fudge Whirlygig between the two of you and then go ahead and each get your own, like always.

I didn't do much of anything for a long time after Mama died, except take care of Daddy, who didn't even know how to turn the stove on hardly, and get the funeral planned, and put the house in order. Then I found out I was pregnant, and school started back up again in the fall, so I was working at my job in the principal's office until just two weeks before Annie was born. I didn't have time to say boo or boohoo, say nothing of sit down at the sewing machine and make a tablecloth I didn't really need.

I did a good job on it, today. I was more careful than I usually would be, thinking of Mama and what advice she'd give. I ironed the hem over twice in a good straight line, which was easy because of the stripe in the fabric, but even so it gave me a satisfied feeling. I had to go answer the phone twice, and I left the iron sitting on the board set to "Cotton," something I wouldn't do with the baby in the house, even though she isn't crawling yet. When the hem was ironed flat, I opened up the sewing machine and stitched it up with lavender thread, which I had to go hunting for and change on the spindle. I almost didn't bother, but then, thinking about Mama, I did. I edged the hem along steady, neither too fast nor too slow, just the way she taught me when I was a little girl making outfits for my dolls. What hit me like a stray fly ball while I was doing that—Annie'll be a little girl wanting to use the sewing machine one day soon, and I'll be the mama showing her how.

I was pleased with my hems—the stitches were even and I managed to keep a good straight line, except for once when I wandered off in thinking that it was about time for Annie's bottle. The next thing I did was to iron the whole thing out, as much for the smell as anything. I do love the smell of a hot iron. It makes me feel peaceful, probably because Mama ironed, and Grandma too. I thought to myself while I worked that I should do more of it, but that I won't, probably.

Next I spread the cloth over the dinette in the breakfast nook just the way Mama had suggested, and set a vase of gladiolas in the middle.

I stood there real still for a minute, and all of a sudden, I had to get busy again.

I went and did up all the dishes, and wiped the kitchen counters clean, and damp-mopped all the floors. I scrubbed the shower and the bathtub and the toilet, then I moved on to the laundry basket and ran three loads through, and folded everything as it came out of the dryer and put it away, which doesn't sound like much when you say it, but is hard to do with a baby in the house. When the laundry was done I started organizing the canned goods in the lazy Susan, but then right out of the blue it was like I could hear Mama's voice in my head. "You're wearing yourself out, Beverley Louise. You act like a pack of hounds is after you, which it isn't. Sit down a minute."

I realized she was right. I sank down at the kitchen table to enjoy the breeze that had picked up and eased through the house, making the wind chimes in the front hall sing, and I wept for about an hour.

Mama and I used to talk every day, if not in person then on the phone, which both Daddy and Harlan professed to find ridiculous, but if once I didn't call her or she didn't call me, Harlan'd start hovering around me in the kitchen or wherever, saying, "Aren't you going to call your mother? Isn't it about time the phone rang? Are you feeling okay?" I just know Daddy was at home doing the very same thing.

There was nothing big we had to talk about, mostly. It was just to ask how are you doing, and how long do you boil fudge, and would you think I should put that new blouse I got last week in the wash, or should I have it dry cleaned. She'd call to tell me there was a sale on canned vegetables at Kroger's and we both ought to stock up, and I'd tell her I couldn't make up my mind whether to paint the bathroom pale blue or something more risky, like chartreuse, which really I was only interested in due to the name.

None of it was anything you'd give two seconds thought to. I'm not sure now if I remember how to make her dill pickles, which there are none others like, and I never wrote the recipe down. I guess I just figured she'd always be there to tell me. But now she isn't here, of course. I'm on my own.

I wouldn't say this to anyone, but I don't understand why we couldn't have just gone on the way we were forever, with her and Daddy living out there on the farm where I grew up, and me and Harlan in our place just outside of town, and Annie getting bigger and taking baton, or learning the Texas two-step, or going to college, or whatever. I know that doesn't make any sense. I know we all have to meet our maker one day. But I wish it all the same.

Just as I was drying out a little and thinking that dollars to doughnuts Harlan won't notice the tablecloth, and wondering if it'll hold its starch once it goes through the wash, Lorene came driving up. I looked at the clock and saw that it was after four. Harlan gets home at four thirty, and I hadn't even thought about dinner. I hustled into the bathroom and rinsed my face with a cold cloth, then went and got my baby.

Lorene was grinning. "We had fun," she said. "Didn't we Annie-girl? Aunt Lorene's going to take you again next Wednesday, and the Wednesday after that, isn't she? And we'll have all kinds of a good time, won't we?"

Annie pursed her lips and smiled like the cat who ate the canary, which made Lorene and me both burst out laughing.

"How about you? Did you have a good day?" Lorene asked as I lifted Annie out of the carrier.

I thought about telling her—how lonesome I felt, and how I sewed the tablecloth, and how I cried. But then I just said, "Yes. Yes, I did."

Lorene gave me one of those looks of hers and a quick hard hug with her arm wrapped around my neck, and then she was gone. About five minutes later Harlan pulled in. I propped Annie on my hip and smoothed the tablecloth with the palm of my hand as I walked by it, and went outside to meet him.

THE WANDERER

Behold, thou has driven me out this day from the face of the earth; and from
thy face shall I be hid; and I shall be a fugitive and a vagabond in the earth;
and it shall come to pass, that every one that findeth me shall slay me.

—Genesis 4:12

The Vagabond docked last Monday night. Rick tapped on the diner's
window and pointed across the bay, and I looked up from my work to
watch Tim's boat cut through the water and swing up to the dock. The
bay was still and the reflecting sun made the hull shine like new silver.
Once the boat was moored in its familiar spot on the opposite shore, it
almost seemed as if it hadn't been gone at all.

I went back to my cleaning up, but everything had changed. We'd
been anticipating Tim's arrival for days, looking for the small dot that
is *The Vagabond* to appear on the eastern horizon, so that winter could
officially end and the too-short sprint through spring begin. His arrival
means that the water is open and the ice out, that summer is hover-
ing so close it might as well already be here, that it's time for Rick to
remember the fish batter recipe. It means we're about to fall headlong
into a time of endless work and stifling heat, frustration and moun-
tains of dirty dishes, exhaustion and never catching up, not even for a
minute. But despite this we both feel an uplift of anticipation when the
boat sails in, pulling summer in its wake.

Summer used to be such a simple thing—school vacation, a garden
and camping trips and cotton dresses. Now it's so much more compli-
cated. The season's freewheeling exterior hides a harsh reality that ev-
eryone in a tourist town knows—there's no time to look back or down,
no time to think or have hopes or ideas. There's only time to work.

Summer is whitefish and French fries and fresh lemons and cole-
slaw, plate after plate of it and feeling like you'd die to have your own
helping, but there's always another customer in line and so it's a cheese
sandwich in bed at the end of the day instead. Summer is bare, sandy
feet, but never being on the beach at any normal time like noon, but
always at the edge of the day—before dawn or after dark, in tired mo-

ments slipped in when the work is done or close enough to done to pass. Summer is frayed nerves and short tempers and trying to smile anyway. It's when the only people you really understand are the ones working the same way you are, because they're hanging off the end of the same short rope, looking at the same bottom line. It's a time when money rolls in so fast it actually accumulates, and you make the mistake of thinking it means something and will last.

Here in the diner summer is defined by whitefish. I think we could sell nothing but fish and chips and whitefish sandwiches from noon until midnight seven days a week and still not run out of people asking in hopeful anticipation, "Do you have fish today?" So Tim brings fish and Rick fries it and I carry it out with its tartar sauce and chunk of lemon, and that is summer. It sounds so simple, and is, in a way, but in another way it isn't.

I can still picture a dinner shift last July—a typical night, a good night for fish. Tim brings in another fifty pounds and finds us up to our elbows in people and so picks up a sharp knife and a cutting board and skins fillets while Rick fries and I wait tables, and we swing along that way for a while, surviving the summer one meal at a time. I remember a boy with a good view of the fish-cleaning operation watching with interest and finally asking, "Is that fish fresh?" Tim gives the kid a look that could wither steel but wisely just tells him yes. Then the boy wants to know where the fish come from. "The lake," Tim tells him, straight-faced, and I have to bite my lip because it is such a perfect U.P. answer. The lake, of course. But it turns out the boy really wants to know something else, who caught the fish and how and why, and he asks all this in an imperious manner I think he must have learned from his father. Tim tells him, "I did, with my boat. That's where fish comes from, from people who make their living fishing." I can't smile this time because this too is a U.P. answer, but one fraught with hard feelings on many sides. After the boy is busy eating, Tim says to me, "Everybody wants fish, but nobody wants the fisherman."

I know that's not entirely true—we're glad to know the fisherman as well as the fish, a lot of people are. But he's right—people want fish but not fishermen, lumber but not loggers, freedom without responsibility, good schools but not taxes, restaurants but not the smell of onion rings drifting out the vents. People want to have their cake and eat it too, that's nothing new, and what can you do? Go about your business and watch the seasons turn.

So *The Vagabond* has docked, bringing summer with it—a time of chronic exhaustion as well as adrenaline, a time when everything but work falls away. Tim's days seem like ours—putting in long hours through every crisis that arises, trying to make the most of a short, important season, cut off from family for the sake of work—and so we feel at ease with him. It's soothing to be around someone just as tired and busy as we are, someone who is trying just as hard, with just as variable success, to remain good-humored about it. It makes me smile, a little, when Tim is as cranky as Rick, and makes me wish things were easier, but they're not.

We admire Tim and his crew for the hard work they do, for their offhand courage in the face of Lake Superior's dangers. We're already weary of the annual flurry of complaints about commercial fishing, especially Indian fishing rights. I don't claim to know what's best for the fishery, but I do know what people want to eat, what it's like to work for yourself, how it feels to be the topic of negative conversation, how the short run can be so overwhelming that the long run hardly matters. I've read that at the turn of the century commercial fishermen were lifting three hundred thousand pounds of fish out of the water around Grand Marais in an average season, six hundred thousand pounds in a record year. That makes me believe that if the fishery has been depleted, it started long before *The Vagabond* sailed into town.

I know that summer is here and the show must go on. It's a mixed bag, as with everything in life, good and bad hopelessly tangled together so you can't tell which is which and have to take them both together and hope for the best.

Sharon Dilworth

THE POSSIBILITY OF WOLVES

Rorie's husband, Yannick, was a clown. Though he had once tried out for the red juggling team of Ringling's Barnum and Bailey Big Top, he had never actually worked for a circus. Yannick was more of a performance artist. He saw nothing exciting about grease-painted faces or nylon silk jumpsuits with button bows. His own style had a lot to do with exaggeration and his collection of costumes and tricks included a five-foot Styrofoam cowboy hat, dozens of phony oversized arms and legs, red velvet tear-away pants, two pairs of stilts, exploding roosters and moose heads, plastic prop hammers, six tricycles, an indoor-outdoor trampoline, and yards and yards of tumbling mats.

Yannick's hero was Houdini. He idolized the man—loved the way he could escape from anything. Yannick would have preferred this kind of entertainment, especially the chance to be internationally famous, but there was no market for escape artists. Houdini's acts took time. The longer acts, like when he freed himself from bank safes or straight jackets, took hours. People were skeptical these days. They no longer believed in the magical powers of the individual and demanded to know the secret of the trick.

"If I reveal one trick, the audience would catch on to all the others," Yannick complained to Rorie on one of their first dates.

"Is it all that simple?" Rorie asked.

"See?" Yannick said. "You can't stand not knowing."

It was early fall and they were sitting outside her apartment in broken-down, mismatched lawn chairs. The early evening air was cold, and they wore mittens to hold their beer cans.

"What I'd really like to be is the first person to tightrope walk across Niagara Falls," Yannick told her. He was balancing his beer can on his chin. From where she was sitting Rorie couldn't tell if it was full or empty until it spilled.

"I saw someone do that already," she said. "On television."

"You sure?" Yannick asked. They were undergraduates at Northern Michigan University. She was a fourth-year social work student and

Yannick was a theater major. He spent most afternoons working out with the gymnastics team, but rarely showed at meets. He was practicing tumbling, trying to perfect standing front flips with no running preparation.

"I think so," Rorie said. "*The Ed Sullivan Show*. When I was a kid."

"Oh thank God," Yannick said. "I'm absolutely terrified of water." Then he paused. "So was Houdini."

Rorie had heard of Houdini, but she didn't know anything about him.

"Well, I don't have any real proof he was afraid of water, but he got terribly seasick every time he crossed the ocean."

Rorie's backyard was built into a hill, and Yannick was trying to stand on his hands. The incline was steep. Yannick over-negotiated and kept flipping over backward, landing on his back.

"I'll get it," he said. "I'll get this right." He practiced walking on his hands over and over and over again until finally he could do it perfectly.

Rorie and Yannick got married the summer after he graduated from Northern. It took him six years to get through the program because he was so uninterested in going to classes. Rorie had finished the year before and had a job working for Marquette County on a government-funded program that brought art programs to rural schools. When Yannick got his degree in theater and speech communication, they moved south to Sarasota where he went to clown college. They spent two years down south. The seasonless months drove Rorie crazy, but she liked the people there. Everyone was a transplant. People moved in and out of their lives like customers through a turnstile at an amusement park.

Yannick specialized in juggling and tumbling at clown school, but didn't make any of the professional auditions. Rorie was glad he wouldn't be working for a circus. The acts hadn't changed much over the years. The caged animals, the sawdust, the cotton-candy trucks, and the tattooed workers were out of sync with the rest of the world and this depressed her. The circus traveled by trains or buses in the middle of the night and set up in the seedier sections of town. She did not want to live like this.

They moved back to Marquette. Supported by a grant from the Michigan Council on the Arts and a small bank loan, they went into business together—*Buffo's Brigade of Clowns*—even though Yannick was the only clown. Rorie took care of the business end and, soon after they installed their toll-free number, 1-800-BIG-CIRC(US), they started getting jobs. Marquette, almost five hundred miles north of Detroit, was an untapped area. Yannick was one of the few clowns north of the Mackinac Bridge, and Buffo's Brigade of Clowns, according to the Michigan Bell Yellow Pages, was the only entertainment company in the Upper Peninsula.

Yannick trained hard for everything he did. He understood the promise of getting the show just right, but more importantly he understood the use of mirrors and smoke screens. Constantly aware that things weren't always what they seemed, he understood the potential for a trick not working.

Familiar with the way he worked, Rorie later came to believe that Yannick spent the year before he moved out training to leave her. She thought he used their numerous fights and arguments as dry runs until he could be sure of a perfect getaway. He started small, arguing about empty ketchup bottles in the refrigerator, mixing white and dark T-shirts in the washing machine, and not getting the car gassed up. The arguments came more frequently, more intensely, and they became more abstract. Near the end, just before he left, she had no idea what they were fighting about. She could see the irony only after he was gone, but refused to enjoy any part of it. She would not be an appreciative audience for the failure of her own marriage.

Business had been bad the summer before he left—their worst three months since they started—Yannick was miserable. He had always had an incredible ego, and the long time with nothing to do drove him crazy. The only gig he had in July was for the Burga-Roo Restaurant chain in Negaunee. Yannick stood in the drive-through line and passed out balloons and discount hamburger coupons to any car with small children. The company asked him to wear a large smiley face. Burga-Roo was starting a chain of restaurants in the Upper Peninsula—this store was their first, so there was no telling how many jobs it could lead to. Yannick painted large circles all over his face—not exactly a grin—

and he looked more ridiculous than happy. He spent the afternoon sucking the helium out of the balloons and talking in a high, squeaky voice to anyone who would listen.

The next morning, he was intolerable. He woke up angry, and as the morning progressed, he got more and more restless. He had not quite washed all the greasepaint off his face, and all during their argument, Rorie wanted to lean over and wipe the traces of color from under his eyes, the long streak of blue from above his lip.

Rorie had said she was going to Mass that morning, but decided after a shower that she wasn't in the mood for church. Her change of plans irritated Yannick. She had been raised Catholic, but only went occasionally when she felt like singing or seeing people all dressed up. It was a sort of ritual that she didn't care for all the time. The day was hot and muggy, and Yannick started bitching about her not going.

"You said you were going to go, so you should go," he said.

"It's ten thirty," she said. "Mass is half over."

"Church is only an hour long?"

"Fifty minutes," she said.

"Christ," Yannick said. "That's just a waste of a wonderful building." He pushed his coffee cup to the center of the table. It was half-full and she drank it.

"The length of the Mass is hardly my fault," Rorie said.

"I think a spiritual life is important," Yannick said. "It gives a person added dimension."

"What do you know about spirituality?" Rorie asked, trying to keep the conversation light. "You're only a clown."

"I hate when you try to be funny," Yannick said.

"I forgot," Rorie said. "You're the comedian in the house."

She looked out the kitchen window and asked him why he had left the lawnmower outside when it was supposed to have rained the night before.

"There's nothing wrong with the lawnmower," he said, and she had to admit he was right about that. The lawnmower was standing there exactly where he had left it yesterday afternoon.

"But that's why we have the garage," she said. "So everything won't rust."

"Is that why we have a garage?" Yannick asked. "I thought we had one because it was here when we moved in." He began tearing strips off the newspaper and cutting them into shapes. He was not doing this for any reason except to annoy her. She had been on a recycling binge and liked to keep the newspapers folded so that they fit into the blue bins the city picked up at the curb every other Tuesday morning.

"You change the subject when you're stuck and can't think of anything to say," Yannick accused her.

"Doesn't everybody?"

"We were talking about your spiritual life, and when you feel defensive, you start talking about something you think I did wrong."

"We were talking about my lack of a spiritual life," she reminded him. "Wasn't that the problem of the morning?"

The coffee granules had soaked through the filter and ruined the taste of the coffee.

"God, you're so easy to read," Yannick said.

Rorie stopped rinsing out her coffee mug. "What's that supposed to mean?"

"Just that," Yannick said. "You're the most predictable person I know."

Yannick agreed to go for a walk, and they went down to the beach barefoot. Lake Superior was only half a block from their house. MacArthur's Cove was crowded with sunbathers. A Frisbee game was in progress. The players had a cooler of beer, and a few of them waved to Rorie and Yannick and called out for them to join in. Rorie waved without saying anything, hoping they could come back and play after their argument. Team sports frustrated Yannick, but Rorie felt like doing something physical.

Rorie and Yannick walked north towards Presque Isle, the small state park at the far north end of the beach, where the college kids hung out. They were silent for about fifteen minutes and then Rorie asked him what was wrong.

"You live your life from day to day without going any deeper, and you're happy with that."

He was definitely having an affair. This crazed, nonsensical talk was definitely that of a man being unfaithful to his wife, and Rorie began imagining who the other woman might be.

"I'm a complicated person," Yannick said. "Being a clown means I have two lives. Maybe more. I have levels of interest. Things that you don't know about."

"What is it exactly we're arguing about?"

"I know everything about you," Yannick said.

"You should," Rorie said. "We've been married for six years."

"You don't have any secrets," Yannick said, and Rorie immediately thought of everything she had ever kept from him.

"They really wouldn't be secrets if you knew about them, would they?" she asked.

"Don't you think people are more interesting when they have secrets?"

With the strong northerly winds, the lake acted like it was guided by tides, and Rorie moved up the beach to stay out of the water.

"Actually," Rorie stopped walking. "I do have one secret."

"I don't believe it," Yannick said.

"Oh yes I do."

"What is it?"

"The secret is that this conversation is making me sick," Rorie said.

Yannick made a noise, low in his throat. Rorie half-expected him to scream. Instead he ran toward the lake and dove into the water. There had been a lot of rain the last weeks in July, and Lake Superior was breath-stopping cold. He was not a good swimmer, and he thrashed in the water, making whitewater waves on the calm surface. For all his movement, he didn't go anywhere, and after a few minutes he stood and walked up the beach.

He was shivering and Rorie went over to him. He stood with his arms folded across his chest.

"I don't understand what we're arguing about," Rorie said. The water had smeared the greasepaint and he looked like he was crying colors.

"Of course you don't," Yannick stripped off his T-shirt and stood there in the sun, trying to warm himself.

"Tell me," she begged.

"No," he said. "I can't."

At that moment, Rorie no longer believed he was having an affair. Sleeping with another woman would not cause this much frustration. Not in Yannick. They had been together long enough that an affair would not necessarily mean the end of their marriage.

Yannick balled up his T-shirt and threw it onto the white sand. He was in perfect shape. He had been lifting free weights for almost three years now. His nonfat, no-meat diet made his skin glow, and he looked better than he had when they got married. She kicked his T-shirt into the lake, but as soon as he walked away she leaned over and picked it up. The cotton material was heavy and she stretched it over the rocks to dry.

They were tired of working together, she decided. They had been in the clown business in a town too small to support it way too long. She should give him some room and more time alone. Maybe separate vacations this summer and then they could decide what to do with the business. He could hire someone new and she could go back and work for the county or do something independent of him. This would give them the distance they both needed.

The note Yannick left on the kitchen table was simple, "Gone. Back later." But he had signed it "Love, me."

Things had a way of working out; maybe it was best to leave him alone until he got himself out of his foul mood. She told herself that everyone fought. It was hard to live without arguments. They had a good marriage—better than most people's. Their life, because of Yannick's clowning, was filled with games and fun. These games defined almost all aspects of their life together—even in bed. Rorie had not had many sexual encounters before Yannick and sex was not something she considered fun, but all that had changed when she met Yannick.

Yannick was the one who usually initiated the games when they were in bed. Rorie could only remember one time when she told him she had a game they could play. He had been excited and asked her what she wanted him to do.

"Let's say this scene takes place after a war," Rorie had told him. She didn't have it planned out, and though she knew where she wanted it to end up, she wasn't sure how to get there.

"What war?"

"That doesn't matter," Rorie said and then she changed her mind. "A war that involves torture."

"Torture?"

"The enemy has cut your vocal chords," she said.

"Why?"

"Does it matter?"

"If I'm going to do this right, it matters," Yannick said. "Now come on. I always give you your full story."

"Okay. They needed some information and you refused to give it to them."

"Gruesome," Yannick said. "This sounds really gruesome."

"Ready?" Rorie asked. She had taken off her robe and got into bed. Yannick had stood there looking confused.

"So what do I do?" Yannick asked. "What's my role in the fantasy?"

"I'm your wife who hasn't seen you in five years and you have to make love to me."

"And?"

"And you can't talk." Rorie had laughed at that point, but it still took Yannick a few minutes to catch on that she was trying to get him to shut up when they made love. Yannick thought it was hysterical and it became one of their best jokes. One of them only had to say war, soldier, or vocal chords to get the other to laugh. She wanted to remind him that there had been a time when they had had fun together. No matter what had happened, they always had fun doing it.

That had changed; Rorie was no longer having fun.

Yannick moved out on Halloween night. Rorie had become an expert on trivia and was well aware that Houdini had died on October 31, 1926, in Metropolitan Detroit's Grace Hospital. "An escape artist dying on Halloween?" Yannick had once said. "Think of the odds of that happening. It's too perfect." So the first thing Rorie thought when she came home from Jan's costume party, the one Yannick refused to go to—clowns didn't dress up on Halloween—and found Yannick's practice room bare, his clothes and books moved out of their bedroom, was that Yannick was playing some kind of trick. It couldn't be random. It had to be a joke. But there was nothing amusing about his disappearance.

She was stunned by the conceit of his leaving. To be an egomaniac in the clown business helped a performance, and Yannick was always honest about his desire for attention, but this was too much.

After Yannick left, Rorie had problems sleeping at night. She stayed up drinking wine and watching the passing car headlights illuminate the dark house.

Yannick sent her two postcards. They had no stamps or postmarks on them. She found them in the mailbox long after the mailman had come by, so she knew he had put them there himself. The first said that he was sorry and that he'd call her as soon as he could. The other said that he was a bad person, that he had always been a bad person and that he was sure he was going to get punished for treating her so poorly. The handwriting was Yannick's, but the writing was smaller, as if he was paying too much attention to the words. Rorie was almost sure he was drunk when he wrote them.

This made her think he might be up with his father in L'Anse. She sat on the stool next to the telephone and tucked her feet in the folds of her bathrobe.

Yannick's father answered after four or five rings.

Rorie said her name a couple of times, and when she was sure he understood who she was, she asked if he had seen Yannick.

"Is he gone?" his father asked. He repeated the same question several times until it sounded like a song. "Is he gone? Is he gone? Is he gone?"

"He left a week ago," she said. She was not embarrassed to admit this to him.

"He's not here," his father said, and she could not tell if he had been drinking. "Do you want me to call you if he shows up?"

"Could you?" Rorie said, and she began to cry.

"I'll find him for you," he said, talking about his son as if he were a dog. And without saying anything else, he hung up.

Yannick's accusations about her lack of spirituality might have been true. But what Rorie didn't understand about spirituality, she did know about secrets. She knew what it was to keep a secret from someone and she understood why you protected the person you loved with silence.

Her secret happened the winter before they were married. She had been bothering him about taking her home to meet his parents. They had already started talking about the wedding and she thought it'd be a good idea if they told his parents. She wanted a big wedding in her home parish in Detroit. She would be the first of her high school girlfriends to get married, and she imagined a large reception with everyone drinking and dancing, everyone having a good time.

L'Anse was only a hundred miles northwest of Marquette, and Yannick went back on weekends and during the semester breaks. He worked at one of the local diners whenever he could. The tips were good, and it was worth the two-hour hitchhike there and back.

"Are you embarrassed?" she asked over pizza and beers in the Tip-It-Inn one night. "It's so cliché to be ashamed about where you come from. No one likes their hometown."

"I never hear you complaining about Detroit."

"I'm not really from Detroit," Rorie said. "I'm from Warren."

"Warren then," Yannick said. "What's wrong with Warren?"

"It's flat," Rorie said.

"That's it?" Yannick laughed. "That's all that's wrong with Warren?"

Two days later, when Yannick got a call to work a Sunday breakfast shift up at Palosaari's Pastries, he asked Rorie to go with him and they hitchhiked up together.

Rorie knew L'Anse meant "bay" in French. She knew the cut the Keweenaw Bay made into the land mass was the largest on the American side of Lake Superior, but the small, lonely town she saw when they got there was nothing like what she had imagined. The place, with its wide treeless streets, was cold and empty. Most of the businesses were boarded up along the main street, and the houses were covered in sheets of cloudy plastic to protect them from the wind, but it gave the impression that they were only half built. The town looked abandoned and lost—a long time ago—to the past.

Rorie already knew about Yannick's hesitation to talk about his family. Yannick seemed irritated at her questions about his home life, as if he were embarrassed. She knew his parents did not live together and that his father drank too much.

No one was home at his father's, but the front door was open. It was a small cabin, two rooms with a screened-in side porch half-filled with snow.

"He wanders," Yannick said as if this explained everything.

They stayed out past closing time at the bar, and she complained on the way home that she might not have a chance to meet his father.

"He's bringing you into the diner tomorrow," Yannick explained. "He'll take you around and show you the highlights of L'Anse."

"I thought you just did that," she said.

"I showed you the bars," Yannick said. "There's a lot more to see of L'Anse, I think." They laughed, and she didn't say anything more about it.

Yannick's father was sleeping on the couch. The place was ice-cold. Yannick covered his father with the blanket off the bed and they slept under a cotton sheet in their jeans and sweaters.

Yannick woke up the next morning to the sound of car tires on the gravel. He pushed back the sleeping bag covering the window and swore. It was daylight, but just barely. "My ride to work is here," he said and put on his clean but wrinkled white shirt and a pair of khakis. The room was warmer; the heat must have kicked on in the middle of the night, and Rorie was awake only long enough to pull off her shirt and pants. She didn't hear the car leave and she didn't hear Yannick's father come into the room. She was aware of a strange smell close to her face. The odor was rancid and she pushed it away with her hands.

He had his lips over her breast and was licking her nipple. She cried out, but before she could hit him, he grabbed her hands and held them at her sides. He licked her nipple until it got hard and she turned away so she would not have to look at what he was doing. She felt his tongue sliding down her stomach. She could feel his legs on either side of hers and she stayed still so he would not think she was moving with him.

"I don't see girls like you around here," he said.

"Get off," she begged. "Get off me." She closed her eyes and pushed to get him off, but he was heavy and determined. She felt his hair between her legs, his lips and tongue pulling at the elastic of her underwear; she screamed. She bent her knees and kicked him off the bed.

"Go away," she screamed at him. She pulled the cotton sheet over her head because she was too afraid to look at him.

When she was sure he was gone from the room, she got up and dressed as fast as she could. Her ski jacket was hanging on the back of the chair in the other room, but she went out the front door without it. She walked to the cabin across the way and knocked, but the wood door, splintered near the lock, was open. Except for the snow piled under the missing glass panes in the window, the cabin was empty.

Yannick's father made a lot of noise coming out of the house. He looked into the passenger window of his truck, then turned around and looked under the tarp covering the bed of the truck. When he saw her on the porch of the other cabin, he tossed her coat across the drive as if he understood that she did not want him near.

She sat on the stoop of the other cabin and kicked her foot against a large rock until she could feel the skin on her toes breaking. The air was cold and she put her hand up to her mouth and breathed through her fingers to warm the air before it got down to her lungs. She would call the bus station when he left and ask what time the bus for Marquette was. If he locked the door, she would throw something through the window.

"You can't walk to town from here." He kicked the snow from the tires. "It's seven miles. You'll freeze to death."

Rorie stayed on the stoop, the cold cement already numbing her butt. He turned then, his eyes were glassed over. "I'll take you to Yannick," he said.

She got in and sat as far from him as she could. The gear panel was on the floor between them, and every time he leaned over to shift gears, she flinched.

She did not know the way into town, and when he pulled off onto a side road, she swallowed the panic in her throat. This was her fiancé's father. He could not really mean her harm, she told herself. Still, she wrapped her fingers around the door handle, ready to run when he pulled the truck to the side of the road. There was a clearing off to her side; a plow had recently come through and packed the snow.

"Two years ago," he said, "we had more snow than anywhere else in the country."

In the center of the clearing was a thirty- or forty-foot-high sign. It was three feet wide and bright red. The inches were marked off in large dark letters. "1977–1978 RECORD HIGH SNOWFALL," it said at the very top of the sign. There was a large arrow pointed to the number—390.4 inches.

"One year," Yannick's father said, and she could smell the peppermint schnapps across the cold truck. "All that snow fell here." He was nervous. "Don't tell Yannick," he stuttered. "Don't tell Yannick. Don't tell Yannick. Don't tell Yannick."

Rorie nodded, but she would not look at him.

"Say it," he pleaded.

"I won't tell Yannick," Rorie said, and she put her face to the cold glass of the window and let the frost bite her tears from her eyes.

"Thank you," he said and started back to town.

Because she had been raised to be polite, she told him he was welcome.

"Don't take it personally," Yannick said. His father had dropped her off at the corner. Neither one of them said good-bye, or Yannick thought Rorie might be upset that he hadn't come in for breakfast. "Sundays aren't his best days."

Rorie started to say something, but Yannick was busy carrying out orders and it took him a few minutes to get back to her table.

"You and Dad get along okay?" Yannick asked. Rorie did not know if this kind of thing had ever happened before, but when she looked at Yannick she saw that he was adding figures on his note pad and was just making conversation. She knew him well enough to know that he was not suspicious.

"He took me up the road and showed me the snowfall sign," Rorie said. The coffee was making her queasy. She bit a section of the crust from the toast Yannick had brought over, but it was cold and she could not swallow it. She spit it up into her napkin and folded it beside her plate.

Later that afternoon, when he got off work, Yannick insisted they stop to say good-bye to his father.

"It's late," Rorie said. "We should get going back."

The sky was losing light and she didn't like the idea of standing on the highway in the dark. He told her five minutes wouldn't matter. She didn't want to go back to the house—she never wanted to see his father again—but she couldn't let Yannick know anything was wrong.

His father was standing at the stove in the kitchen. "Dinner. Dinner. Dinner," Yannick's father said, motioning to the pots in front of him.

"We don't have time," Rorie said quickly. She could not sit down to a meal.

"She's afraid of the dark, pop," Yannick said. He put his arm around his father's shoulders. "We better not stay."

His father cleared away the plates he had set on the table and turned off the burner under one of the pans. His movements were large; the kitchen shrunk with his weight and clumsiness.

"Food. Food. Food," he said, as if this were not obvious.

"Listen, bud," Yannick talked loudly as if his father had gone deaf. "We're going to hit the road. Rorie's not used to hitchhiking. They don't do this kind of thing in Detroit."

His father mumbled for them to wait. If they couldn't eat there, then they could take the food with them. He opened the cupboard over the sink and rummaged through the stack of newspapers. She could have predicted that he would knock everything over, and he did. Yannick was right behind him, and he held him when the weight of the falling papers almost knocked him over.

He found a couple of brown grocery bags and dumped the chicken into one of them. He spooned mashed potatoes and green beans and corn into the other. He had not sufficiently drained the water from the vegetables, and the paper bags soaked through quickly.

"Crazy old man," Yannick said when they were halfway down the drive. Rorie knew that he was embarrassed about his father, but she could not think of anyone else's feelings at the moment. She was near panicked in her desire to get out of town.

A semi-truck, going north, blew by. Yannick held her and then they crossed the road and stood on the berm. The sky was losing the last of its light. The brown paper bags were dripping with grease. The bottoms soon would get too wet and they would burst open.

"This is bad," Yannick said. The highway was empty—they were standing on a long stretch with no bends or curves and she could see that no one was coming south—but they hadn't been standing there that long. They had to give it some time.

"What's wrong?" she asked.

"Wolves." His bag was already starting to leak through. She could see a yellowish liquid dripping on the snow. She held her bag away from her body, not wanting anything to get on her.

"Let's throw it away." Rorie started to toss the bag into the ditch, but Yannick stopped her. He had turned so that his voice went into the wind. But when he motioned her to follow him, she did. The snow was crusted in the steep ditch and their weight broke the surface with each footfall. The winds had swept most of the deep snow from the open field, and they walked another hundred feet or so before stopping near a large tree.

Yannick crouched down at the base of the tree and cleared away the snow and ice until the frozen earth showed.

"What are we doing?" she asked.

"Burying the food," Yannick said.

"Why?" she asked. The wind had already frozen her chin, and she tried to move her head so that it was more protected in her scarf.

"So the wolves won't get us."

Rorie looked around. The sun was now gone, the sky faintly pink at the horizon line. They were all alone, and she was no longer afraid.

"Don't they have wolves in Detroit?" Yannick asked, though he clearly knew the answer.

"No," Rorie said suddenly, feeling that everything was going to be all right. "We have Hudson's and Saks Fifth Avenue and J. C. Penney's, and a bunch of car factories. Gas stations, lots and lots of people, but no wolves."

Yannick dug for a few more minutes, but the ground was frozen and would not give. Rorie brushed some snow away from a thick root and set her bag down there. Yannick continued digging with the side of his gloves, but the tough earth did not move. He stood up and set some pine branches over on top of both bags. The chicken was still raw and she could smell the uncooked meat when they turned back to the road.

This was her secret. It was not the kind of thing a son should ever hear about his father. In the six years she was married to Yannick, she never learned anything more about the possibilities of wolves attacking people on highways in the early evening light, and she never broke her promise to her father-in-law.

Matthew Gavin Frank

ENDNOTES FOR CUDIGHI

Though cudighi was brought to the Upper Peninsula of Michigan by Italian immigrants from the Lombardy region (debatable!), it is the French, after whom so many Upper Midwestern towns are named, who claim ownership of its invention by claiming ownership of the invention of all sausage.

Loosely translated from the Italian, means *fuck you and your tarragon.*

Though the act of smoking meats as a preservative measure was initially popular solely with the Romans, the French claim ownership of the salting method responsible for the first hams and sausages. According to the text "Heptameron," by Queen Marguerite of Naverre (1492–1549), a poor Pyrenees pig stumbled over its trotters and fell into the headwaters of a natural salt spring stream on the outskirts of the town Salies-de-Bearn. The clumsy beast drowned, its body rescued by a team of herdsmen, and eaten by the townsfolk during an impromptu feast. Blown away by the flavor the salt spring imparted to the meat, the locals began to mimic the salting procedure, and word, as they say, got out.

So much depends on the word *clove* and the word *cinnamon* and the word *nutmeg* and the word *allspice* and the word *garlic* and the words *red pepper* and the word *anise* and the word *fat* and *salt* and *salt* and *salt*, which, though it can be excruciating, can stanch an open wound.

In this way, not only were the horses saved, but Père Jacques Marquette himself, without the spices the explorers used to savor their sausage, would have bled out that night.

In the Upper Peninsula of Michigan, this time of year, shivering, words are exiles, and exiles bastardized. In this is new language, and the names of the sausages . . .

Here, in the winter, those who descend from Lombardy take their sausage with red wine similarly spiced with clove, cinnamon, anise . . .

Though cudighi's origins have been traced back some six thousand years, the art really gained a foothold during the Western Roman Empire when the ruling class's palates demanded a more refined cuisine (they went so far as to legislate ways of preserving pig joints), and was elevated to operatic status in France after the Empire's fall in the fifth century. Originally, as now, the sausage dealt primarily with pork, which, according to Galen, a second-century Roman doctor (of Greek origin), first entered into the human diet via cannibal cultures, as the meat of the pig most closely resembles that of the human in flavor.

In hot climes, we eat each other traditionally; in cold ones like this, we do so only desperately.

Here, we must question the nature of "true" in *The Last True Wilderness of the Midwest*, implying the falsity of other trees, trees elsewhere, Indiana trees and Minnesota trees and Illinois trees. The trees in Ohio are bald-faced liars and the Iowa trees are imported. Somewhere, beneath these, the first true wilderness shades the silkworms, and, should they have dined on beet greens, their red thread, and the rainwater going rank in the shells of their halved cocoons.

In Lombardy, the poplar questions its existence, wonders if it shares *popular*'s origin.

The cocoon predicts the casing.

The poplar, in the worst of its dreams, is of the people, but not of Upper Michigan.

Natural casing, nature of.

To naturally case something, another thing must first unnaturally be uncased.

Cudighi is a coat made of sheepskin.

A parka stuffed with the feathers of so many dead birds. One may wonder, heart-burning past midnight with too many cudighi sandwiches, where all the birds' meat went. All of the bills, blood, brains, feet.

So much depends on the grain of the grind.

Coarsely, we squeeze into our jackets and our brains tell us that we're warmer.

We are ready for this world, and its towns and restaurants and trails and bicyclists and old drunk men with dead wives named Mona Lisa, and Lake Superior to poach us beyond trichinosis.

This is the true wilderness of the Midwest.

Encasing a region in a slogan helps to make its winter more bearable.

We remember the Treaty of Lodi with hot tongues and freezing lips. In the Wooden Nickel, Paolo throws a dart at Aarne.

Because this is a small town, the meth lab, by definition, is close to the Walgreens.

In the Upper Peninsula, I saw a cauldron of considerable size only once. In it, a grad student of mine was boiling the head of a doe. *Preparing it,* were the words he used. The cauldron's feet were held in place with the ice. The fire couldn't melt all of it. I think he detected my shock, but mistook its source, and suggested we go have some lunch. I ordered the cudighi on a hot dog bun with poppy seeds and coleslaw. He had the whitefish sandwich with sweet potato fries. I put both meals on the university credit card.

Some believe *cudighi* is an endearment for *cotechino*, a sausage from Gavello, Italy, a hamlet whose population has been steadily decreasing since 1951.

Cudighi as cute exodus, as baby-fied exile to a seven-month winter.

As a cruel mathematic: as bovine regurgitation + a juvenile penchant for self-reference + a phlegmatic *hello* . . .

Cudighi as indifference toward equality.

Cudighi, the addition of.

Say *cudighi* in Italy, and no one will understand you. It is ours now, the last true ours of the Midwest.

Loosely translated from the Italian, means *the lavender is shit*. We must be careful. The lavender is shit.

Greek mythology further details the importance of the pig, citing that Zeus, as an infant god, was sustained by the milk of a prominent sow.

"A coarse grind is fine."

I overheard someone say that the smell of cudighi cooking is *celestial*. Juice spitting through the casing. Her comment predicted the aurora borealis that drew green lassos over Lake Superior. The story of the aurora borealis, as rendered on the Channel 3 Nightly News, predicted *. . . went missing . . . last seen on his snowmobile at the Mt. Marquette trailhead*, which predicted the commercial advertising *two-buck Ladies' Night cudighis*. The frost on our bedroom window looks churchly.

We must be careful.

In Italy's Emilia-Romagna region, a hush falls over the village of Ferrara. Talk of its indigenous *salamina da sugo* rarely breaches its borders, though this anarchic sausage is seen by some as a precursor to the cudighi of Michigan's Upper Peninsula. Perennially crowning the Christmas tables of the Ferrarese, the mysterious and controversial dish remains out of reach for the rest of the world, allowable only via reinvention in another last true wilderness.

The salamina cum cudighi style of sausage was first documented in the fifteenth-century letter from Lorenzo il Magnifico to Duke Ercole II d'Este. Apparently, the first to produce the product were the "porcaioli" of the Trentio and Bormio mountains. Eventually, they migrated into the Po valley, and then into the area that was to become Ferrara. Not a single discovered document mentioned salamina da sugo again, until 1722.

Capturing the artistic heart and palate of writer Antonio Frizzi, salamina da sugo became the object of his poem, "Salamoide."

Frizzi writes, "I mix the pig's liver with its meat, put an iron on top, and step on the iron."

Frizzi went on further to speculate that the pigs destined to become salamina are born carrying the spirits of all dead women. In tasting it, he wrote, one has difficulty separating flavor from verse.

Often invoked as an incurable aphrodisiac, the salamina (or salama, as it is often called) was a popular meal at wedding banquets and brothels. The dish was reputed to soften the skin and add life to the blood of newlyweds, as well as prepare the "ladies of the night" for their customers.

The Slow Food Movement, which, among other revolutionary tasks, takes it upon themselves to rescue "endangered" foods from the global-warming-esque jaws of overregulation (from governmental departments of "health"), flies the salamina da sugo as one of their primary flagships. This is, indeed, a nearly extinct breed of sausage, stirring the Slow Food Movement to educate the masses via protest in an attempt to lift it from certain death.

Today, the salamina remains commercially illegal, reserved for back-alley gourmands, and cultish, hooded dinner parties, and those of us Upper Midwesterners who take it in numbed form, lifted from the frozen food tubs at the EconoFoods.

The dish begins with the grinding of the "less noble" but more flavorful parts of the pig: liver, tongue, belly, shoulder, chin, top neck, throat lard, cheek, thigh. The ground meat is then coupled and cured with an array of spices—types and amounts differ with each producer. Typical spices include salt, pepper, nutmeg, cinnamon, clove, and garlic. Red wine (approximately two liters per ten kilograms of meat) is added to the mixture—usually a Sangiovese, Barbera, or Semisecco del Bosco Eliceo. Certain producers also add rum, grappa, or brandy.

The mixture is then packed into a pork bladder, tied with twine, and traditionally divided into eight segments. In a well-ventilated, dark chamber, at about fifty-degrees Fahrenheit, the salamina is hung to ripen and age for at least one year. During this time, the salamina is periodically brushed with olive oil and vinegar.

Once sufficiently aged, the salamina will bear a protective coating of white mold. Prior to preparation, the mold is rinsed away and the cased meat is soaked in lukewarm water for at least twelve hours. After the soaking session, the salamina is placed inside a cloth bag, which is then tied to the center of a long wooden stick. The stick is draped across the top of a large cauldron, so that the salamina bag is hanging in the middle, away from the pot's bottom and sides. The cauldron is filled with water, and the salamina cooks for about four hours at a low simmer. Once ready, the salamina is cut from the bag and gently removed from its casing with a spoon. The salamina's wine is released during the cooking process, yielding a viscous and spicy sauce.

Like our wilderness and our winter and our sausage, we are barely legal and stubbornly clandestine. We are the Culinary Underground, gathering in windowless spaces, camps in the woods, reading by candlelight, ancient farmland recipes, and passing samples of banned foodstuffs. We, and the salamina and its cudighi offspring, will survive in the coldest attics of the world.

This part of the world is confusing and beautiful.

Try it with mustard.

ELEMENTS OF THE PASTY

It's not like this with Cream of Mushroom soup and La Choy Fried Onions. In the pasty, in the singular shell, dinner shares space with dessert. We start with dinner and eat downward. It's not like this with Hot Dish, with casserole, with pizza with a Saltine crust. In the pasty is an eating toward. In the pasty is difficulty breathing, is eyes adjusting to the mineshaft dark and to the daylight, is anticipation, is harbinger, is a whole new world beyond the chuck and the rutabaga, is apples-and-cinnamon, is an eating toward, and an eating toward sweetness.

———

My uncle has a bumper sticker that says FUCK CORNWALL, THIS IS MICHIGAN. If my uncle doesn't have this bumper sticker, then he has black lung, and if he doesn't have black lung, then he's depressed due to a lack of light, and if he's not depressed due to a lack of light, he can call this only soul-sickness, can only lament the ways in which we're not jacketed in pastry dough brushed with egg yolk, a crust that will protect us from birds who scream from the dark, from the lack of air that, in the beginning, seemed to exhilarate.

———

This is goal-oriented eating. The meat as a means to an end. Macerated plums on Thursday. The brake to a shaking hand. In the bath of the headlamp is the pasty and the hand that holds it. The batteries here are strong. Once we bite through the crust, release the steam, the heat, the wet, something of the ghost and something of the future, things begin to go cold, dry, the batteries here are the only things that are strong. Tomorrow, I want to lie in bed all day. It's good to have a goal.

———

In Michigan's Upper Peninsula, from 1843 through the 1920s, pure native copper just about leaked from the earth, exploded from it, and towns were established and boomed, and folks ate food and drank liquor and men spread their legs and women spread their legs and with food and liquor and spread legs made descendants who can visit these towns in the name of communion and reunion and union and none, and we call these gatherings *heartfelt* and we call these gatherings *historical*, and we use words like *ancestry* and *inheritance* and we stand on the rock piles and bluffs and tailings of Central Mine and Gay and Mandan and Cliff and Delaware and Phoenix and we eat pasties not because we need to, but because they are some sort of souvenir, some kind of shaft that leads, definitively down, toward something like heritage, something makeshift and collapsible and we pretend that these towns are not popularly preceded by the word *ghost*.

———

The old Phoenix church, in 1858, was called St. Mary's. Later, it was disassembled and rebuilt and renamed The Church of the Assumption.

———

We assume there are meanings in names.

———

The Ontonagon Boulder, of the Upper Peninsula's village of Old Victoria, is a 3,708-pound massif of native copper. It can now be found in the Smithsonian Institute's National Museum of Natural History in Washington, DC, where, should a tourist decide not to read the exhibit's plastic 3 x 5 placard, he or she will wonder about the specialness of this big, ugly rock.

———

Ontonagon, in the Chippewa language, translates as "Lost Bowl." Regarding the pasty, I'm not sure what this should mean.

According to a travel brochure titled, *Visit the Upper Peninsula of Michigan's world-famous "Copper Country,"* Old Victoria is "a very picturesque ghost town."

———

The atomic weight of copper is 63.55 g/mol. The atomic weight of iron is 55.85. The atomic weight of sulfur is 32.07. The atomic weight of gold is 196.97. The average pasty—a baked pastry shell, half of which includes a savory dinner of stewed meat and root vegetable, half of which includes dessert—weighs two pounds. The average human lung weighs about 14 ounces, so much heavier than this underground air, so much lighter than the pasty.

———

While many immigrant miners in the Upper Peninsula were from Cornwall, many more were Finn, Austrian, Croatian, Italian, Canadian, and Swedish. Each group impacted the pasty's regional evolution, with seasoning, with ingredient. Culinary arguments were fierce. Regardless, each version varied little, and each version was easily portable, heavy and hearty, but clutchable in one hand, and each version, in the cold of the deep, could be heated up on a shovel held over the candle flame of the miner's headlamp. The pasties are cooking. The canaries are screaming. Someone coughs.

———

The U.P. pasty, when compared to the Cornish variety, contained larger chunks of vegetable, a higher ratio of vegetable to meat, encased in a thinner crust.

———

The U.P. pasty as thin-skinned, even in all of this winter, the weather closer to the blood.

———

The U.P. pasty as a little of this, a little of that, as Yiddish, as Fanagolo, as Esperanto, and the language through which we all can communicate up here/down here, as a means to understanding, as overused symbology, as cliché, as Kumbaya, as all things savory sharing space with all things sweet. As reminder. As anchor.

———

Often, a homestead requires leaving home, and then never leaving the homestead. A life of two places. For the subsequent generations, it requires never leaving home in the first place. The pasty as perspective, encased in a hard crust. As riding a snowmobile before you can walk. As your great-grandson doing the same thing. As *I remember when I . . .*

———

An 1861 proverb proclaimed that the more ingredients one crams into the pasty, the more protection one has from the devil, as the devil may fear that he may end up as just another ingredient for the filling.

———

On the playgrounds of the turn-of-the-century U.P., schoolboys would sing:

> Matthew, Mark, Luke, and John
> Ate a pasty five feet long,
> Bit it once, bit it twice,
> Oh, my Lord, it's full of mice.

The pasty sits fixed in the hands of the miner, poised, poisoned.

———

Breton may have said, *They lowered a humpback into a copper mine to determine the quality of its air. The human lung can hold only six liters of breath, which is nothing compared to Lake Superior. Where are the headlamps when you need them? My uncle took them into the mine. He says, Whales are the canaries of the ocean. He says, The pasty is no kind of savior.*

———

Regarding the Quincy Mine Shelter, from the aforementioned brochure, "Hopefully this historic site will be restored." An eating toward. Before we die, we take the elevator up. It takes a few seconds to recognize the sun.

———

The pasty as doubling back on itself, as a confused plot line, as a figure eight, Möbius strip, infinity, a late bite downward, toward the sweet, the sweet being closest to the hands.

———

In the candle-shadow of the pasty and the birds and the shovel, coughing, we can't tell where umbra becomes penumbra becomes antumbra. We can't tell hands from feet. We can't tell if that's a shadow dying, or a man. We can't tell if the body is broken, or celestial.

———

So, we eat.

Steve Hamilton

WATCHING US

When I turned the key, I didn't hear anything. Not even that little clicking sound you might hear when the alternator is shot. Just nothing. I sat there in the car, watching my own breath, saying to myself, I am dead. My life is over. This whole thing has been a big mistake.

I got out of the car and went back up the path I had dug from the house. I couldn't help but wonder how long I could survive if I stayed outside. It was twelve below, cold enough that I was already starting to lose the feeling in my fingers, but I did the math anyway and finally came up with better odds inside the house, even though Joanne would be there waiting for me.

It was the worst winter I had ever seen, and even for the U.P. it was apparently on the wrong side of normal. The snow came hard and fast like it meant to wipe out any trace of us. Then somehow after it snowed for a few days it would warm up just enough to melt the top inch or two. Then another day of bitter cold and the top of the snow would become like white stone, until more fresh snow would cover it again. So it continued, layer after layer. I stomped the snow from my boots as I entered the house. Joanne came from the kitchen to look at me.

"It won't start," I said.

"Did you put on the engine warmer like your uncle told you?"

"No," I said. "I didn't think it would get this cold again. It was over forty yesterday."

She shook her head and went back to the kitchen, leaving me standing there in the hallway. I took my boots off slowly. I felt old and heavy and useless, not sure what to do next. Like it was my fault the weather was this bad or that we had ended up here in the first place. Like this had been my plan all along.

I went into the kitchen and stood behind her while she looked through the cupboards. "It's supposed to warm up again tomorrow," I said. "I'm sure it will start then. If not, I'm sure one of the neighbors will give us a jump."

"The nearest house is a half mile away. I don't think he even qualifies as a neighbor."

"Everybody is a neighbor up here. That's one thing you have to admit. If I go out to the road, the first car that comes by will stop. Besides, we have enough food, don't we? I can go to the store tomorrow."

She shrugged her shoulders and left the kitchen. I went down to the basement. It was my uncle's summer house, so naturally everything I laid eyes on belonged to him. The outboard motor, the patio furniture, everything he had brought inside for the winter, because that's the kind of thing you do if you have your head on straight. Everything was buttoned up tight, and it would have stayed that way until spring if I hadn't called him. We're losing the house, I said. We have no place to go. I know you've got that place up north. Up in Ishpeming.

"We don't belong up here," she had said to me the first day we were here. "We don't know anything about this place."

"It's not so bad. The people are nice. We have a place to stay. For a while, anyway. It's not forever."

"Winter feels like forever," she had said. "Up here, I'm sure of it."

Hard to argue. But at least we could stay warm. Problem was, my uncle didn't have a lot of firewood. Even if you're like my uncle and you're ready for everything, you don't buy a lot of wood if you're going to lock up the house by Labor Day. We'd have to buy our own, he had told me. We'd better get right on that, too, if we didn't want to freeze to death.

But the money didn't go quite that far. So I poked around and found the pile of scrap wood next to my uncle's workbench. I collected an armload and brought it back upstairs. Joanne was in the living room now, sitting by the wood stove.

"What in the world are you doing?" she asked.

"I'm going to burn some of this lumber. We've got plenty."

"Oh, now this is too much," she said. "That's treated lumber you're putting in there, you realize that. If we don't starve to death first, we'll die from the fumes. And then in the springtime they'll find our dead bodies in here. That'll be a damned pretty sight."

"Well, I guess it won't matter much to us if we're dead."

She left the room. She was running out of rooms to walk out of. I went back outside and shoveled a path from the back door to the bird feeder on the back of the porch. My uncle had plenty of birdseed on hand. If we weren't here, the birds wouldn't be getting any of it, so that was one thing in our favor right there. One thing I was doing right.

The snow was nearly up to my waist, more snow than I'd ever seen before, and it was nearly impossible to get through all of the frozen layers. I had to stop every couple minutes to catch my breath and straighten out my back. I used to be in shape, I thought. I used to be an athlete.

Later, after a make-do dinner from the last of the cans, I sat in the living room watching television while Joanne did the dishes. I sat there and listened to her work at it until she finally spoke.

"Hey, come in here," she said.

"What is it?" I said, going into the kitchen. For some reason, she had turned out the light.

"There's something in the backyard."

"What is it?"

"I don't know. Take a look."

I looked out the window above the sink. I couldn't see anything except the bird feeder and the woods beyond it.

"Where am I looking? I don't see anything."

"It's right there, right in front of the woods."

When my eyes became adjusted to the dark, I made out a shape. "Now I see something. What the—"

"I think it moved," she said. "It must be an animal."

"Hold on." I went over by the back door and turned on the back porch light. "Can you see any better now?"

"I see a pair of eyes now."

I joined her at the window and looked out at the two glowing red dots in the darkness.

"Can you see those eyes?" she said. "It's like it's watching us."

"I'm gonna get the flashlight."

"Don't go out there!"

"Don't worry. I'm just going to shine the flashlight on it from the back porch."

I got the flashlight from the closet and went out the back door. The air smelled like we would be getting more snow soon. I went to the back of the porch and pointed the flashlight toward the edge of the woods.

It was a deer. I should have figured as much. My uncle had said there were deer all over the place. We just hadn't seen one until now. But why was he just sitting there on top of the snow, not a hundred feet from the house? The deer's eyes kept glowing in the light. I thought I saw it twitch its ears a little bit, but aside from that it was just sitting there with its legs folded under its belly. It was just planted there, perfectly still, looking back at me.

I went back inside. "It's a deer," I said. "It's just sitting there."

"Why would it be doing that?"

"I don't know. It's the damnedest thing."

"Well," she said, "at least we know what it is now."

"It doesn't make any sense. Just sitting out there in the cold like that."

"Maybe it's resting."

"No, I don't think so," I said. "It could be hurt."

I went back to the door.

"Now what are you doing?"

"I'm going to make some noise, see what it does."

"Be careful."

"Don't worry," I said. "I'm just going to stand on the porch and yell at it."

When I got back out there, I stood at the back of the porch but couldn't decide what to yell. What do you say to a deer?

"Hey!" I finally said. "Hey there!"

The deer did not move. I yelled louder. "Hey! Hey you! Hey! Hey!"

The deer sat there like a sculpture in the snow. I went back inside.

"It's not moving," I said. "It's gotta be hurt. There's no other explanation."

"You're probably right."

"I can't see its legs, but it must have hurt one of them. Maybe it got hit by a car and made it off the road and into the woods and this is where it stopped."

"Maybe. But it's a long way from the road."

"We should call somebody," I said.

"Who are you going to call?"

"I don't know. The wildlife people."

"The wildlife people?"

"You know, the people who take care of wildlife and things. The nature department."

"I'm not sure who that would be," she said, "but I imagine they're closed right now, anyway."

"Maybe they have a hotline for after hours." I got the phone book and paged through it. "It would be a state office, right? Let's see, yeah, right here. This must be it. Department of Natural Resources."

"What are they going to do? Send out a guy to look at a deer?"

"Sure, why not? They've got to have some sort of animal control department."

Joanne went into the living room while I called the number. It rang for a long time. Finally, I got a recording. "Can you believe that? They say I have to call back during normal business hours! Like an animal is only supposed to need help from nine to five. Seriously, can you believe that?"

Joanne didn't say anything from the other room. She was staring at the television.

"Maybe I should call the police," I said.

"Do not call the police."

"I think I should call them."

"For the love of God," she said, "listen to yourself. You are not going to call the police to tell them a deer is sitting in the back yard."

"We have to do something."

"Why?" she said. "Why do we have to do something? Why can't we just let nature take care of itself?"

"You've got a heart of gold, Joanne." I went to the back door and started to put my boots back on. "A real heart of gold."

"What are you doing?"

"I'm going to look at it."

"You've got to be kidding." She got up and came into the kitchen. "You're kidding me, right?"

"I'm going to go look at the deer, and if it looks hurt, I'm going to call the police."

"You are not going out there. What if that deer has Lyme disease? Have you thought about that?"

I stopped in the middle of pulling a boot on. "Lyme disease? Are you serious?"

"Yes. You can die from that."

"You get Lyme disease from a tick."

"A tick that's been on a deer!"

"Please, Joanne," I said, "like a tick is even going to be alive in this weather and it's going to jump off that deer and find a place to land on me."

"Then what about rabies? Maybe that deer is rabid and that's why it's just sitting back there. You know there's lots of rabies going around. Raccoons and bats and all sorts of animals."

"You may be right," I said. I took my boots off. "Now you're talking some sense. We could have a rabid deer back there."

"If it's still there in the morning, we can call somebody. Okay?"

"Okay," I said. "Okay."

I was glad that we hadn't gotten into a big fight about the deer. The house was small enough already. We both sat in the living room and watched television for a while, until I finally said, "What do deer eat, anyway?"

Joanne looked at me.

"I'm just wondering," I said. "I'm just wondering what deer eat."

"Leaves," she said. "Berries."

"That deer is probably starving out there."

She looked at me again.

"I was just thinking," I said. "Maybe we should, you know, just throw some food to it. From the back porch. I mean, it would be perfectly safe."

"Will you just leave it alone, for God's sake?"

"You don't have to jump all over me. I was just thinking that there wouldn't be any harm in throwing some food to it."

She got up from her chair. "I've had it," she said. "I'm going to bed. You can do whatever you want. You can feed it, you can bring it inside and make up a bed in the guest room, whatever you want. I don't care anymore."

I sat there until she was gone. I sat there in the flickering light of the television and looked at the floor. Finally, I got up and went into the kitchen.

"Leaves," I said as I went through the cupboards. "Berries? What kind of berries? Strawberries? Blueberries? Hell, it doesn't even matter. We've got nothing here. Old Mother Hubbard went to the cupboard."

I went to the kitchen window and looked out. All I saw was my own reflection. I turned off the light and looked out again. I could barely make out the shape of the deer. I could see just enough to know that it was still there.

I grabbed the bag of stale bread that I had been saving for the birds. I turned on the outside light and went out onto the back porch.

"I'm sorry," I said to the deer, "but this is all we have."

The deer hadn't moved. I took out a slice of bread and threw it toward the deer. It flew about halfway there and landed on top of the snow. I tried throwing another slice like a Frisbee and then another. The bread was landing close, but not close enough for the deer to reach, assuming that it could not stand. I swore into the cold night air and smashed the last two slices of bread into a doughy ball. When I threw it, it went right past the animal's ear. The deer shook its head like it was shooing away a bug.

"I'm sorry," I said. My shoulder hurt from the throw. When I was in high school, I could play sixty minutes of football. Offense, defense, special teams, every single play. Now I couldn't even throw a piece of bread without hurting myself.

"I'm sorry," I said again. "I don't know what else to do. I don't even know why we're here. How the hell did we end up in the Upper Peninsula, in the dead of winter?"

I went inside and went to bed. Joanne was already asleep. I thought about waking her up, asking her to tell me what I had to do to make up for things. How we could put it all behind us and start over.

I didn't wake her up. I left her alone.

I woke up sometime later. I couldn't see the clock radio, but I knew it was the middle of the night. Corn flakes, I thought. We have corn flakes. I got out of bed, careful not to wake her. When I had found my pants and shirt, I stood by the bed for a minute and watched her sleep. I watched her sleep and listened to the sound of her breathing.

I went into the kitchen and got the box of corn flakes. It was still half full. I put my coat and boots on and went outside. The deer was still there. I knew what I had to do, because you can't throw corn flakes. From the back of the porch, I looked at the snow. There were six steps down from the porch to the ground, but the snow was so high it covered all but the highest step.

"I'm going to come out there," I said as I took the first step off the porch. "I'm just going to see how you're doing, and I'm going to give you some food. I'm sure you don't have rabies. A deer with rabies doesn't just sit there like that. You'd be foaming at the mouth and running around in circles or something."

The hardened surface of the snow held my weight as I took my second step and then my third. "Everything is going to be okay," I said. "No reason to be alarmed."

On my fourth step, I burst through the snow, my right leg disappearing all the way up to my waist. The sound ripped into the cold silence of the winter night. I pulled my leg back out and winced. The deer looked at me.

"Well, that hurt," I said. "That was no fun at all."

I started walking again, as carefully as I could manage. I put each foot down slowly and tried shifting my weight onto it. When it held, I took my next step. The problem came when one foot was planted and I went for the next step. That little extra weight on the planted foot was what the snow could not bear. Every third or fourth step, I went through again.

I made slow progress until I was finally within twenty feet of the deer. It hadn't moved but the way it was watching me made me stop. I looked at the deer, at its long neck and dark eyes.

"My God," I said. "You're beautiful."

My uncle said he had gone deer hunting a time or two. I could not imagine how you could see this animal and want to shoot it.

"I have some food here," I said. "I'm just going to come a little closer so I can set it down."

I took another step. In one sudden, smooth motion, the deer rose on its thin legs and bolted into the woods. It took the wind out of me just seeing it.

I stood out there for a long time after the deer was gone. There were a few snowflakes in the air. The air was so cold it hurt just to breathe it. Where the deer had been there was now just a faint depression in the snow. No other trace. Nothing else but the cold and the silence and the way the light from the house lit up the trees on the edge of the forest.

Maybe there's still time, I thought. I could do something new tomorrow. Something to help take away the anger. The resentment. Why can't it happen that quickly? Just like that? Whoosh, it's gone.

As I made my way back toward the house, I discovered the trick to staying on top of the snow. The trick is pretending that you're fast and light and nimble. Even if it's not true, you make yourself believe it. One step after another, I made it all the way back to the house, never once crashing through to the ground.

Sue Harrison

UNA CORDA

Mary let herself into the opera house with the key that Mrs. Orten had pinned to the front of Mary's skirt. The opera house turned cold during the days, so Mary took off her hat but left on her coat and gloves. Then she fetched a handful of dust rags from the mop closet.

After she finished with the ticket office, she pushed through the double doors that led into the music hall. To her surprise the electric stage lights were on, and a boy was sitting at the pianoforte, its top wing lifted so that it looked like a bird unsettled in its nest. As if Mary were his cue, the boy began to pound frantic music into the white and black keys.

The notes roared up the aisle and rudely pounced. They flayed Mary's skin, ate through to her bones. She fell to the runner that carpeted the floor, lay there until the music finally stopped and drained away to far corners.

The silence healed Mary's bones, and, when they'd knit themselves into a reasonable union, she sat up. The boy stood beside her. His skin shone so pale that, had she come upon him in the night, he might have made her believe in ghosts. His hair was white, and his eyes were pink, but most of all she noticed his hands, so beautiful that Mary's chest hurt when she looked at them.

"What was that?" Mary asked.

"What was what?" The boy spoke like a heckler, mutinous and angry.

"What was them notes you played?"

"The third movement of Ludwig Van Beethoven's Fourteenth Piano Sonata, Opus 27, number two. Some people call it *Moonlight*."

"They're wrong, them people," said Mary. "There ain't no moonlight in it. Not one candle's worth."

Barbara Henning

ON HIGHWAY 23

On Highway 23, heading north toward the Upper Peninsula of Michigan. It's raining beautiful rain, pine trees, deciduous, now pine, now foggy and the little trailers and trucks leave a trail behind them of smoke and water, the wipers going back and forth, pretty continual the rain today, but a lightness in the northern sky   constant   incessant perennial Over the Mackinac Bridge, I pass a big truck with logs on the back, the sky still gray, and the ethereal span of the bridge, white and green pillars, delicate and tall, reminding me of Genny Kapular's yoga instruction: lift your diaphragm, like delicately lifting a lady's handkerchief on two pillars dividing north from south   freestanding   Halfway over, the rain stops. I grew up around water, I think, as I turn into the Welcome Center. Sitting on a picnic table, I read a brochure. Michigan didn't want the U.P., but to become a state they were forced to take it. Too cold, too rough, a place only Indians would like. Give it to Canada, the folks in the Lower Peninsula said. I'm speeding through farmland with giant sprinklers on wheels slowly progressing across the fields, water, and something that grows very low for August, maybe a root of some sort. Then a sign for a disaster kit, and I start imagining invaders coming in tanks, but now if anyone takes over, it will be through ownership. Just then on the right, a chain fence with a sign, HALLIBURTON, and a parking lot full of trucks and machinery. Monumental government contracts. Work for the locals. War. Profit. Greed   *only a bird will wonder*   Surrounded by miles of Michigan timber.

TURN RIGHT

After you pass Orchard Restaurant, turn right on Sandling. Straight up you'll see a clearing and an old brown broken-down barn. Turn there, the directions say, and then go past the house and turn left, park, and walk another fifty feet to a little broken-down shack, and behind it there's another newer-looking cabin with a tin roof. One room with a big stove in the middle, old furniture, table, cabinet, no running water, no toilet, but on the other side of the drive an outhouse and in the main farmhouse, Susan can take showers every few days. She's collecting rainwater for washing and hauling drinking water from the farm. I look out over the meadows. Stein says that civilization began with a rose is a ... Quiet, the way the trees blow in the wind, the rustling of leaves, the wind bending the long grass   distance   solitude   stillness

We hike around the meadow and stoop down to look at little fungi growing in different colors and shapes on the edges of the path. Some are white and look like carved and feathered radishes and another is yellow with little buttons on top. We stop and pick raspberries, and later I eat so many that I'm no longer interested in raspberries. There are a few things I want to ask Susan, but for one reason or another I don't think of them until I am driving downstate, like why she is living on four hundred dollars a month, and how does she plan to stay in this uninsulated cabin in the winter when there is a three-foot snow cover for months on end solitude   stillness   distance

Jennifer A. Howard

ALL IMPERFECT THINGS

Clara's ex calls and tells her the pediatrician found a murmur, a little hitch in their daughter's rhythm. When he says it, Clara's own heart stops for long, mothered seconds.

"Lots of children, most children even, have them," he says. Speaks kindly for the first time since she left him. "You had one when you were little," he says. Clara has never heard this, doubts her mother told him any such thing. She doesn't argue. If anybody understands the history of her own imperfect heart, it's him. Her heart loved him, and then it stopped. She lets him think she already knew this, that as a child her heart's scattered cadences alarmed somebody else. It might even be true, might explain Clara's mistakes. But her daughter's five-year-old heart must be too young to be broken.

The next time she's with her, during their weekend together, Clara rests her ear against her little girl's chest. She wants to take her baby's heart in her hands and pet it till it calms. To blow gently on it till it cools.

Clara calls people so they'll worry with her. Nina says her son had a murmur, too. "They grow out of them," she says. "Little hearts beat in all sorts of crazy rhythms, but they settle." Clara wonders why hers did not, why she couldn't relax into the metered world of marriage. She thinks how she'll teach her daughter to better diagnose the impulses of the heart.

They say the sputters and catches are normal. Clara stands next to her ex and watches the pediatrician watch the computer screen. "She's fine," he says, trying not to be bored by yet another innocent murmur. There's no hole between atria, no leaking valve. "She's functional," he says. Then they get in separate cars, her girl heading home with her dad, and Clara scraping the ice off the windshield alone. She exhales for the first time in days, in a visible cloud.

Nina tells her not to worry. "Our bodies aren't robots," she says. "There's no such thing as perfect regularity." This is the friend who took Clara in when she moved out. She holds Clara's cold hand, later, presses two fingertips against the fragile inside of Clara's wrist. "Everybody has a heart murmur," she says, "if you know how to listen."

Jonathan Johnson

NOTES FROM THE END OF
MY OCCUPATIONAL LIFE

I had three pizza boxes built when the door buzzer went off and a man walked in and said his car was on fire. He was fat through the chest and gut and had on a tie and blue overcoat and galoshes, which he stomped on the rubber mat.

I looked out the window but saw no car.

"It's right up the street!" he said and kept stomping. "I need water."

"Yeah, yeah! I got it." I ran to the back where I put the mop bucket in the sink and cranked both hot and cold on full.

This incident didn't make the newspaper, even in this tiny city up here on the far northern end of the country where nothing much happens for weeks at a time. But it's a big part of why I don't work anymore, why I've decided it's safer for my spirit and body to walk the streets and stop into this warm café where they know me and let me drink my decaf by the window for hours for a dollar, including refills, and watch the old people creep their long cars down snow-packed Third Street, and write in my notebook.

It was early in the evening, before five, which is why I was there alone still, but this far north it was dusk already. I remember the red, white, and blue Domino's sign was on and shining against the darkening sky out the tall glass door and windows. I'd just started to fold that day's flat sheets of precut cardboard into pizza boxes. This is what we were to do when the phone and counter were dead, which is how it'd been until the man in galoshes walked in.

"Do I need to call the Fire Department?" I shouted to him from the sink.

He didn't answer so I stepped out front to ask again. There I saw he was stuffing bullets into an open revolver and had a little wooden box, a gun case with purple velvet lining, open on the counter.

This was something entirely outside my realm of experience, but I knew instantly to run.

"I only want to love you, Sweetheart!" he called out as I hit the back door.

I ran past the dumpster and slipped on a patch of ice hidden under the snow and smacked my elbow on the pavement. He came through the door behind me as I scrambled to my feet.

"I only want to love you," he said again.

I rounded the corner of the building and headed toward the front. I knew I wasn't going out into the field where train tracks ran behind the store and where I, where *we*, would be invisible to passing traffic. But when I hit the front parking lot there wasn't a car on the street so I spun around to go back inside. I locked the door shut, grabbed the phone as I went by, and ran into the back again and dialed 911. My elbow throbbed with my heart.

And now an old woman just interrupted my recollection with, "Sir? Sir?"

"Yes." I looked up from my notebook.

"Will you carry out two hams for me?"

"Oh."

"Hams," she said rummaging in her purse, "out to my truck."

"Sure, I can do that."

From her purse she pulled a smaller coin purse, which she unsnapped. She pulled out two dollar bills and thrust them toward me.

"No," I said. "No, no."

"Oh yes," she said, and thrust the two bills toward me again. "Please."

"Not this week. Maybe last week. But not this week."

"It's Christmas," she said.

"I know." I stood up and took her fist with the money in my hand. It was a cold hand and the skin was loose on the bones. I put my other hand on her shoulder. "In thirty years maybe someone will carry the hams out for me. No money."

"Well." She smiled, took back her hand, and stuffed the bills back in the coin purse. "That's very kind of you."

I took the two white boxes from Jamie, the college girl behind the counter, who winked at me, which was worth a hundred times those two dollars, though I am always against it for money these days. I opened the door for the old woman and carried her two hams across the street toward her pickup. It was sunny and cold outside and I'd left my jacket on the back of the chair at my table.

"Would you like them in the cab or the bed?"

"In the bed would be fine, where they'll stay cold."

"On the snow is okay?"

"Oh sure, they've been in the freezer."

"Well, Merry Christmas."

"Merry Christmas," she said. "And thank you so much."

Now, having recounted that, I'm glad it happened. I'm glad a moment of grace interrupted my story about this nut in galoshes chasing me out and around and back into Domino's, where I crouched in the back room under shelves stacked with five-gallon buckets of tomato sauce and whispered into the phone while he knocked on the glass door. "I know you're open for business, Sweety," he yelled. Though he was puffing from the chase, he had a lilt to his voice.

"Sir," the 911 dispatcher said. "I've got officers on the way, are you inside?"

"Yes."

"God damn it!" The nut yelped and smacked the glass. "God damn it!"

"Has he fired the weapon?"

"No."

"Are there any other people in the vicinity?"

I looked up at the convex mirror we use to see customers at the counter from the back. His arms were open against the door, the gun in one hand, the other hand flat against the glass, and he was peering in. "GOD DAMN IT!" he screamed.

His shape was distorted in the mirror, his short arms extended from his fat torso, which looked even bigger, and his head was enormous, his face contorted in weeping frustration like a baby. The gun, off at the edge of his image in the mirror, looked tiny. I saw no other people.

"I JUST WANT TO LOVE YOU!"

"I don't see anyone else, but I can't really see out very good."

He stepped back from the door, aimed the gun at the lock, and fired. I must have closed my eyes in that instant because I didn't see any flash, just heard a boom.

When I looked again there was a hole in the glass surrounded by circular and radiating cracks, like the splashes made by meteorites on the surface of the moon when you look up at night. He fired twice more into the glass, but the glass held.

"Sir?" I heard on the phone through the ringing in my ear.

"I'm okay," I said. Water cascaded over the lip of the sink and onto the tile floor. It was still gushing full-blast out of the faucet.

"What's your name?"

"My name is David Shepard."

"Keep an open line, Mr. Shepard," the voice said. "I'll be back in just a few seconds. I have to talk to the officers. Keep an open line. Don't hang up."

I could no longer see the man though the shattered, moon-surface-looking glass, but I kept my eyes on the mirror. The water ran across the floor and into a pool above the drain where it swirled down into a tiny vortex. I felt my pulse in my elbow. The pulse of the living.

"Mr. Shepard, the police are outside now."

"Already?" I looked up in the mirror and moved my head from side to side to see out the wall of windows on either side of the door, but I didn't see any police, just the human form in that blue overcoat looking much farther away than he'd been. "No, no police."

"You're doing great, Mr. Shepard. They are there, right there. Just hang on."

"I'm okay, really," I said. "You're very encouraging, but I'm okay. Let's just not have any bad outcomes." At that moment on the phone I felt polite and helpful. Capable and civic, even. It's only been since that I've come to think of myself as nearly a victim.

I heard the screeching sound of tires jumping the curb and saw lights flashing in the mirror. "Okay, okay. Here they are."

The dispatcher told me to stay where I was, but I got up and went to the doorway between the back room and front counter. I peeked around the corner and saw two cops swing open their doors and squat behind them. They pointed their guns at the man.

"Put it down now!" one of them shouted.

The man looked away, toward the burning signs for the Ramada Inn, Dick's Family Foods, and Taco John's, the twin rows of amber street lights that ran down either side of Washington coming closer and closer together toward the vanishing point where downtown ended at the lakefront.

A second car came into view from the other direction. It stopped, and the two cops in it also got into position behind their doors.

"Put it down!"

The man tossed the gun and it went off as it hit the ground and everyone flinched. One of the cops hit the man from the side so fast I hadn't seen him coming and another one was on top of them both a second later. The other two stepped from behind their doors and aimed their guns down at the wrestling pile as they trotted over. In seconds the man in galoshes was hogtied on the parking lot surface, and I thought how cold his face must be against that snow and ice and asphalt.

I had just one more job after Domino's before I achieved this current state of repose and was done working forever. That spring, thanks to a call on my behalf from our neighbor Ron Anderson, who'd known me all my life, I got my shipping papers and union card and signed on as a deck hand on the Algoma Steel ore freighter *Charles E. Wilson*. *The Chuck*, the crew called her. We did three-day runs hauling iron ore from Lake Superior ports like the one here in Marquette to Ohio, and sometimes in Ohio we'd take on coal for the return trip to the power plants up north.

The Chuck's crew were bigots and bullies. The first trip after I signed on I was already regretting it. I've never heard our neighbor Ron Anderson utter a racist word in his life, or any unkind word for that matter. He's a lifelong union Democrat, and since his retirement off the boats, whenever my mother has been in the hospital with this or that infection or complication from her diabetes, he always blows the snow out of their driveway and never says a thing about it, so I was unprepared for the redneck character of the *Chuck's* crew.

"I'm a racist, boys, so I love hockey!" the captain said once as he plopped his overloaded tray down on the table and pulled up a chair in the galley where we were watching the Stanley Cup semifinals on TV. "The only black thing in sight's bein' chased by guys with sticks."

The guys at the table all laughed. One of them actually said, "Aye, Captain." *Aye, Captain!* Like one of the crew on *Star Trek.*

It was Burn, Bernard, the deck hand I often worked beside and one of the only other young guys around. He had red hair and a face that alternated between sullenness and delight, with few expressions in the middle. He brightened quickest when he talked about his truck or made comments about women or blacks or when the captain was around. When the game broke for the next commercial, Burn asked, "What do you think of hockey, Shepard?"

They all looked at me. I'd been the only one not laughing with the captain. I still hadn't spoken a word to most of the guys there and had only interacted with Burn to the extent necessary for a couple shifts of work on deck. I sure wasn't going to let the little punk lure me into making some kind of stand.

"Well," I said. "What I don't get is this whole icing, off-sides thing. How the blue line works."

"And you've lived in the Upper Peninsula how long?"

"My whole life."

"Oh, wow," Burn's eyes danced around at the other faces. "Wow!" The captain was shoveling in his food and made no sign that he was listening.

"I like hockey and all. But ever since I was a little kid that's made no damn sense," I said.

Burn shook his head. "U.P. boy stumped on the rules of the game." The commercial playing on the TV was for Bayer aspirin.

"Okay, so explain it to me then," I said.

Burn studied the TV. "No thanks." The skin of his face flamed red with his hair. A heart monitor filled the TV screen.

"No, really, I want to know."

"I bet."

"I want to clear up the difference between off-sides and icing once and for all."

"I'm not the one who grew up in the middle of Hockeyland, USA."

"Well, that's true, I guess. So help me out." I caught a couple half-grins from around the table.

"You sure you're a white guy, Shepard? Do you blush?"

"I just want to know the difference. Off-sides, icing."

On TV a doctor was standing in front of the heart monitor with the little line that bounced up and down, and the doctor was saying that he gives Bayer to his patients to substantially reduce the risk of a second heart attack.

"That's you, Shepard, a real brain wave." He pointed at the screen and grinned. The captain glanced up from his tray, and Burn gave another shake of his head, as if we were old buddies and he were giving me an old-buddy-type ribbing.

"Because I don't know off-sides or because I don't know the difference between an electrocardiogram and a brain wave?" I asked. A few chuckles.

Burn didn't look at me but kept his eyes focused on the TV, still smiling, still flushed red. "No," he said slowly with mock patience. "Because you use words like electrocardiogram."

"I see."

"Do you, Brainwave? Do you really?"

Like Burn, most of the crew had nicknames or altered versions of their real names, and for the next few days, Burn saw to it that "Brainwave" became mine. He used the nickname for me around the rest of the crew at every opportunity and shortened it to just "Wave" after he'd gotten used to hearing himself say it.

I'm trying to hold all these thoughts together, keep the memories flowing, but I've got to stop again and tell you that I just saw my parents cruise by in their rusty Oldsmobile. They had on their puffy, winter parkas, and my father was behind the wheel. My mother was watching the storefronts and houses pass. She has only one foot now so spends a lot of time seeing town from the car, especially in winter. For years my family lived in a state of unspoken dread over the amputation we feared was coming, but she's a person of extraordinary grace, my mother, even more so now that the horrible imagined thing finally happened. As her physical life has contracted, her awareness of and pleasure in that life

130

have grown. When I told her about the racist captain on the *Chuck*, she said she should be a sea captain, like Ahab. "I could tell people it was a whale that got my foot," she said.

The sun has come out and must be reflecting off this café window as they didn't see me wave when they passed just now in the Olds. They were smiling, talking to each other as they drove up Third, from my father's office toward the IGA, I suppose. He will be off for Christmas now, but he usually stops by his office anyway to check his phone messages and maybe get some time on the Xerox machine. He loves his work.

Despite this, he has said he understands and supports me now in this time when I'm "between things." Which is how he refers to my not working, though it is a permanent commitment I've made. But I do appreciate his patient outlook on me, a son swearing off labor for life must be hard to get his head around.

I don't live with them. When I made this decision I'm trying to recount for you now, I also decided that I would accept the consequences. In the summer, I stay in a little camp trailer in the woods up Big Bay Road. It's paper company land, so the DNR leave me alone. I fish the Dead River just below the old dam, which is as far as the salmon coming up the river can go. You're not supposed to sell these fish, but I've got a deal worked out with Mel's Fresh Fish in town to buy what I can catch and fillet out for two dollars a pound. I clean and fillet them on a stump outside my camper and leave the guts there with the heads and spines. At dusk, I sit inside my screen door and wait for the raccoons to crawl through the balsam saplings and underbrush and the crows to fly down from the high branches of white pine. This fall a bald eagle, wings fully extended, talons spread, dropped silently into the middle of the crows and raccoons and grabbed a salmon head with the spine attached. He pumped his wings twice—I could see the air pass over those feathers—and flew over me. The spine dangled from his grip not three feet above the camper. The raccoons looked up from their meal for just a moment, but three of the crows took off cawing after the eagle.

But that's in the summer and fall. About a month ago I moved for the winter into the Janzen Hotel downtown, where you can do two hours of chores in the morning in lieu of rent.

I know the faces of so many of the people who pass this café window in their cars, the coroner from the hospital in his red pickup, the girl in the Escort who runs marathons (I used to see her on her training runs up Big Bay Road), the folk singer from The Village Pub in his minivan, more and more old people. They are all my brothers and sisters crossing in the cold. That's how I think of people here, and it's an outlook I'm determined to keep.

The person on the *Chuck* who didn't follow Burn's lead in calling me Wave was the cook, and over the next couple weeks, I came to think of him as a friend. He was a widower whose wife had been killed in an accident driving downstate to pick him up five years earlier, when the boat had taken an unexpected lay-up in Detroit for engine failure. He was at least my father's age and his nickname was Mole. I never called him that and wouldn't use it here except that it was the only name I ever heard him go by.

Still, I could see where he came by it. He was short and blocky and pasty-skinned from working inside all day. His white hair was cut into a flattop so that his thick neck seemed to go halfway up the back of his head. Like a mole he had small eyes, and his little plump hands looked like paws at the ends of his short arms. He wore a white apron and a T-shirt, exactly what you'd expect from a ship's cook, and he spoke in a loud, friendly voice.

I'd been avoiding mealtimes in the galley, where Burn had seen to it that I'd be sure to be needled. Instead, I'd take a sandwich to my cabin or, if it was decent weather, out on deck where I'd write in my notebook. But I wasn't eating Mole's hot food—his meatloaf and mashed potatoes and pizza and cooked carrots—and he was concerned.

"David my boy," he said once as we stood outside staring at the flat lake. "You're not gonna waste away on my watch. You tell me what you'll eat and I'll get it fixed."

"Wild game," I answered. "I'd eat anything wild."

Mole had spoken with great fondness of hunting grouse and deer. Wild game hunting. Which was how he'd learned to cook. His mother wouldn't go near anything he'd shot, so he taught himself. I loved to picture him as a boy of ten or twelve chopping onions and sprinkling them onto a pan-frying deer liver.

I had said I'd eat wild game to remind him that he'd told me about his boyhood growing up in Marquette, our mutual hometown and love, decades before me, and that I'd remembered. As much as I avoided conversation with most everyone else on board, I wanted Mole to know I valued his company, that I listened those nights out on the deck when he'd smoke and talk and the moon would blow itself to bits on the lake.

He thought about it a minute, rubbed a paw hand over the stubble on the back of his head, and said he thought he might be able to get some meat when we put in to Marquette, our next port after we offed our load of coal in Duluth.

"We're in for over four hours," he said with serious consideration. "I could go by my place and get some venison out of the freezer. A couple of steaks and a roast. That might be just the thing to fix you up. No wait! Even better, there's geese in Duluth."

"Geese?"

"Yeah, they warm their feet in the lake around the river mouth. The power plant discharges warm water there. It's just up the beach from the dock." He took a drag on his cigarette and blew smoke through his pursed lips into the night air in a kind of thoughtful sigh.

"Yeah?" I asked absently. I hoped it didn't show that I wasn't at all interested in where he was going with this.

"Yeah, well." He flicked his cigarette over the rail. "I shouldn't eat that shit anymore anyway, at least not all glazed up and with a tub of scotch alongside, how I used to. But that's how it's meant to be eaten."

"No?"

"Nope. Got practically no gut left. They took out half my esophagus and almost all of my stomach a dozen years ago. Built me a new one out of the top of my intestine, and it works okay as long as I stay away from grease and alcohol. And coffee, too."

"Cancer?"

He nodded. "Ayep. And it's not a kind too many beat. The doctor at Mayo told me that if the surgery healed, and it hadn't spread, *and* I didn't develop infection, maybe, maybe. . . . But here I am."

"Infection" was the word that snagged me in what Mole said. Not "cancer," like it would be for most people. Infection was the enemy in my house. Against infection my father knelt and sprayed saline solution from a syringe into the little round abscess wound on my mother's pale foot while she propped it on a pillow on a chair.

"Course," Mole continued, and I could see him smile, his white teeth in the moonlight. "I could just bake it in something like a ginger, garlic, and honey sauce, something light. We'd eat it up, just us. And," he leaned in to whisper, though we were perfectly alone on that deck, the sound of the hull one constant wave cresting beneath us, "I've got a bottle of Merlot stashed away. One glass certainly wouldn't kill me."

"No, I wouldn't guess," I said back in my own hushed voice. Alcohol on board was grounds for termination, and Mole had confided in me about his stash, along with his cancer and his deceased wife. Disinterest was no longer an option. I've never hunted before, and though I was half serious when I'd said I'd eat some wild game, I couldn't imagine killing some poor goose in Duluth.

That's exactly what I went out to do the next morning, though. I snuck up on doing it, went to bed telling myself no way, woke and told myself no way again, but how would you anyway, just hypothetically? Then I had my bed sheet and figured it'd never work so what the hell, I could tell Mole I'd tried. While thousands of tons of coal spilled into the dock chute from the end of the conveyer belt on the *Chuck*'s crane, I walked up the beach carrying the sheet toward a dozen or so geese. They turned their heads from side to side to eye me with each eye, but they didn't move away.

It was cold and early and the beach was deserted. Though the power plant's smoke stack and the mountain of coal and the rusty ore dock and ship towered over it, the beach area was a park, with a parking lot and lawn with benches facing the water.

They were plump, plush-toy-looking geese. They hadn't yet shed their thick winter coats of feathers.

"It's okay there," I said and slowed my walk. These were tame birds. Hand-fed, like the ones in Marquette, I guessed, by little kids and old folks. By people like my parents. My mom even feeds them now from the widow of the car.

"What do I have for you?" I asked and extended a closed fist.

The geese straightened their necks and turned toward me.

"Yeah. What is it? What have I got for ya?"

The biggest one waddled a couple steps closer, stopped, and hissed once, his tongue like a tiny finger pointing at me out his open bill. The others congregated behind him.

"So you're in charge, big fella." I kept my fisted hand extended, and with my chin and other hand I unfolded the sheet.

The geese turned around and trotted a few feet up the beach.

"This?" I said and took the sheet in both hands. I noticed that I was trembling. "This is nothing." Tiny waves pushed up onto the beach beside us, and when each retreated it left a silky sheen that just started to dissolve down into the sand when the next wavelet tossed more water up.

I wrapped the sheet around my shoulders. "It's a cape," I said. "A white cape for an evil superhero. How do you like that? But you don't know." I walked casually toward them, then away and up the shore. I took the sheet in both hands again and held it out in front of me, and I turned and walked back past them. I walked the fifty feet of beach in front of them six or seven times.

They edged up the beach and onto the lawn. A couple of them bent their necks and started to feed on the grass. They gripped it in their beaks and gave almost imperceptible tugs with their heads to pull it loose.

I walked toward them with the open sheet. This wasn't going to work, I was becoming fairly certain and relieved at the thought. But as I got closer, they didn't startle, they didn't hiss or move away. The ones eating didn't even stop. The biggest goose walked over toward me, as if he was going to speak and ask me what the hell I wanted.

I dropped the sheet over him and fell to my knees and pushed my arms onto the ground tight on either side of the squirming bulge.

The air erupted with honks and flapping wings. I wrapped the sheet in around him. He was struggling and trying to peck through it, honking like the others who turned toward the lake and rose quickly away from us.

I wrapped him tighter and he bit me on the knuckle through the sheet.

Once he connected with that bite, he went at my hand until I got a good grip with my other hand on his neck up by his head. My hands hurt from the pinches of his beak and I squeezed on his neck.

The honks of the other geese were far off now. I twisted on his neck and he pushed back against the torque.

I wanted to let him go. I stopped and thought I would do that, but when he let out another honk from under the sheet, his voice was raspy, like a half gasp that I took to mean I'd already crushed his windpipe, so I twisted hard and quick and kept twisting 'til I'd turned his head completely around once and his neck was tightly wound like a wrung towel.

I couldn't look at what I'd done, so I wrapped the sheet and tied it into a bundle and sat down on the grass beside it. Mist was rising where the warm river water fanned out into the lake.

I remember saying, "Oh, God fucking damn it," and holding my face in my hands and being surprised to feel that my cheeks were already drenched in tears. I wished that I hadn't done the thing, and I wish that still. I wish I could put him back with the others, wherever they went. When I looked up they were gone.

Though I have of late endeavored to live by a principle I wouldn't have thought myself capable of, namely, to dedicate myself to each of my days without the relinquishment of self-control required to work a job, I have also always considered myself a pragmatic person. In fact, I sometimes think that my not working is the pinnacle of pragmatism, the culmination of thirty years of my personal mental evolution toward practicality. I am that happy.

But even before I came to this decision, I was pragmatic. So after I'd killed the bird, I knew the bird was dead. And I figured, pragmatically, that I might as well make Mole happy. Anything else, leaving it there on the beach for the waves to claim and the cold lake to envelop, for instance, would have been wasteful.

I carried the bird back to the *Chuck* and put it, still wrapped in the bed sheet, on the steel counter in the kitchen.

"I'll be damned," Mole said. "David, my boy, you got one."

"Just like you said." I smiled at him.

He untied the knot and unwrapped the sheet.

The goose lay on its side with its neck arched back and its tongue showing through its agape beak. Its eye was open. The sun shone straight through one of the small round portholes. Mole had to squint up at me.

"You okay?"

"Yeah. It was just a little fucked up doing him in is all."

"Mmm." Mole turned his eyes down from me to inspect the bird. "The gettin's never as good as the huntin'," he said.

We were finished offloading coal by nine that morning, and the *Chuck* left Duluth at 9:07 for Marquette, scheduled to arrive just before midnight. As a deck hand my duties included coiling the cables and ropes used in port and hosing down the deck, which I did with Burn as the skylines of Duluth and neighboring Superior sunk toward the horizon behind us. Burn was going on about his truck, a little white Mazda with smoked-glass windows and a ten-speaker stereo. He kept it garaged at his mother's house down in Trenton. I made only the slightest gestures of acknowledgment. I guided the wrist-thick cable through my gloved hands onto its turning spool and nodded or grunted "hmm" at more or less random intervals as he talked.

"She's bad, Wave, bad to the bone! Under fifteen thousand miles for ten grand. Ten. Probably hot, for all I know, but I got legal document and no one's telling me different. Legal document, and that's all I have to say about it."

When we were done with the ropes and cables, we sprayed the coal dust from the deck with hot water through fire hoses that were loud enough that Burn had to shout for me to hear him, but he kept on with "I still have to get a bigger motor. A six cylinder instead of a four."

"A WHAT?" I shouted, making arcing passes with my hose along the deck beside him as he did the same.

"A FOUR CYLINDER IS WHAT I HAVE NOW! I WANNA GET A SIX!"

"A SIX *WHAT*?"

"FORGET IT!" he hollered in disgust.

"OKAY. TELL ME LATER," I returned and gave him a big nod that time.

After the little clusters of downtown buildings—buildings that looked like model railroad buildings, children's buildings—disappeared, the giant bluff above Duluth descended with its rows of radio towers. In that cold, early May air, steam from the wet steel deck and railings rose in the sun.

Once the deck was hosed, we had to go down into the holds to clean out the remnants of coal. The first hatch was removed and we put on masks and respirators with air tanks, like firefighters going into a burning house. We walked down the stairs and chipped bits of coal from the metal grate treads as we went. When we got to the bottom, we rattled coal from the long chains that hung down. Far overhead the square of blue sky passed with its occasional high cloud, and it occurred to me that we were standing below the waterline. It was like scuba diving, as if I'd dived into a wreck and was looking up through the open hatch to the bright surface of the water hundreds of feet above.

That night I ate the goose with Mole out on deck with wine he'd poured into empty Coke cans, and we watched the coastline for the lights of our town. It was the first food I'd had all day, and I could feel a tremble in my hand as I held the fork. Under the moon the distant line of trees along the shore was darker than the water. The tender, sweet meat dissolved easily into my mouth, and though the warm, red wine in the Coke can tasted of metal, it went to work quickly on my brain, so that later, when we'd eaten our fill and the wine was gone and the glow of Marquette rose ahead, I closed my eyes for long stretches and opened them to see again that fistful of lights. There was five hundred feet of water beneath us as we passed a couple miles northeast of Granite Island, and the spin of that close lighthouse answered the tiny, distant blink of the one in Marquette.

Mole was talking about his wife, telling me about her paintings. "Watercolors. Houses and old buildings around town." We both had shore leave that night because Marquette was our home port, and Mole said he wanted me to come by his house and see his wife's paintings. "Do that for me?" he asked. "They're up on the walls, in every room." His voice hung in the dark air like a ghost.

"Yeah, I can come by." I pulled strips of meat from the pile of goose flesh and bones between us. Mole had cooked it as he said he would. The remaining meat was cold but still moist with ginger, garlic, and honey sauce and the grease of the meat's own juices.

"She'd take pictures of the old houses on Ridge Street or of broken-down hay barns out in Skandia. You should see them."

"I will."

"It's how she spent her time when I was gone."

"Yeah."

"Sometimes, in nice weather, she'd just set up her easel right there. Not use a photo but the real thing itself. On the shoulder of a back road or right on a neighborhood sidewalk. Half the big old Victorians on the East Side have her paintings of them hanging inside. People would stop and watch her work. Word got around and everyone down there had to have a portrait of their house by Carolyn. I used to think she wanted one of those houses herself. Our place is over on McClellan, not exactly the historic district. But now I think she was happy just painting them. She never talked about moving. She's even got one of Vango's Lounge."

"No kidding. Vango's."

"Oh, sure. It wasn't just the old houses. Like I said, old barns, too. Well, sir." Mole stood up. "I'm gonna go in. Get the roasting pan and these dishes done before we dock. If you're done, I'll slice up the rest of this for lunch meat."

"I'm done."

"Good to see you eat something, Killer. I'll find you later. We can share a taxi."

"Yeah. Out here, I guess, if we're still tying up. Or after, in my cabin."

Mole gathered up our plates, the roasting pan, the Coke cans, and our forks and stepped inside. The metal door clunked shut behind him.

Killer.

There was a light breeze, and I sat out as we made our approach, the long minutes toward the red light at the end of the Upper Harbor breakwater, which we finally passed. We slowed, and our spotlight flipped on and fixed on the end of the dock where the American and

Canadian flags fluttered.

Killer.

I was stuffed and could smell the grease on my hands and taste it on my breath. I didn't want to see Mole's wife's paintings, didn't want to have to walk through that empty house in the middle of the night with him and nod and make admiring comments. I was tired. Not sleepy. But tired of even his kind company. It was for his company that I had strangled the goose.

When we were tied off, I went in and found Mole in the rec room watching TV with a couple of the guys. We were early into Marquette and Jay Leno was still on. I told Mole that I thought I'd better take a rain check on his place. I lied and said I'd told my parents I'd try to stop by tonight and I didn't want them waiting up any longer than they had to. Like most of the crew, I kept an old bicycle aboard, and I told him I'd just ride into town on my own. Mole didn't seem to mind. "Next time in I'll have you over," he said and looked up from the TV for just a moment. "No problem." He didn't mind—or he was very good at not letting on.

I did go by my parents' house, but I didn't go in. I rode my bike into the schoolyard across the street and stopped there. The curtains were drawn, but there was a light on in the living room. They would be watching the *PBS NewsHour*, which my father always taped while they watched the regular prime-time shows and played back after. They never bothered with the local news. As I said from the start, there never is much local news. Schoolkids convert an old bus to look like the Space Shuttle. Sometimes there's a car wreck, like the one that killed Mole's wife. Sometimes a strike at one of the mines.

Or my parents could well have been on the phone with my brother Michael down in Ann Arbor. His first year of law school was hard on him, his first time away from upper Michigan adding to the stress of study. He'd stay at the law library 'til late at night then go back to his apartment and call home. My parents had two phones spliced into the jack behind the little table between their easy chairs, and they'd both get on the line at the same time and the three of them would talk sometimes for two hours. They'd reassure him that Mom was fine, the abscess on her foot was healing (whether it was just then or not). Michael would tell them about crazy old Professor Owens in Contracts, or his new friends, or sometimes how he was lonely and overwhelmed and wanted to just come home and be a legal secretary.

My parents would talk him through these rough nights. My father would say he'd leave right then and drive down to get Michael if he absolutely had to get out.

"I'm with you, son," he'd say. "Whatever you need to do. We're both very proud of you down there, but if you need to come home and regroup and maybe take stock, we can do that. If it's grinding you up."

There would be a long pause, then I would know my brother was crying from the way my mother would break in and say, "Listen, listen . . . Michael? Listen to me. Oh, kid. You're stressed out. We know that. It's okay."

I wanted to go inside their house with its one lit window and ask them for just that kind of absolution. They think of the Marquette geese in the park along Lakeshore Drive almost as community pets. They wait for the spring goslings to appear covered in fuzz. They would have recognized the brutality, the wickedness of grabbing such a creature and wringing its neck. They might even have understood why I did it if I'd told them how I spent most of my free time alone in my cabin or eating alone on deck, and that Mole was the only man I talked to.

Of course they would have understood. They would have sympathized. My mother would have told me to fix myself a root beer float or bowl of raisin bran. And my father would have said, "You can always come home."

But then they would have known forever what I'd done, what I was capable of. They'd have known I was rotting inside, alone out on that boat. Not down in a beautiful law school with stone buildings and leaded glass windows and leather books and the shade of oak leaves in the quad, but out on an ageing, ugly, steel-hulled freighter that smelled of chewing tobacco and rusty, powder-fine dust of iron ore.

Above all, I didn't want what had become my working life to be true in any broader context than my own experience. I didn't want to be someone who hadn't been able to go back to work at Domino's, who couldn't bear the thought of strangers all day coming through that door that was still taped over with cardboard when I went by to pick up my last check. I'd pretended to my parents and Roy Anderson next door and a few friends around town that I'd signed on to the *Chuck* for a romantic adventure, a youthful self-indulgence, but the truth was it was an effort to keep me from falling apart.

I only want to love you sweetheart.

I spent many nights on my bunk, twenty miles off shore, surrounded by the dark—dark cabin, dark lake, sky dark as an endless pupil looking right at you, dark as a wound—hearing the man in the galoshes say those words.

I didn't go to my parents' door and let myself in. My mother was babying that foot, keeping it elevated even those times when the home health nurse had said it looked better. She and my father were fretting about Michael. They didn't need me telling them this shitty thing I'd done or telling them that I heard the words of the man with the gun when I was alone on my bunk.

I rode my bike out of the schoolyard across from their house and two blocks over to B and G's Corner Store where I brought a two-liter of 50/50 to the counter and asked Della for a pint of Captain Morgan's from the shelf behind her. The price under the row of Captain Morgan's said seven dollars in big red numbers, but it was the only rum I knew by name, and the shelf was too far to read the other bottles. Della had gone to high school a couple of years before me and had worked at the B and G since. She was petite. Blond hair framed her round, open face, and there was always a flirtatious energy between us when I came in. She called me "Mister" and I called her "Missy," but I never did anything about it, never asked her out. She'd started wearing a wedding band a year or so earlier, so I figured I'd blown my chance.

"Now don't drink this all at once, Mister," she said as she slid the bottle into a paper sack.

I wanted to ask her if she was happy. Not so much with being married, but just in a more general way, working the B and G, living in Marquette, but I couldn't imagine a way to phrase the question that wouldn't sound condescending or at least maudlin. So instead I asked, "What makes you think I'm gonna drink it at all, Missy?"

"Just a hunch."

"I'm actually buying it for the carload of teenagers who are waiting down the block."

"Hope you're getting a good profit."

"I got to see you, didn't I, Missy?" I said and walked out with the pint in my coat pocket and the two-liter tucked under my arm.

I rode down College to Seventh and continued along beside the cemetery. The occasional tombstone flashed back a streetlight from polished granite as I passed, and I wondered if Mole's wife was buried in there.

I crested the hill and rode down through the little park, toward Washington Street and the red, white, and blue Domino's sign. I sat down on a bench back in the trees, opened the 50/50, poured some out in the grass then poured in the pint, capped the plastic bottle, and swished it around. The mix was sweet and fizzy going down, and a warmth rose from my throat after each gulp.

I am not much of a drinker. Even these days. People assume I am sometimes because I don't work and I live at the Jantzen Hotel and they see me so much, walking around town. When I have the cash, I'll stop in to Vango's or the Third Base and have a beer, but usually just one. I want to keep as clear-headed as possible now to get my thoughts down on paper. That's where my sense of purpose is currently, where my work ethic has gone.

But that night I'd left my notebook on the *Chuck*, a dumb move because I was thinking more and more about not going back there. So I sat on my bench and drank my drink and watched Timm through the glass wall of Domino's. Timm had worked a couple shifts with me. He hadn't crossed my mind since I'd quit, but I was happy to see him in there, glad to have some other memory come into my head besides Mr. I-Only-Want-to-Love-You-Sweetheart.

Timm was tall and lanky, friendly in a zany, spontaneous way. Sometimes he'd answer the phone, "Timm's Famous Pizza." Sometimes he'd turn up his Al Green tape on the boom box and sing along as we spread sauce and cheese and mushrooms and pepperoni on pizza dough. He was a theater major at the university, and often he'd rush in late after a rehearsal with makeup still on. His face would be orange, like a sunburn, and his teeth would look unusually bright by comparison as he'd flash a grin and say, "So'd ya miss me?" He spelled his name on the schedule board with two *m*'s, and after I got to know him I called him Timmmm.

Of course he was gay, but I didn't care about that. He never mentioned it, and no one ever dropped him off or picked him up from work. He always walked.

Now he was working with some girl who must have been hired since I'd left. Maybe my replacement. There was new glass in the door, of course. It'd been months. A delivery car I didn't know swung into the lot every ten or fifteen minutes. It was a big old Cutlass, idling there with a Domino's sign on the roof. The driver would come back out and set the pizzas on the passenger seat and slam that heavy door and chug off.

The other businesses along Washington were dark, the signs above Dick's Family Foods and Taco John's dark, the office lights off in All-state Insurance Agency. Only Domino's was lit, making it look as though Timm and the new girl were on stage, talking on the phone, building pizzas and putting them into the oven. Once as they passed each other, Timm took her hand and gave her a little twirl. She curtsied and he bowed and they went on working.

She was young. So was he. Her black hair was back in a ponytail and her bangs showed under her Domino's baseball cap. Light, late-night traffic passed between me and them.

I sat there and watched them like that for a long time, as they made pizzas and laughed, and customers and the delivery car came and went with boxes of pizza until they shut off the sign and locked the door and rolled out the mop bucket. I thought about going down there, saying hi to Timm and meeting the new girl, but my head had started to spin from the Morgan's on top of the wine of Mole's I'd drunk with the goose, and I knew if I tried to talk, I would slur my words despite my best efforts and my breath would smell like the drunk I was just then.

I must have nodded off because I was startled awake by a burst of light. I could see nothing but light filling my brain, and I heard a voice falling over me from the angry trees, *hello, hello*, a shadow coming toward me, above me, my father here to take me home where I could slip between the cool sheets of my childhood bed.

"Sir, time to wake up." His hands were on his belt. I shielded the light with my arm. There was the silhouette of his gun, his hat cresting over his head.

"I thought you were someone else."

"Why don't you try to stand up for me."

"No problem."

"And how about grabbing the top of that bench."

I did as I was told.

"Any weapons or needles?"

"No."

"Park closes at ten o'clock, sir," he said as he patted my clothes. "Okay, you can turn around. How about some identification?"

"Sure, sure." I opened my wallet and handed him my license and my new union card.

He clicked on his flashlight and studied both cards under the beam. The light flooded around our feet.

"You off the ore boats?"

I remembered my happiness at thinking, just before I drifted off, that if I slept until dawn I'd miss the *Chuck*'s shove off.

"David?"

"Yeah, I'm with you."

"You can't stay here. I could run you as it is for drinking in the park." He tipped his flashlight beam toward the empty fifth of rum and 50/50 on the ground beside the bench. "Why don't you toss those in that trash can and let me give you a lift back to the boat?"

With my bike in the trunk, we drove down Washington and onto Lakeshore. I sat in the back, and Officer Kelly, as he introduced himself, glanced at me every so often in the mirror.

"You're not going to be sick, are you?"

"No, I'm fine. I was just . . . I used to work at Domino's back there."

"You were the one there on that firearm incident, weren't you?" His eyes in the mirror looked young. His hair above his ears was shaved to his scalp.

"I'd just—I was alone."

"I thought that was you. That guy was an A-number-one head case. My heart juiced the whole rest of the night on that one."

"Mine, too."

"And then the weapon discharges when he tosses it. Went into a tire on a car parked across the street."

"I remember." I felt myself drifting off again.

"So you don't work there anymore?" he asked in a louder voice.

"Yeah." As the road rounded the point by the lighthouse, I could see across the bay to the pulsing lights answering each other on the twin, Upper Harbor smokestacks, and then the lights of the ore dock and the *Chuck*, which was lower in the water now, weighed down with all those billions of pellets of iron ore in its belly. "I quit right after."

"I can see it. That guy was flipped, but he made bail, if you can believe it."

"Made bail? No way he made bail."

"'S how it works, my man."

Then I didn't feel drunk at all. I wanted back on my boat, in my cabin and offshore. Or on deck with Mole watching the lights of this town drop over the horizon.

"Well, that's just fucked. Bail?"

"Bail. But he ain't comin' back. He's gone."

"Does anyone know where to?"

"He's dead, man. Big dead. Splashed his skull all over a room out at the Oak Inn."

"He killed himself?"

"Yeah, officers that took the call said he'd put down a sheet of Visqueen on the floor first. Sometimes they do that, have that kind of consideration and presence of mind. Left his license on the end table. The phone was off the hook beside him, so they wipe down the receiver—this guy's blood is everywhere—and they hit redial and his wife picks up. They'd been fighting on the phone and he says, 'Oh yeah? Listen to this.' She thought he'd kicked in the TV or something. She said it sounded like busting glass. She said she hung up and went back to bed."

I was freezing cold in the back seat of that cop car, shivering again.

"He got his gun?"

"I don't know, must have had another one or bought it when he got out. I can't imagine he got the same one back, even if he did get bail."

"He gets out and they keep the gun?"

"Evidence, my man, evidence."

My job before shoving off that night was to seal the hatch covers, forty-foot square sheets of steel that had been lowered by boom back over the full holds. The clamps that rimmed the covers had to be tightened before we could leave with a load, even in calm weather. This I did with Burn, who smiled when he saw me and said, "Brainwave! You're fucked up. We'll make a sailor of you yet."

We started side by side. He tightened his clamps one after another in one direction and I worked the other way so that, according to procedure, we would meet on the opposite side and continue around, checking each other's work. But by now I was barely able to stand, and I'd finished just seven of the eighty clamps when I looked up and there was Burn, done with all of them, all the way around and right beside me.

"Whew!" he said and waved his hand in front of his nose. "You smell like a bar. Better lay low." He checked my seven clamps, then moved on to the next hatch cover as I made a half-hearted show of checking all of his clamps should the captain be looking down at us from the bridge.

When I'd gotten around the first cover, I looked up and Burn was two hatches farther away. I could see he was working faster, really twirling his wrench on those clamps to make up time for doing it alone. There was another pair of men working the same task from the other end of the ship, and if he kept up his pace, he'd be close to meeting them in the middle.

Like most of the rest of the crew, Burn was on the tubby side, but otherwise, bent over his work in the artificial light, he could have been mistaken for me. Same brown coveralls and orange safety vest, same yellow hardhat. If the captain were looking down from the bridge, or if someone were watching from up on top of the ore dock, Burn and I would be a couple deck hands, distinguishable from each other only by the fact that one was working away at a good clip and the other was moving with slow, deliberate motion.

In retrospect I'd say that if there was a specific moment I've made a key life decision, that was it. I stood drunk on the deck of an ore boat, free, released, without guidance or companionship, the ungoverned agent of my own grace, my breath rising as clouds into the gold glow of burning halogen.

I didn't tell Burn I was going. I just went inside to my cabin, where I took off my safety vest and coveralls and hardhat. I folded the coveralls and vest and put them on my bunk, then put my hardhat on top of that. I shoved my clothes and notebook into my duffel, along with my Walkman and tapes and the little framed photos of my parents and Michael. Just before I left, I took out my union card and set it beside the hardhat on the vest and coveralls. I left the cabin with my bag and bike.

The hallway listed slightly from one side to the other with my head, and the *tick, tick, tick* of the bike sprocket sounded hollow, like it was coming up from a well, echoing off those metal walls painted with countless years of light green. Outside Mole's cabin I dug my notebook out of my duffel and pulled the pen from the wire spirals. I flipped to a blank page and wrote, *Mole, I will be by to see Carolyn's paintings one of these days.* I folded the note, but there was no space to slip it under the door, which made a tight seal with the floor, so I rolled it into a tube and tucked it into the door handle.

I walked my bike down the stairwell, through the porthole and down the gang ramp to the dock.

I passed a pair of shoremen who nodded at me, then I was through the cyclone fence gate. I got on my bike and peddled with surprising steadiness back to town.

Since then, I have occasionally considered descending again into some work, maybe start up with a few classes at the university. There is nobility in labor, in purposefulness, I know that. But I also know that my pragmatic side wouldn't have it for long. Like the diver in the wreck, I'd have to surface again. I write like this for hours every day, and spring will come eventually, when I can move back out to my camper with the salmon and crows and raccoons and maybe even the eagle again.

And soon now, I'll be heading out into this cold, sunny day to join the good people of my town moving up and down Third Street, all of us on the brink of forgiving ourselves. Michael flies in tonight from downstate. I'll go by to see him and my parents later. But first I'll walk down Hewitt or Michigan or Ridge Street to the lake, past the same steep houses that Mole's wife painted. The beach will be empty and the wind will blow through me, but the lake won't be frozen over yet, not for another couple weeks, so I can watch the wisps of spray lift off the waves right as they curl over, right as they change from rise to fall and tip toward shore.

Linda Johnson

I KNOW HOW LEMMINGS WINTER

Anything that resembled our old life has been packed into boxes and into the small spaces of the car. Useless items packed in a rush: the dog brush without the dog, Mother's Austrian silverware, her bottle of Chanel No. 5 perfume—last year's Christmas present from Father, almost empty.

We four children know enough not to talk loud or ask too many questions; Mother's hands are gripped on the steering wheel, guiding the Chevy wagon over the snow-packed road. Ten hours. Father could have made it in seven. Never before have I seen the Mackinac Bridge like this, lit up at night in the falling snow, suspended high above the black water—Mother weeping, steering too close to the railing.

Summer up north. Father would buy smoked trout in St. Ignace; Mother, in the passenger seat, would unwrap the butcher paper on her lap, pulling apart the flesh, handing us chunks to eat while Father drove on: the good, strong smell of smoked fish on our faces and hands all the way to the cabin.

But Mother crosses the bridge and goes right on driving past the lights of St. Ignace. No hot bowl of soup. No trout. She pulls off at the rest stop and we children run to the toilet and back to the idling Chevy, clumps of snow stuck to our shoes. Then she turns north on I-75 into the wilderness and I sense the gloom of separation, leaving behind the land mass that I have called home for fourteen years, only our headlights shining onward into the falling snow.

Weeks have passed without word from Father. I hoped he would send money, perhaps rescue us. Nothing. Mother does not disclose how much money she has in her purse, but it is not enough to dry clothes at the Laundromat in town or pay the required thirty-five cents for hot lunch at Brimley School. We get reduced lunch for ten cents and a new wardrobe from the Salvation Army Store. Mother has no bank account. No credit. She has filed for divorce through the Legal Aide office in Sault Ste. Marie. She has applied for government commodity food. The family home in Mt. Clemens has not sold. Mother applies for a librarian position thirty miles away in town. No word yet. She is not in a pleasant mood.

Wind is master here along Whitefish Bay; it howls all night long, whipping snow everywhere. It whips through your bones. No life outside. It is a death sentence, this cabin a dot along the deserted Lake Superior shore. Snow has drifted into deep, sweeping curves covering the roofs and doors of the scattered cabins, the summer people long gone.

Dollar Settlement. Our cabin stands in the open, in the middle of a three-acre parcel of snow. Fifty feet behind the cabin, Lake Superior, which is immense as an ocean, churns violently cold and relentless, slamming grotesque icebergs against the bank.

Before daylight I hear the scraping of the Chippewa County snowplow along the two-lane road—a lonely lifeline. Across the two-lane an artesian spring trickles into a ditch. It is our water source. We crack open the ditch with an ax and scoop cupfuls of water into metal buckets. On the hill above the artesian spring the forest: spruce, red pine, maple, birch, oak.

Uphill we struggle through the waist-deep snow. My little brothers, Eddie and Nick, shimmy up the trees like monkeys to break off dead branches. The high, dead oak limbs burn best. I collect the precious fallen branches. Mark, sixteen, directs the piling of the branches onto the blanket; he is smoking a Pall Mall that he must have stolen from Father before we left. Together we drag home the load of kindling, tripping over our own deep tracks in the snow. The split wood we ordered from Don Hiekkela is green. He tells Mother it is green. No matter, she orders six cords. Green, blue, red, what difference does it make? We learn that green wood, unseasoned wood, hisses and smolders and smokes up the cabin when the stove door must be opened to feed the languid flames.

From the road our snowed-in cabin appears as a child's drawing: white hat sloping down, square face, two slit eyes—not built to look out, but to shut in. Moved in the early twentieth century from Canada, the cabin was pulled with a sled and team of horses across the frozen bay.

It is a remnant of better days, busy lumbering days. The cabin and I are both remnants of better days; we are exiles on this icy shore.

Inside, everything is dark and heavy. Oppressive. Large, hand-hewn beams brace the low ceiling. The walls are built of rough pine boards of irregular size. They are aged, heavy boards, some three feet wide. Downstairs in the corner stands the wood stove: the center of our life.

A crooked set of stairs leads upstairs to two cubbyhole bedrooms. There is a crawl space with mice droppings and squirrel nests. I hear the rodents scratch in the walls at night. Do they bite? Long into the night I lay awake with a watchful eye.

Mother calls from downstairs. "Time to get up."

I crawl out from my nest of blankets in my nightclothes: flannel nightgown, knee socks, my brother's woolen sweater, red beret pulled down over my ears. I am never warm in this place. All night long my shoulders and back are cold. There is no dry wood to burn in the night stove. The blanket tacked over the window is frozen against the ill-fitting pane. I step carefully into the small room that my brothers share, the floor slick from snow that has seeped in through the rafters. "Eddie, Mark, Nick, time to get up." They answer with muffled groans.

Mother stands beside the wood stove in her long ocelot fur coat and matching hat, slicing potatoes into a cast-iron pan. Big-boned, tall, and blond, she commands presence. The breakfast table has been pushed close to the stove. It is covered with a linen tablecloth and set with Mother's Austrian dishes, blue-and-white plates with matching cups and saucers. Linen napkin and silver knife and fork lie at each plate. Ice is sculpted into patterns across the small windowpanes. The window sashes are frosted over.

"Good morning, Mom."

"Good morning. You do plan on fixing yourself before breakfast? A beret is not meant to be pulled over the ears like that."

"Yes, Mom. I'm going to the outhouse."

I put on my coat, push my feet into cold boots, and pull open the back door. The outside thermometer reads minus twenty-four degrees Fahrenheit. The bay, no longer open, lies white and frozen, jagged ice sculptures stretching out like a moonscape. All is still. How far out could a girl walk before she freezes? Five miles, ten? How solid is the ice?

Footprints have broken through the drift leading to the outhouse. I see the patterned sweep of Mother's fur coat, but do not attempt the walk. I squat just outside the cabin door, then cover up the yellow snow like a cat so Mother does not see, then rush back inside.

Mark pulls on his cap and zips his coat over his long underwear. "How's the path this morning?"

"Deep."

Mark is short for sixteen, his voice barely cracked, his face smooth like a boy's. He is skinny like his brothers. Their ribs show; they call each other the most minute names: amoeba, protozoa, corpuscle.

Partitioned with a blanket, the washroom is a four-by-four corner. I light the candle. An empty washbasin stands on the bench, two buckets on the floor: one holds clean cold water, one holds slop. I dip out one cup of cold water, brush my teeth, and spit it into the slop bucket. I have carried in my allotted pot of warm water from the wood stove and pour some into the basin, reserving half for rinsing my hair. I undress and wash quick, beginning with my face and hair, then with a wash cloth continue down to my toes—never quick enough; the water has turned cold. But the ritual of washing keeps me human.

We sit clean and presentable in coats and hats at the breakfast table, beret on my head "properly" as Mother has ordered.

The ceremony of eating begins: "Malztzeit," Mother nods. We return the Austrian expression of good appetite and nod back. Napkins are placed on laps. She has dished out potatoes and an egg onto each plate. They are no longer warm; the fork in my hand is cold, the seat of my chair is cold. Potatoes are palatable cold, but not a runny egg.

My brothers are glum, each filled with his own misery. This morning is the misery of an unfinished cold egg on their plates. I spread the last few bites on my plate so it looks as though I have finished. Mother looks sternly at the wasted egg, then lectures how she has survived the Allied invasion and occupation of Vienna. How at thirteen years old she and her mother ran down three flights of stairs to the cellar during Allied bombing raids. "We were lucky to have tucked in our pockets hunks of cod liver oil bread to eat in the dark." She tells of the stench in the bucket where tenants relieved themselves—how it slopped onto the floor when it was her turn to carry the full bucket up the stairs to empty out into the street.

Her stories do not improve my appetite. Mother lashes out, "We were happy to eat rotten, frozen potatoes and wormy beans. You have no idea. You Americans don't know suffering. You're all alike." We eat her bitterness, sit there gagging, until the last bite on our plate is swallowed.

Outside, the temperature on the thermometer drops to minus thirty-one degrees. Eddie and Nick wander onto private property where an abandoned shed stands. They knock down wall studs with the ax and drag home their prize, which we desperately need for kindling; they muscle the eight-foot boards through the snow with their skinny arms. Grinning. "Mom, look what we found. There's a whole bunch of it."

"You did what—are you crazy? That's all I need. No husband. Now bastard sons breaking the law."

In the next moment she has Nick by his coat collar and a stick from the woodpile in her hand. She swings it, whipping him across the back. Mother loses her grip and he runs away, but she catches him and slams him down into the snow. She continues whipping, cursing in German. Nick has lost his cap in the snow. He is crying.

I pull Nick away from her.

"Out of my way before I smack you, too. I should never have hatched you, none of you. I should never have married the bastard." She grabs my hair and beats me with the stick: my back, arms, legs. She can't stop.

Did I fall or did I know to drop to my knees and throw my arms around her legs? "Please Mom." Her arms slow down, she collapses, hanging onto me heavy, and then the first choking sobs begin.

"What have I done?" she says. She is embracing me. I let her. I return her embrace, but I am floating on another plane, detached in the knowledge that I have controlled her rage by falling to my knees.

Mark, the boy-man, hauls most of the water and wood. When the wind blows and the snow falls, he is first in the morning to put on his coat and shovel the path to the road. He appears a mere stick moving in the falling snow; the snow falling endlessly upon itself, covering his tracks as he shovels, obliterating his effort.

Each day Mark spends more and more hours brooding upstairs in the darkness on his bed. I, too, have retreated upstairs. It is not so much the harsh winter that is intolerable, rather Mother's discontent. Life is so hard: no father for her boys, no money, no lights, no heat. Her teenaged son would soon sneak out nights, stealing her car, leaving the family without transportation. No phone.

At night I hear Mark crawl out of bed, rummaging through the cardboard box of clothing. It does not concern me. Often during the night it is necessary to dig out a coat or extra pair of wool pants. But he slips into my room, kneels, whispering, "I'm going back to Dad's house—come with me."

"He's not there anymore. What makes you think he wants us?"

"I'll find him. Are you coming or not?"

"She'll kill us if we have to go back."

"Damn it, she's killing us now. Are you coming or not?"

I don't answer. We need Mark here. Our mother asleep on the couch downstairs, how can she shovel so much snow alone? How can I leave my family?

"You know what you are—you're a goddamned lemming. Stay then." He returns to his room. I hear him digging in the dark, a zipper opens and closes. The steps creak. I can hear Nick and Eddie breathing, sleeping in the cold room on cots beside Mark's empty bed. They are vulnerable. The chance of escaping by hitchhiking with children is not good. At best, the county sheriff would pick us up. Return us home to Mother.

Will Mark freeze to death on the side of the road? He has no money, no food. Will Mother blame me when she finds Mark's empty bed?

I must have fallen asleep because I did not hear Mark creep back upstairs and crawl into bed. Sometime during the night I do hear a sound—like whimpering—and I lift my head. Mark is crying like a little boy. I lay my head back down, pulling the blanket over my ears, relieved that Mark was forced to come home.

I never did ask Mark how far he had walked that night. I didn't know then that a lemming is a suicidal rodent that migrates in vast numbers, plunging into the sea to drown. Is that what Mark meant—remaining with Mother was suicidal? Is that why I stared out at the frozen bay, tempted to walk out into the whiteness?

Finally, that year in April the unbelievable warmth began to seep into the bay; the ice floes pulled in and out along the bend of the great shore; then one day open water came in to stay. My parents did divorce, but we had survived that first winter in the cabin. For we were still family: one by one we emerged like miracles from the sea, cold and spent, slithering home, pushing up close against the weak fire to dry.

Ron Johnson

THE HITCHHIKER

They had been going at it all afternoon, and now the white disk of a sun was sliding toward the hills on the western edge of the lake, the largest surface area of any lake in the world, but Geri could not let it go.

"Did you fuck her?" she said.

"She was a dance partner. That was it."

"Did she do the hula while you were on top of her?"

Ben stood with his cup of coffee looking at the languid blue water beyond the road. Only in the last six weeks, since after their wedding, had they really began to go at it. And he was sick of it. Glancing secretly at her face, her drawn mouth, brown eyes that had once been soft and inviting now hard, he said, "I didn't ask for this."

"Neither did I."

And after a moment. "Did she ask for it, or did you?"

"You won't let it go, will you."

"How can I when you never told me about her?"

"There was nothing to tell."

"Right."

She stormed out of the front room, boot heels clicking on the tiles of the kitchen until she stopped at the coffee pot, cup in hand. As she was pouring, the pot jiggled enough to slosh a few drops over the brim onto the counter, and seeing her hand shaking, he felt almost sorry for her. She couldn't help herself, just like he had not been able to the other day when he had answered the phone and her ex needed to talk to her. All innocent enough, a paper that had not been dated at the divorce needed to be resigned, not her fault, but the tone of her voice had set him off, the conversational lilt to it—like two old friends who had known each other for twenty years. Well, wasn't that the truth of it? And then some. It wasn't that she would ever go back to him, for she was in love with Ben now. It was just the idea that for over twenty years Geri had been married to this guy with the decent voice on the phone, evidently many of those years as happy as most married couples until he had one affair too many and things had started falling apart.

Wiping the coffee spots away with a paper towel and tossing the wadded ball like a shot into the waste can, she turned away from Ben's gaze to look out the kitchen window at the lake.

The irony of it was they had gone to the Marquette Art Fair looking for a wedding present for each other. With the scramble to set up the ceremony and the preparations for the honeymoon and his extra afterschool debate club coaching, they had not been able to find the right piece, so had agreed to wait until the art fair. But when they had turned the corner of a booth, April had been standing there. With her open smile April said, "Hello, Ben."

"Hello." He had turned to Geri behind him, and taking Geri's forearm carefully in his, brought her forward. "April, this is my wife Geri."

He was watching Geri of course, her quick hard look at April before turning away, not saying hello.

"Congratulations, Ben." April smiled again at him, eyebrows arched in surprise. Actually with April there was quite a bit to look at: her white chemise that showed her deep cleavage, her blond hair up off her neck, the kind of smile that made people want to say hello. Yes, April looked better than he remembered, taller, blue jeans as tight as ever. No way she looked fifty. That was the hell of it.

"And nice to meet you, Geri," April added. But Geri just gave a stiff nod, turned, and started walking away, and with a shrug of his shoulders, Ben had followed Geri out the booth and back into the milling crowd.

They had left without buying anything, silence thick between them on the drive out until he made the turn east on M-28 at the stoplight where a hitchhiker stood with his thumb out. The man wore a stained white T-shirt with a red do-rag, probably in his early forties, although he had some hard miles on him—he might have been younger. Over a muscled shoulder that carried his ink draped a small backpack. "If this wasn't such a good place to hitch," Ben said, "I'd pick him up."

Geri looked at the hitchhiker a long moment as they passed, not speaking.

"Bet he's going to St. Ignace," Ben said. "Or someplace below the Bridge. Wouldn't do him any good to drop him at our driveway."

But she remained looking out at the trees they were passing.

Maybe if he gave her enough time, she would get hold of herself. Seeing the hitchhiker might have helped: when Geri had left her first husband she had had no car, and during one of their long talks she had told Ben that for a couple years, until she got on her feet, she had hitched everywhere with her kids, placing both of them before her when she stood beside the road. Even a woman in a car by herself would stop.

They had told each other everything then, when Ben had first moved in, spending those months talking, often hours at a stretch. As if they had their fifty-some years to catch up on and had to tell—and hear—it all: the events, the people, the lives they had lived without each other until now. Often they talked through the middle of the night, lights out after making love, lying in bed with each other's body near enough to reach out and touch.

During one of those nights a few weeks ago, lights from a passing car crawling across the bedroom wall, she had said that if she wasn't so much in love with Ben, she wouldn't be fighting with him, and Ben believed her. He believed her because he knew it was true for himself. But she had been in love with Ben first, committed to him, and it had taken several months for Ben to come around. During those months he had continued driving down to Milwaukee to see Nancy on long weekends and had kept up on his friendships with women in his dance class. After all, hadn't he told Geri about Nancy on their first date? That hadn't seemed to bother Geri then. And hadn't he broken it off with Nancy as soon as Geri filed her separation papers? But Geri couldn't now forgive herself for not dating other men at the same time. And he suspected that wasn't the whole truth, that Geri could not forgive him for not falling in love with her when she had fallen for him. What the hell could he do about that anyway?

Go figure. Just when he had committed to her, and they had married, it had starting coming out of her.

But yet it wasn't that simple either.

When she first told Ben of her ex-husband—from her second marriage—Ben had been relieved that the man was stand-up, had actually split their property fairly, enabling Geri to buy this modest house with its breathtaking view of the lake that Ben had grown so fond of.

Why did he get so bent out of shape about this ex?

Maybe because this man had actually been so very decent? The first man, Geri had said, who had treated her fairly in her life—except, of course, for his women on the side. It didn't help that this ex made over three times as much as Ben and had for all the twenty years Geri had been with him. It was complicated, all right. Ben had never expected to be in a complicated situation like this at fifty-six years old. Wasn't that supposed to be something younger people had to deal with?

But now Geri pulled out a pan and went to the fridge, removing a package of steaks. She was a great cook, the best cook he'd ever been with, and he knew she liked cooking for him: this was a good sign.

Maybe now they could get back on track.

And he held that thought until dinner was laid on the table. Sitting down to the bowl of steaming rice and the steaks and green beans on their plates, she turned on him. "Why can't you just level with me?"

She stared at him, waiting as he dished up his rice and carefully put the serving spoon back in the bowl. "That's all I ask, just level with me."

"I have. I told you she was my dance partner. I didn't sleep with her."

"Did you drive her to the dances?"

He had to be careful here. "Sometimes."

Her jaw set. "Didn't it ever occur to you that I was sitting at home waiting for you to call?"

"I've told you: it took me a while to know what I wanted."

"Was that the only place you went? To dance?"

This was trouble. But he had to go with it. As she dished up her rice, not looking at him, he said, "We went to a movie. Occasionally."

"More than once?"

"A couple times."

"Dinner?"

Ben didn't say anything.

"You did, didn't you!" She was standing now, pushing her face across his plate, the serving spoon with its stray grains of rice gripped in her hand, her knuckles white. "You son of a bitch!"

"Listen: we didn't have sex."

"You dirty son of a bitch!"

Here we go again.

He stood up from the table: looking down at the steaming steak and rice and green beans, he felt it getting away from him. What had he done to deserve this? "It's not my damn fault that April happened to be at the art fair. I have no control over that." Now this good meal was ruined, and he realized he was shaking with anger over that.

Take it easy, he told himself. "I need to take a walk."

Geri came around behind him, between him and the door, sticking her face into his, brown eyes wild. "You dirty son of a bitch."

He grabbed her shoulders in both hands and propelled her to her chair at the table, setting her down before her plate.

"Don't you shove me around, goddamn it!" She hopped up, the serving spoon still clutched in her hand, circling around again between him and the door. "How could you!"

Anger boiling out of him, he grabbed her upper arms and pivoted her out of his way. She screamed, "You're hurting me!"

Yes, he'd grabbed her too hard: he released his hands, the vise grip of his fingers, and she crumpled to one side with the serving spoon slipping to the floor, then catching her balance, she ran—face broken in anguish—to the bathroom, slamming the door, the click of the lock jamming home.

At the backdoor, knob in hand, he paused to look back at the dining table. The meal on the table before the empty chairs seemed sad— his anger suddenly sucking away to an emptying void, only its hollow residue remaining. In his very lungs, it seemed he couldn't breathe right.

How long had he stood there looking at the table before slowly releasing the doorknob? He walked over to pick up the spoon, carried it to the sink where he set it gently on the stainless steel.

At the table, sliding the plate and silverware to one side, he sat. Out the window over the lake the red angry ball of a sun was now dropping toward the hilltops. What had he done?

In the thirty-two years before Ellie had died, they had disagreements but never shouting; and then after she passed in those few years with

Nancy there had been a couple of quarrels, some heated exchanges over his dance partners, but he had never manhandled a woman before. It sickened him. How could he have done it? He hadn't suspected that was in him. When Geri had told Ben about her first husband socking her—he always went for an eye, Geri had said—Ben had felt superior to the man, the father of Geri's kids, in a different category entirely: Wasn't Ben someone who knew how to treat the woman he loves? But now here it was: he hadn't measured up.

Strange: if she had hit him, or slapped him, something physical, he would have simply walked away. What is it about a woman's words that gets to a man?

After looking out at the lake for a long while—all that water, over a hundred miles of it beyond the horizon—the food on the plates cold, he heard the toilet flush and the sound of the shower running. Walking slowly up to the bathroom door and leaning against the jamb, he waited until the shower stopped, and through the door he told Geri he was sorry he hurt her.

And he was.

Maybe she heard that in his voice, for the door clicked as it was unlocked and out she came, glancing at his face as she hurried past with her wet hair and dryer into the bedroom where she closed the door behind her.

Well, now what?

Was she packing her suitcase?

The whir of the dryer started, and he walked over to the kitchen, standing before the sink and looking out over the lake with the bloated sun in its redness dropping onto the hilltops.

Soon out she stepped with her hair combed, now wearing tennis shoes and a halter-top, the car keys not in her hand.

She approached the table, stopping to look down at their plates. "You hungry?"

"I don't think so."

"I'm going to put mine in the microwave." Carrying her plate into the kitchen, she stepped a wide berth around him and slid her plate into the microwave.

At the table, he sat. Surprised but thankful for her quick change of mood.

Now an ore boat was way out, downward bound, a pencil line of smoke dissipating into the rose-tinted sky.

The microwave beeped and she removed her plate. "You want yours heated?"

"Go ahead."

She slipped over around him, again keeping her distance, scooping up his plate quickly, and walking over to insert it into the steel box. Setting the timer, she stood waiting, looking over the sink out the kitchen window. "You see the boat?"

"It's too far out to make. Maybe the *American Mariner*?"

"Maybe."

Maybe. That was good enough for now.

While Ben picked at his steak, watching the laker, she really went for her food. Something seemed to be settling in her now, something beyond Ben, and yes, he was thankful for that.

But he also resented it. How was it that she could get beyond it so easily? Was it her experience with her first husband? One time she said he had almost killed her, smothering her with a pillow. Maybe after something like that, her response to what had just happened wasn't the same as his.

And there in the last rays of the sun, the hitchhiker was walking quickly down the side of the road. Long strides, this guy who looked so worn-down consumed with relentless energy. What was with him anyway? Was he leaving a woman? Going back to one?

A green van appeared and the hitchhiker hung out his thumb, still walking backward as the van swept by, then whirling his body determined like a dancer to follow as it disappeared out of sight behind the line of pines near their driveway.

"He's been walking a while," Geri said quietly.

"Must have. Or someone dropped him off near our driveway."

The man walked past the ore boat visible in the distance behind him, heading in the same direction. Crossing their driveway and mailbox, the man slipped into the line of evergreens out of sight.

"If he doesn't get a ride in the next half hour, he's going to have a long walk. Won't be many who will pick up someone at night." His own voice sounded hollow in his ears.

Geri looked at him as if she had never seen him before in her life—as if Ben were a complete stranger. "It's easier to walk than to wait," she said matter-of-factly. "You've hitched before."

"It's been a long time."

For a moment she stood with the cold bowl of rice in both hands, and then walked into the kitchen, where she inserted it into the microwave and washed the serving spoon in the sink. After looking out the kitchen window at the laker for a long minute, she said, "You know what I wish?" The timer on the microwave beeped but she did not move, still watching the boat. "I wish I could give that guy a ride."

"What if he's going all the way to St. Ignace? You'd be driving all night."

Geri frowned.

There it was: he'd said the wrong thing.

He tried again: "I wish I could give him a ride too."

She glanced at him, taking him in as she sat. She picked up her fork and knife and started on what remained of her steak.

He could feel the resentment easing out of him. Now he was able to cut into his steak also.

When she turned to him, her brown eyes were soft. "Why don't we?"

"What do you mean—drive him to St. Ignace?"

Geri looked out at the laker, weighing what she was about to say, and turned to him. "Well, maybe just up to the motel at Sand River. We could take him that far."

That put a different spin on things. Now she was with him, he didn't want to change that. But he didn't like the idea of picking up the man with Geri in the car. Ben might do it himself, expose himself to whatever the hitchhiker was, but he wouldn't do that to Geri. And he couldn't tell her that either, not now.

"What do you say?" she said, still looking at him, simply asking. Maybe asking for both Ben and herself?

"What if he doesn't have enough for a room? You know yourself, he might not have that kind of dough. What would it take, fifty bucks?"

"Probably." She looked back out at the laker as Ben chewed a piece of steak, then turned back. "What about dropping him off a sandwich and some water. If he's going to be walking all night, at least we could do that."

The question in her eyes, Ben took a deep breath. "Maybe so."

Geri hopped up from the table. "Good. Let's catch him."

He cleared the dishes and, as she made a peanut butter and jelly sandwich, grabbed one of the plastic bottles of water in the fridge. While she rummaged in a drawer for a plastic bag, Ben watched the laker in the gathering twilight, its lights visible now, looking like a floating building in the far distance, the profile of the hull indistinct as it neared the darker line of evergreens.

Would bruises be on Geri's arms in the morning, the imprint of his fingers?

How will that feel?

"I'm ready," Geri said.

He walked into the bedroom and picked up his wallet from the dresser, checking his cash. He'd forgotten about the fifty-dollar bill he had put aside for the wedding gift, folded beside the twenties so he wouldn't spend it by mistake.

After he climbed into the car and sat behind the wheel, he turned to her. "You know that fifty for our wedding gift? He could get a room with that at Sand River."

She looked back at him closely, and smiled.

"We won't pick him up. You hand him the money and the food. Tell him about the motel."

Again she smiled at him, and all that life he'd lived without her was gone, lifted from him. And from her: he could see that from the way she sat in the seat beside him as he turned the key and the engine caught.

How could that be?

L. E. Kimball

DEADFALL

She woke, tried to roll over, but her arm was trapped beneath his massive body.

He smelled of sweet grass, and sex.

Her arm was long past prickly; a dead weight attached to her shoulder. Was it part of her body or his? She tugged, heaved backward with no luck. Rather than wake him, she left it, wondering how long a limb could remain bloodless before it died.

It was 1957, a prickly time in general. While she would come to terms with the human way of the world, and its inevitable turning—with the dead weight and the deadfall—she had not come to terms *to date*, and was as stuck with things in the topography of her mind as she was stuck with her arm trapped under the big Anishinaabe man beside her.

Perhaps it was her original failure to bond that had caused her to be temporarily stuck in her mind.

It was her biological mother, not Rona Ansgar, who had left her. She was not abandoned on someone's doorstep or left by the side of the road; her mother had taken her across town and relegated her to the local refuse dump.

She was a month old.

She had lain there for over a day, it had been estimated (weather mild in June), under a copy of the *Newberry Gazette*. She escaped notice of the foraging bears, lying in a relatively clean sandy hollow, her head against a fallen cedar tree, with the good piney scent masking the garbage, the incubating warmth of the sun penetrating through the classified section that first day, and the lunar gleam of moonlight rocking her to sleep that starry night, the rhythmic beat, the earth's heartbeat in her ears, along with the gentle rustling of the newspaper. It had sprinkled about dawn, which had wet her lips, rainwater rich with nitrogen, phosphorus, boron, copper, iron, manganese, and zinc, fortifying her like mother's sweet milk.

As that day in the dump gave way to darkness and it in turn gave way to light, her body, predominantly water, slowed its processes, matched the diurnal/nocturnal pull of the earth and then the lunar pull of the moon. And all of it: the rain, the sun, the moon, the easy wind, smiled on her, infused her with a sideways look at the world, and a high good humor that would last all her days.

Time passed, but only so much of it. If more time had gone by, she would have joined the other soluble ions that had been broken down by the steady decomposition of (more) time and returned once again to the great body and soul of the earth.

Which would have felt right to her and okay.

Instead she was rescued in the year 1937 by John and Rona Ansgar, who named her Norna—which was Norse for "fate"—and took her home. But she had bonded not with the flesh and blood of her own human kind, but with the loamy eternal coolness of Mother Earth herself. As if she had skipped a step somehow or never left the heavens at all. Had gone instead straight from heaven to Earth. And despite the loving care of her adopted parents—and though Norna would love them dearly all of her life—the earth, the source of all life, would stand surrogate, always, between them. The bear cubs, the fishes and beavers, the June bugs and mayflies, became her siblings, the rocks and trees, flora and fauna, all part of her extended home.

As a toddler, she would wander off and the Ansgars would find her half a mile away, chest-deep in some crick or tributary playing with a water snake or a frog. She swam like a river otter, moved with the three-gaited lope of a coyote, and her voice had acquired a whippoor-will quality.

When chastised about leaving "home," she'd look bewildered. The word would mystify her all her days.

"Don't you love us?" the Ansgars would ask her. "Don't you want to live here with us?" they'd ask.

"Of course," she'd answer, not understanding the searching looks on their faces. Not understanding their not understanding.

She left school in her thirteenth year, though she read voraciously and was possessed of an intellect extraordinary to most people. The women of Newberry, the do-gooders, talked about her now, in this year of 1957. The townspeople would punish her but never disown her; after all she was theirs. They talked about how she had disappeared into a wigwam with "that Indian" this last fall and how she hadn't come out all winter, it now being mid-February. Even though the shack was off the main road and close to the falls, the townspeople knew all about her, and she was aware that they knew and that they talked. She let their derision run off her back like the spring torrents she was longing for.

It was not true she hadn't left the wigwam since fall. She went out at night often to hear the wind howl through the river valley, feel the snow swirl around her face, see the stars blink at her like long-lost cousins. Much later, she would recognize these months for what they were: a young-adult hormonal depression. But at twenty years old, she was not sure if she *could* or *would* emerge from that wigwam or if she'd stay there, suspended, forever.

She wasn't aware, for instance, that Britain had just exploded a thermonuclear bomb in the central Pacific, that Dr. Seuss had written *The Cat in the Hat*, or that the world's largest suspension bridge (which was five miles long and had taken three years to build), had recently connected her world of the Upper Peninsula of Michigan with the Lower. But if she had, she would have seen the irony of all three things.

Because these days it was as if there were nothing more in the world than the big Anishinaabe man's hairless chest against her breasts, his thighs between hers, his shoulder-length hair that ended up in her mouth, slick with something her imagination said was bear grease, but was probably Brylcreem.

"Put your hand here," he'd say. "Put your mouth here."

Her mind would become hyper-focused on a patch of his hide or her own until nothing else existed except that patch, and that was what she liked most, the disappearing into that infinitesimal piece of flesh.

Given all this, it wasn't surprising she hadn't noticed it at first, so oblivious to things, so turned into herself and their sexuality, was she.

So what exactly was it? What was it that had pushed her to the realization that this *was not the same man coming to her every night*?

It was none of the obvious things: The fact that he wore one set of clothing when he went to work at Newberry Mental Hospital (Upper Peninsula Asylum for the Insane), came home in other clothing claiming he'd had to change in order to run the trap line; the fact that his appetite for both sex and food seemed to vary wildly from day to day; the fact that his shoes disappeared twice and he claimed he'd had to buy new ones.

How could she be fooled?

You would think that if anyone could know him intimately, it would be she, a keen observer of life; that she of all people would know. Norna was colorblind, but rather than relying on her other senses, she was even more focused on the blackness or whiteness of things.

Perhaps anybody can be fooled.

For instance, what does it mean to *know* somebody?

Did it mean you recognized their heart and soul? Was their being like a contained body of water in which you lost yourself, diving until you were immersed in the entire essence of it? Is there a connection between two people that can never be quite the same connection between two others? Did it mean that, in this case, he became predictable to her? That she knew how he would behave, say, in a dangerous situation? How private he was, how selfish, how generous? Did it mean that she recognized the taste of him (garlic and tobacco late at night), his smell (tobacco again, sage and lye soap mixed with old flannel wool from a shirt several years too old)? Did knowing him mean she had memorized his body? Would she recognize, anywhere, his wide, square hands, knobby knuckles, hairless smooth fingers with skin the golden color of maple syrup in sunlight?

Norna didn't even presume to know him like she knew her own heart.

No, she thought. She would settle for knowing him enough to tell him from someone else.

———

You might wonder, *and she wondered herself* through the years, why she stayed if she was convinced that there were two of them?

Much contributed. This would not be the last time there would be more than one man in her life, and she would be accused of a certain lack, a failure within her character to make commitments. She would never defend or explain this. It was untrue at the time and untrue later. It was, rather, the necessity within her character to *over*-commit—and not lightly or often, usually due to unusual circumstances—to more than one person at a time. Commitments that would not end when the relationship—as most people defined one—ended. A commitment much as a mother commits to more than one child. Timing, to her, *wasn't* everything, and ultimately it became about her investment.

She would not be fool enough to fall for their double standard, the one that said that women were immoral at worst, unromantic at best, to care for more than one person, while men could and would love the masses.

In her lifetime, Norna would love and be committed to twelve people. Five women including her daughter; five men, which included four lovers; her parents. Sex wasn't relevant. That people considered her shallow, frivolous, impulsive, or promiscuous didn't occur to her, and if it had, she would have found it laughable.

A personality in such stark contrast to someone who would leave another person in a dump.

———

The wigwam was like this: the stove was in the corner of the shack-like dwelling, and when fully stoked, burned too hot on certain days, and forced them to leave the door open for air; conversely, it would die down in the middle of the night turning them to huddled, frozen chunks of flesh on the ground.

They were warmer naked, they found, clasped together in one down sleeping bag, topped with animal furs, lying atop a bright blue air mattress, their bodies forming a frigid *S* pattern; sometimes on their left sides, sometimes on their right, he sometimes behind her, sometimes her body wrapped around his.

They had a table made from the stump of an enormous white pine, several wooden folding chairs, a shelf that held a cast-iron frying pan and miscellaneous cooking utensils, and various Indian rugs. On the wall over their beds, she had hung her only possession, a Scandinavian quilt given to her by her adopted mother, Rona Ansgar.

They bathed, hauling water from the Little Two Hearted River, carrying it in a large tin feed bucket. After warming it on the stove, they would stand in another metal bucket and dump water over themselves in dipperfuls, soaping first and then using the water as rinse.

She would not call herself bored, though the days got long. She'd spend them doing daily chores, reading or moving the furniture. She'd tilt the log table onto its side and roll it from one end of the shack to the other, settling, finally, with its placement under a particularly wide gap that served as window and offered the most light.

The next day, she'd roll it again.

She preferred to view the stars through the slits, and though the wind and snow drove through the cracks on bad nights, she was loathe to seal off the wigwam completely.

————

It wasn't every other night she'd notice the switch. It seemed, looking back, that they didn't split their time with her equally; one of them came to her about two-thirds of the time. Some might think (and friends later suggested) that he was just ambidextrous, so the fact that he'd insist on some nights that she lie within the embrace of his left arm, which left his right hand free to stroke her—sometimes the reverse—didn't necessarily mean anything. Moreover if they *were* identical twins, some might think, it would make more sense that they would both be right handed or both be left handed, possessing the same genetic markers and codes and tendencies toward the same physicalities. But Norna believed that hand orientation wasn't pertinent in *this* case, and she believed she knew the reason for it. And no matter what the people of Newberry (or friends she was to make subsequently) said later to dispel the notion, she was never able to fully lose the thought.

And the thought was this: *they'd been joined together in the womb.*

She'd seen the slight scars on their opposite thumbs. Instead of floating free in amniotic fluid in probable positions of front to back, or above and below, they were instead mirrors to each other, each with the opposite hand free. Which she knew had joined them mind to mind and heart to heart. This would require that each rely upon the other for use of the opposite hand, dependent on the other for mobility and access to that side of the womb. They likely touched each other's faces in curious adoration, pulling each other close, but they must have, on occasion, shoved each other away just as passionately, in a mad claustrophobic frustration. She imagined the struggle for who would exit the womb first.

Ultimately even this wasn't what convinced her they were two: it was that until she'd spent many nights with them both she'd had an incomplete joining, a partial experience sexually and emotionally. She knew it took both their hands and both their hearts to satisfy her.

So she devoted herself to the study of him *or them*. Because she so desperately needed a distraction. She was twenty years old and twenty-year-olds fall in love as it serves as distraction from themselves. No one has the stomach to confront themselves at that age, and maybe they never do.

And they both became "Sam" to her. Two sides of one, like moon and sun, part of the same day.

And though she accepted it, she resented it, too. She found herself hoping that he might cut a finger or contract an obvious bruise along the trap line, which, healing slowly, would be conspicuously gone on the other man. She hoped he'd get lice and cut his shoulder-length hair, do something that would enable her to trap him like one of his animals, a coyote in a snare or a beaver in one of his wet traps. It became important to catch him up in the lie, to reveal the deceit, and to at last confront him with it, and that is to what she devoted herself this elusive winter of 1957. But it was not to be.

Conversation was spare, at least at first. And that was okay with her, since the first things she concentrated on were the physical characteristics. Norna knew ambidextrous people preferred one hand for certain tasks. They might switch back and forth batting a ball or golfing, but they tended to use one hand while eating. It seemed Sam ate most of the time with his right hand, but not exclusively. So she'd watch and when she saw him eating with his left hand, she assumed he was "the other" and she'd attend closely at those times to the intimacies between them.

But that was harder than it sounds, since it was at those times she most returned to the earth; sex was nearly like dying, or at least not existing, the closest she came to abandoning that false sense of order and purpose to things, the closest she came to just "being." Prayer, in the sense that the Anishinaabeg practiced it, was a close second, she thought. Or for them, it could be argued, it was the same.

How soon the trappings of the world intruded after sex! And she suspected that this momentary erasing of self was something that appealed even more to the male psyche. An end in itself, a dying over and over like a mayfly mating, where females, of course, had yet to produce and nurture life. For most of them, a beginning.

As Norna's suspicions grew, and she found physical identification inconclusive, she began promoting more of a dialogue between herself and the big Anishinaabe man. His name was Sam Gabow. He would confide a spirit name later that winter.

"How crazy are they?" she'd asked him once of the inmates of Newberry Asylum where he performed custodial duties nightly.

"*Windigo*," he answered, the Anishinaabe word. "My people are afraid of those who are *touched*, but they don't fail to recognize their gifts, the special knowledge the rest of us lack. They are usually either great healers or see things others can't."

"Women, too?" she asked, of the inmates.

"Oh, yes, at least as many in there."

"Tell me about them," she said.

And he'd gone on to tell her about a woman named Rose who claimed her husband had had her committed so he could marry a third cousin who'd arrived a few years back from Ontario. "It is pretty much *his* word against yours, and all they have to do if they choose is drop you off in the bin," Norna pointed out to Sam. She asked him if Rose'd seemed all that crazy, and he said he'd watched her one day, an enormous red-haired woman with chalky-white skin, pick up a black carpenter ant and put it down the front of her shirt as she lay on her bunk, crossing her arms over her chest protectively, as Sam put it, "like she had an infant or maybe a million dollars shoved down there." Another time she had hung her head out the window and howled like a mad wolf, shouting "God Save the Queen." Though, who knows how crazy you'd be, Norna pointed out, if your husband had you incarcerated like Ann Boleyn in order to marry someone new.

"White people always ask questions," Sam said. "Anishinaabeg wait until the answers are revealed."

"I want to know about the trap line," she'd said.

He didn't answer.

It was early March now and The Day, always changeable this time of year, was driving snow, more nearly hail, at the door of the shack. She had him backed up against the wall of the wigwam. She was naked; most women feel at a disadvantage, but not her.

"What is it about this trap line?" she asked. "Why do you do it?"

She'd been living with him for months and this was the first time she'd asked.

"I only work part-time at the asylum, but I'd probably do it even if I didn't need the extra money."

Verbalizing reasons for running a trap line always proved tenuous for the Anishinaabeg, she found. So many factors. They retained hunting and trapping rights, which somehow made it more acceptable for the Native American; the intrinsic right to do it seemed to distract from the *why*. The wigwam, a "temporary" structure (built out of scrap lumber and pieces of slanted corrugated metal to serve as roofing, and constructed on state land), was in accordance with the hunting and fishing rights bestowed upon the Anishinaabeg under the Treaty of Washington written in 1836.

Norna helped in the shed; she was good with the fleshing tools. Sam would come in with his catch—maybe a coyote, a red fox, a raccoon— she'd insist on working with him in the shed (a lean-to attached to his wigwam, the proximity of which decreased the likelihood of the catch being destroyed by investigating bears; though there were nights they'd have to come screaming out of the shack, pots and pans banging like steely thunder in order to protect their catch).

There was no freezer or easy way to protect the carcasses, so the animals would have to be tended to immediately. As soon as an animal's fur was dry, the big Indian made the cuts from one back foot to the anus around to the other back foot and removed the skin like you would a bulky sweater. Coyotes were reluctant to lose their hide and had to have more cuts made on the forelegs before it could be peeled off their reluctant forms. But it would be Norna who would stand at the fleshing beam, holding the skin in place with her belly, clasping the two-foot-wide metal tool in each hand, pushing the flesh away from her in a scraping motion, the fat mounding in front of the tool like pinkish-gray rice pudding. This would free him to adjust the stretching boards, and when Norna was finished with a pelt, he would then tack or nail the skin to the board.

Sometimes they'd skin a rabbit; he'd clean it, hand her the meat, rabbits so cat-like in size and shape, and they'd make stew, using wild sage and bits of bacon and vegetables, wild mushrooms. But whether he was selling pelts, hunting for food, or fishing the streams, she saw the prayer in his eyes, thankfulness that this time the creatures of the world had sacrificed for *them*, conscious of how easily it could be reversed and how eventually it would be. Recognizing their part in nature as temporary and not proprietary, without sense of entitlement. And when he made love to her, she saw in his face the same soulfulness, the same thankfulness, the same conscious attachment to the act, not a moment taken for granted.

Once in the middle of their lovemaking, they were lifted off the floor, tossed in the wind, and they'd heard the thunder threaten—thunder and lightning in a snowstorm, the odd juxtaposition of electrical disturbance on top of blizzard, the driving blinding snow illuminated by flashes of light that looked like the glare of a knife through a white cloud of confetti. It was the act of joining with each other that was the *strange thing*, and as her body orbited his, it was this strangeness that kept them both safe; they were not part of the earth, nor part of a thundercloud, or the storm, or the electrical field, not one thing and not another thing, and therefore not vulnerable.

They didn't—and couldn't—believe in collective blame.

But it was the animals—specifically their *deaths*—that connected them. His attitude toward sex, she thought, unproprietary or not, was not that different from the animals he caught and skinned, the sacrificial nature of sex, disparate from all things.

———

"What kind of traps do you use for what kind of animal?"

Not an idle question.

He pulled one of the large furs—a blanket made of pieced and carefully stitched muskrat— around her bare shoulders, covering her breasts as if he suspected they would become part of his downfall. She left the blanket where he'd put it, accepted the handicap.

"Wouldn't you rather play poker?" he asked.

The Anishinaabeg loved mystery of all kind.

"What kind of traps?" she asked again.

She listened as he listed: snares, leg-hold traps, Conibear kill traps, Trou de loup traps (the bear-pit type with spears in the bottom of the hole, a trap he didn't use anymore), the old-fashioned boulder deadfall trap—each of them in a variety of locations—dirt holes, culverts, open-water rivers, under ice-rivers, cubbys, hollowed-out logs.

"What do you use most?" she asked.

"Snares and leg-hold dirt-hole sets, since I mostly trap fox, coyote, and raccoons," he answered.

———

Stir crazy.

What happened next might be blamed on her self-imposed cabin fever, her intense desire to know the truth, or the fact that her body had betrayed her and she had been running a temperature. What happened was significant in that it would be the last time she would believe that her "desire to know the truth" could be satisfied by any set of circumstances or reasoning to explain that circumstance. That is, that answers existed in the sense that we think of them. But back then she still believed in answers, and this answer seemed to represent to her, in her fevered state, the answer to everything. The answer to this question:

———

The Day had had the feel of acupuncture, needles descending from the sky in driving sheets, piercing her skull as she hauled wood from the pile and stacked it next to the fully stoked stove, unable to keep up with the relentless wind through the cracks.

They were camped too far north, close to the trap line, but only four miles from Lake Superior in the snow belt, and this would be the start of yet another four-day blizzard that would require digging out every few hours. It had been raging only a couple days, and she'd been out shoveling twice, huddling beneath the hood of the beaver coat she'd made from Sam's pelts. She'd returned to sit next to the wood-stove, chilled through, wondering if Sam would make it in time or be forced to stay in town, leaving her alone to battle the storm, when he arrived in a rare state of inebriation, out with the Potter boys in town it seemed, and when he reached for her she reached back, thinking this was the fastest means to her end. He had extraordinary endurance despite the whiskey, and her offer to move up top was declined as it always was. Superior position for him sexually; emotionally, however, there was more to the proximity between them.

She waited until he fell asleep on his back. She listened to his snoring, how much it sounded like the whistling of the wind through the slats, and she pulled her arm and body out from under him (the dead-fall weight of him), which she accomplished without waking him from his drugged state. She crawled across the wigwam on her knees and added short pieces of beech and a few pieces of coal to the woodstove.

Then she went to work. She wasn't sure what style to use, but had settled on a form of foothold trap, made with strips of wet rawhide (some kind of metal handcuff would have been a closer imitation, but she didn't know how she would get her hands on a set). She wrapped and wrapped the leather firmly around one ankle, knotted it several times, and then, using longer pieces of rawhide, she tied several strips securely through the hole in their enormous log table, then back through the foothold trap, which would serve quite effectively as a "drag." He might be able to move the table, but would not be able to pull it through the doorframe of the shack. She decided one leg was enough, but since he was an animal of the human variety and she needed to harness his brain as well, she rolled him gently to his side and managed to bind his hands together firmly behind his back. The strips would tighten and harden like molded concrete to remediate any looseness in the bonds or inferiority in her knots. Then she covered him so that he would not become cold, and poured herself a cup of coffee from the enamelware pot, thought about who would check the trap line and what time Sam was due at work, and she listened to the rhythm of the earth and Sam's breathing, watched the contours of his body in the sepia shadows in which she saw all things then, looked out at the night and saw the black humped bodies of fallen trees, another kind of deadfall, imagined small creatures, the vast wildlife huddled under them and under the cedar sweepers, thought about the pressing darkness that intensified the storm, and waited for him to wake up. Which he did about daybreak.

He took one big heave in an effort to sit up, bound leg preventing it, and flopped back to his side.

"What the hell's the deal, Norna," he said.

She hadn't considered what she'd say, an explanation for her actions, yet the look on his face (though he'd asked the question) told her he knew what this was about. There was no betrayal in his eyes, no accusation. Was it her imagination or did he understand the nature of the game between them—that since he acted in accordance with his nature, she could only act in accordance with hers. She said nothing and he watched her without speaking. She'd begun to sweat now, her fever rising with the day and the continuing storm. The room swam, and she felt she might fall off the stump on which she sat and she leaned her head and body against the wall; she wasn't sure she hadn't dozed off. When she opened her eyes, Sam was still watching her, but his eyes had become small and fox-like (yet his countenance more bear-like), and she saw him clearly for the first time. And how easily things could have been reversed, and maybe still were.

The big animal shifted in the trap.

He pulled himself up on one knee. Norna loosened his trousers, and held the bucket while he relieved himself.

"Do you think this matters?" he asked her.

"I don't know," she answered.

She wasn't sure if she expected the other Sam to show up when this Sam didn't. If she expected to hear he'd been at work when she knew he couldn't have been. Or if she expected him to confess in order to get her to release him. She didn't know. She didn't even know what she intended to say or do next.

It was hard to tell predator from prey, she knew that. When she'd tied his bonds the night before, she realized it was not merely a measure in self-defense; she recognized every role inside her: victim/oppressor, lover/hater, exploiter/exploited.

"It's not a trap, you know," Sam said. "When you trap creatures, there is a volitional aspect to it … animals decide to walk into the trap."

"Oh, you set yourself right up for it."

He was quiet for a minute.

"True," he conceded. "But suppose I choose not to recognize myself as being trapped. Suppose I choose to accept it as a sort of *vacation*." And when she offered him rabbit stew, he refused, stating that he had decided to fast. "A vision quest," he announced. "You may be happier I've chosen this path since you've made it hard for me to relieve myself." And he smiled at her, making her wonder again who was trapped and who was free, and how it was hard to tell.

"You might give thanks," he suggested. "If one creature benefits, another sacrifices."

"No trust, eh? No such thing as a symbiotic relationship?"

"Happens," he said.

He closed his eyes and she imagined him in his mental wilderness, the place where you see the face of God. Sam referred to Him as The Day, consisting of light and dark, day and night, consisting of all sides of a thing, all aspects of the all-knowing and all-being. And as Norna watched him, she felt The Day envelop her, too, her head leaning against the shaking wall of the wigwam, a fevered weariness overcoming her, pulling her along. But no, maybe it wasn't The Day pulling her so much, it was Sam, wolf-like now, hand held out, inviting her on his quest. Yet, despite his invitation, she was acutely aware that this was a vision quest of her own, that they might start off together, but that was the best case.

Together but forever apart.

It began to seem more like a journey to her than a "place" of discovery or contemplation, which seemed right. And she followed along behind Sam for a while, through clouds, or maybe fog, but then it turned to a raging blizzard, wind whistling through the trees, snow driving in horizontal sheets. They trudged on in the dark, he occasionally looking back to see if she was still there, but taking no responsibility for her welfare. After a while, she seemed to be the groundbreaker, with Sam on her heels, but when she looked back she saw what looked like a pair of bear cubs leaping through drifts, and the two of them looked helpless, motherless, and she had the feeling they were trying to keep up with her. Then she couldn't see them anymore, heard what sounded like a wolf howling—songs of prayer in the night.

She wondered if Sam (*the Sams*) were still back there and if He had seen the face of God yet, because so far she had perhaps only the vaguest feeling of The Day. And then she was at the falls, which had frozen into icicles the size of swords and in which she was able to see her own reflection. And she suddenly had the feeling that she could see The Day in the reflection of her own eyes.

"Norna." She heard her name, several times, and woke to see Sam had dragged the table over to her. She had slipped off her stump and was lying on the dirt floor, her head propped on the woodpile. He was nudging her with his head. "Norna," he was saying. "Are you all right?"

She opened her eyes.

"How long have I been gone?" she asked.

"Twelve hours, maybe a bit less." It was dusk, she thought, or maybe dawn.

She stood, weaved, grabbed the wall. She located the hunting knife from the shelf and cut the rawhide binds from his hands. He grabbed the knife and cut the binds on his foot, then helped her to the door, supported her as she squatted in the snow, then lifted her into bed. He stoked the woodstove, climbed in with her, pulled the furs around them, and together they listened to the storm rage on.

She didn't apologize for her behavior, and it was clear he didn't expect her to.

They survived the storm, or rather, she survived it, and they resumed life in that winter of 1957, she watching him, he providing for her, she helping in that shed of slaughter that somehow became as much her responsibility as his. They made love and played games of chance at night, or she'd read to him aloud, from Rilke, her favorite poet.

She never asked him directly.

She didn't know if Sam had deceived her; didn't know how much she'd deceived herself, and it no longer mattered. Her experiences increased her compassion, caused her to demand less of others. She might in the future and of necessity make decisions based upon apparent circumstance, but she would forever be suspicious of her ability to assess "badness" or "goodness" based on them. Though this gave her a greater sense of peace, life for her would always "beg the question."

And that was good.

———

She had been in Sam's shack since November, and as she knew she would do eventually, she walked out in late March. Sam told her about the origin of the medicine lodge, the story of the North Star, and finally he told her the creation story. It could only be passed, this verbal history, orally, the magic a testament to their intimacy, the extent to which they had surrendered to the trap. This was something that would be lost if told indiscriminately or written down for the eyes of a casual reader.

There would be no record of him or her having been here this long winter of 1957, except that which had been written on each of their souls.

In late March, the first thunderstorm swept through the region marking the end of the *Anishinaabeg storytelling season*, dragging off part of their roof, and creating a distance between Norna and Sam they would never eliminate, but would, paradoxically, never widen.

He helped her pack up the burlap bag that held her books and the few clothing items she had come with, and her quilt. They swept the floor without speaking, sometimes rubbing shoulders companionably, and when they were finished, they left the wigwam together, he walking south toward his trapline and she, without a backward look, made her way toward Lake Superior, and finally west to the town of Grand Marais.

FOR THE HEALING OF ALL WOMEN

Sunday morning. Baraga powwow 2004

July winds blew against my face. The sun felt brilliant. Lisa and I hung our dresses on hooks from the ceiling of her open porch to catch the morning breeze. Lisa's white satin jingle dress was a bit dusty after a day of dancing, but it was still striking. Her hands brushed away the dust. Hundreds of silver cones swayed and sparkled from the sunlight. Her black velvet yoke also hung with her dress. Baby blue and yellow beads: an Ojibwa floral design.

My traditional dress is made with a deep blue velvet fabric. Numerous brilliant water birds are sewn all over; purple, pink, orange, and yellow. A circle of eagle feathers is sewn on the front. This dress is snug around my bust, but overall a nice fit. I picked up this dress from my friend Summer just before I left for Finland and just after my injury.

Two weeks earlier 2004. Sugar Island powwow.
"How is your ankle, April? Still bothering you?" Robelle sat upright in her lawn chair, eager for my answer.

"Fine . . . as long as I dance traditional." I smiled at her, but the question poked at my emotions—it had been three years.

The sounds of the powwow—drums, singing, bells, laughter, crackling fry bread oil—were in the distance. Robelle and I sat at her camping area where we could visit in private.

Robelle was not dancing either. She wore a white top with a skirt that went right to the ground. Robelle never wore a lot of makeup, but her lips had a hint of pink lipstick. Her dark eyes focused on me.

"I just can't dance jingle. Doctor's orders—no 'bouncing.'" I shifted in my lawn chair.

"Yup..." Robelle nodded. "Jingle dress dancing is right out." She brushed her hair away from her face. Her hair was much shorter now than when we first met. It hung just below her shoulders, a mix of black, charcoal, gray, and white strands.

"I can dance when my foot is wrapped." My hands air-wrapped my foot as I spoke. "See, there is this way to wrap your ankle, kind of like they do for athletes when their Achilles is injured. Anyway, I can sort of dance, but then I can't walk. So that doesn't do me much good."

She shook her head. "No, I guess not." Robelle was attentive to my every word.

"I tried it a couple of times, but after a couple of hours, I'm in pain. So I end up taking the wrap off anyway."

My cheeks were warm. Tears started. I stared at my feet so I would not have to look Robelle in the face.

"I can't stand it," I continued. "I can't stand this—being sidelined. This sucks." My throat was starting to get scratchy. "Have…have I done something wrong?"

Robelle shook her head.

"You are in mourning," Robelle said quietly after a moment. "You did nothing wrong. You are in mourning for that dress."

Summer. 1992.

"When you make a jingle dress, you have to be in the right frame of mind." Robelle's voice was soft but her tone was serious. Parental. "You have to be in a good place. Of course it's always a good idea to smudge. I try to keep smudge going the entire time I roll cones."

Robelle wasn't old enough to be my mom, but her voice was confident. Her long dark hair almost reached her waistline.

We sat across from each other at her large dining room table that had been converted to a temporary sewing center. A large abalone shell about the size of a soup bowl was placed between us. Gray sage leaves were made into small round bundles about the size of grapes. These tiny balls of leaves were burning steadily in the shell creating a thin line of smoke. The smell was bitter and gave the air a slightly harsh taste. But it was familiar and felt safe.

Robelle shared with me the responsibilities of a jingle dress dancer as I cut dozens and dozens of Copenhagen snuff can lids. Collecting lids was not an easy task: we often had to answer to looks of confusion upon asking for the lids.

Each lid carried a tart scent of tobacco and metal. My job was to trim the sides of the lid so that I was working with a flat, round piece of metal. Robelle was helping me. We used scissors that were not made for cutting metal. My twenty-three-year-old hands were tired and not as self-assured as Robelle's. The muscles between my right thumb and index finger cramped. My palm throbbed but I continued without complaint.

I held the lid with my left hand and the scissors in my right. I trimmed it in a counterclockwise motion until a slender ringlet of metal was formed and the lid itself was flat. Over and over and over again I cut these lids: hundreds of them. Ringlet after discarded metal ringlet. Vaguely artistic. Prickly against my tender fingertips.

Robelle's method was quick and simple—take the scissors, cut into the lid lip with one turn of the lid. Voilà, flat metal.

Sunday 11:25 a.m. Baraga powwow 2004. Grand entry in less than an hour.

As our dresses caught the summer air, Lisa and I sat on her dining room floor. The thick rug didn't cushion my bottom as I had hoped. Regardless, I sat and began inspecting my regalia accessories. Hair ties: blue, pink, lavender, and white ribbons with a heart-shaped shell at the top. Bracelet: black, gray, and silver beads sewn on to dyed gray leather. The bracelet was already ten years old.

My fingers ran through the emerald fringe on my mint green shawl to clear out tangles from the day before. Various pieces of jewelry, large turquoise rings, bone earrings, and silver bracelets hid in their respective places within a small black bag next to me on the floor.

Lisa was sitting in front of a large mirror propped against the wall. She braided her long black hair. Her hands moved rapidly, twisting and weaving; the tattoo on her wrist caught my eye. *Nemikigokwe.*

My brown eyes caught her brown eyes in a quick glimpse in the mirror. We giggled at nothing special. I wondered if this was what it was like growing up with a sister: trying on each other's clothes and brushing each other's hair.

My tired knee-high deer hide boots needed attention. Two-inch fringe hung from the top of the boots. Temptation hit me. I put the boot to my nose . . . and sniffed. The whiff of the soft deer hide did not hold its sweet smell from years prior.

I turned the boot over to look at the elk-hide sole. "Damn!" The tape was coming off.

Lisa looked over. "A good blow-out this time, huh." We laughed. My right boot had a thin but very apparent rip. The rip was right against the bottom edge of the right sole, just under my big toe. The tear was over two and half inches long. The soles had never torn like this before. I had made a makeshift bandage with white electrical tape the day before, but some of it was coming off already. I checked the clock. Grand entry was quickly approaching.

I pulled out a small roll of white electrical tape from my bag, not sacred, but definitely necessary. I ripped several small strips of white tape to cover the tear. I rubbed my thumb against the smooth tape and thought of my dad—an electrician by trade.

My dad is not Indian. However, he made me these pair of hide boots for dancing when I was very young. He made them just a bit too big. "So you can grow into them," he said. My feet never did "grow into" them. But they always feel the best.

Summer. 1992.

Tobacco stained my hands. My fingertips ached from the sharpness of the metal. A small cut on the inside of my index finger made me wince. I licked the cut immediately. My tongue recoiled: tobacco dust. I hung my tongue out for the taste of fresh air. Robelle took notice.

"Even as you cut yourself now, you are sacrificing yourself for your people. This is a dress of healing for others, not for you." Robelle stood up from the dining room table and went to the kitchen sink. Not missing a beat she handed me the moist paper towel, sat back down, and went on with her teachings.

"This first dress is the only dress that I will help you with. After that, you are on your own. It will be your turn to pass these teachings on to someone else." Robelle continued helping me cut the lids. She was moving much quicker than I was and with what looked to be little effort.

"Each time you roll a cone, it represents a prayer for someone." Robelle put more sage in the shell and lit it with a match. After it caught the flame, she waved her hand over the leaves to create smoke. "This is why you must first be in a good place yourself. Each cone may be dedicated to someone different, or several cones may be for the same person; maybe one who is very sick."

After all of the lids were cut, I rolled each one with needle-nose pliers. Robelle could not help me with this. These were my prayers. The muscles in my palms and fingers loosened with each turn of the needle-nose pliers. I felt inadequate to be "praying for the people" so I kept these prayers in my head.

First, I prayed for my mom. Then I rolled a cone. Not an easy task. Robelle showed me a couple of times how to roll these lids into cones. Her hands moved so confidently that she made it look too easy. I fumbled with the pliers as I turned the metal. I tried to avoid the sharp edges. Pretty soon I got the hang of it and returned to my silent prayers. I prayed for my parents, family, and friends. I prayed for my husband. I prayed for people I knew who were sick. I prayed for my friend's son who suffered from leukemia.

"What if you run out of people to pray for?" *Silly question.*

Robelle had been lining up patterns and cutting up fabric. She looked up for a moment to answer me. "Prayer is a personal thing. Just pray from your heart. It will come to you."

Hoping that I wasn't cheating, I started over with my mental list, but this time I was more specific with everyone's problems. My dad's knees were bothering him again and mom was facing more hearing loss. This time the prayers were tougher but came easier. More and more faces began to appear through my closed eyelids. Some people needed more than one cone. Matt, my friend's son with leukemia, needed at least ten cones.

Sunday at noon. Baraga powwow grand entry.

Veterans raised their flags: numerous eagle feather staffs, the American flag, the Canadian flag, a Vietnam Veteran flag, and several tribal flags. Colors, sounds, and emotions ensued. A well-respected group of singers from northern Minnesota was host drum. Their beat was unified, solid and purposeful. Over a dozen of them struck the drum assertively and with accuracy; their voices precise, high and melodic.

Beads of sweat formed against my back. Sunbeams peeked through the tall pine trees and struck me with a wave of heat as purposefully as the singers struck the drum. The timid breeze could not penetrate my velvet dress. My breastplate hung over my shoulders. My mint-green shawl was placed carefully on my left arm. A slight headache snapped at my temples due to the tightness of my braids. No matter. My feet felt every little rock under them. My toes wiggled, ready to dance.

A buzz started in the grand entry line, dancers stood on their tip-toes to see who had entered the dance arena. Hundreds of women in bright outfits adorned with jewelry, beaded barrettes, and eagle plumes clipped in their hair. Our eagle feather fans circulated the air around us. Grand entry goose bumps.

In single file we entered the arena by age. We stepped with gentle intention, bending each knee slightly. Each step with each drumbeat: the heartbeat of Mother Earth, the heartbeat of our nations.

The jingle dress dancers came in the dance arena behind us women traditional dancers. A more agile dance, these ladies jumped and bounced on the balls of their feet. The steps exact, their motions faithful to each beat. I recalled what it felt like, entering the arena with my jingle dress on surrounded by other jingle dress dancers.

The grand entries where the hair on my arms stood straight up . . .

We entered the circle from the eastern direction and danced clockwise heading into the southern direction. Pride consumed me.

Where are the chills?

Probably sixty or more women traditional dancers were in front of me; some in hide dresses, many in cloth dresses. Another four or five traditional dancers were behind me and the jingle dress dancers immediately behind. My ears sought out the elegant resonance of the thousands of cones shaking the air with a metallic melody.

I followed the traditional ladies into the western direction and raised my fan to honor the eagle feather staffs held by the veterans who were dancing in place.

It felt like lightning cracking against the ground, yet still, I was light and free as a plume.

Gentle steps, knees bent slightly. My shawl swung and the fringe dangled. I moved forward now rounding the circle moving in the northern direction. Because of the July heat, the elder traditional women made the decision to dance in place. Even though I wanted to keep going forward, this was their right. I turned and faced inward. Our line of traditional women turned to dance shoulder to shoulder.

The jingle dress dancers kept going and danced in front of us; vivid dresses with the glistening reflection of sunlight from the cones. The tender crashing of the cones consoled me.

There were over 250 dancers for the afternoon grand entry.

Summer. 2000.

My jingle dress is difficult to wash. The fabric soaked up sweat, smoke, and summer dust. The organic smell really doesn't bother me. But I haven't washed her in at least three or four powwows. It is important to wait for a hot and windy day, not a forecast easily found in upper Michigan. I will not place her in the washing machine because of the cones, and I don't trust any dry cleaners with her.

She is a sacred dress. So I hand wash her. It can be painful when the cones, formerly Copenhagen lids, cut my skin. Because of her cones—365 of them—she is heavy.

I kneel down and twist the faucet on. My white antique tub fills slowly with warm water and my knees ache as they point down with all of my weight. I lean against the tub to pour a cap of Woolite into the water. I drop my fingers in the water to shake bubbles to life.

I smell (or perhaps imagine) fresh cherry-flavored pipe tobacco as I undress the hanger. I carefully hold her with both arms. She hangs as if she has collapsed in sleep. I drop back down to my knees and place her into the tub, as if I am placing a dozing child into bed. The top of the dress lies back against the tub. She looks like she is sitting up, waiting for me to wash her back.

Temperate bath water is soft over my hands. She shifts as if to move on her side. My hands must move fast because she cannot stay in the water long. I carefully select pieces of her, first the stiff arms, then the front of the skirt. I rub the fabric together furiously. I turn her over and wash the back of the skirt. I turn her back again to do the top part of the dress last. This area has painting on it, and I am shy to really scrub this part for fear the paint will be altered or even ruined. I submerge her breast, collarbone, and shoulders into the water.

Detergent bubbles have foamed and covered the entire dress as it is submerged. I lift her back up with one arm and drain the water. I then rinse the dress with cold water. I squeeze bits of her here and there to ring out excess water. I hang her on a line outside to dry. She is beautiful.

She is my third and favorite jingle dress. It has been eight years since I started dancing jingle. I look at her for a while as she blows gently in the breeze. Mainly maroon fabric in color with green, maroon, and pink ribbon. The maroon color is purposeful. It represents the lifeblood that we, as women, give each month. Our moon time is sacred. It is considered ceremony.

The top of the dress, satin eggshell in color at one time, is now a bit worn and faded but still maintains a minor sheen. At the top of the dress are paintings of roses. The edges of each petal are dark pink and naturally fade into a white flower.

At each collarbone a matching pair of rosebuds peek out from their opening petals. This represents the stage of a girl's life: opening up to a new world around her, where she will face changes—her first moon, her first kiss, or perhaps her first fast.

The arms wear matching roses, one fully open, two smaller roses open a bit more than the front ones. One can see the inside petals more. This represents the young women who are not quite adults but no longer children; women who are not yet mothers but who are learning how to take care of young ones.

On the back of the dress there is a full bouquet of roses in bloom. These roses represent the adult woman. This is where I am in my life. I am not a mother, but I do have several children in my life and several women surrounding me on my path. This bouquet represents that collective of strong women at the full bloom of their lives. It helps me remember the women in my life; women who have helped me become who I am. Women who have taught me life lessons, women who have sung with me, sweat with me, danced with me, cried with me, sat silent with me. It reminds me of the women who have laughed with me, prayed with me, taught me, learned with me. These women know who they are. It is for these women and all women that I wear this dress. She is for the healing of all women.

Sugar Island 2004.

"You did nothing wrong. You are in mourning for that dress." Robelle said quietly.

"Yeah, I know." I sighed and concentrated: *No crying.* "It's really hard because I have been working on this hide dress, and I feel as though I am having a slow time of it because I still feel like I should be a jingle dress dancer...." *Oh shit. I'm going to start crying.* "And I can see her all the time. She is hanging right in my sewing room."

I stopped to think about this. *Was she watching me and wondering?*

"Perhaps you need that dress to heal you," Robelle suggested. I looked toward her for her wisdom but didn't make eye contact. "Do you remember when I carried Kristin's dress into the arena?" My head nodded. Kristin, Robelle's youngest daughter, was sick and facing many challenges in her young life.

Robelle continued, "Do you remember how I hung it over my arm and carried the dress like a shawl? Perhaps that is what you need to do. Let that dress heal you now. The people who know you, who love you...they will understand what you are doing."

I simply continued to nod in agreement and looked at the grass below my feet. Robelle and I talked more about our hopes for the future, our own healing. I heard the drums in the distance. The recognizable sound of the drum and Robelle's voice comforted me.

Baraga powwow. Sunday sometime after 3:00 p.m.

The emcees announce the jingle dress exhibition. Drops of sunlight reflect off of the metal cones, beads, shells, and silver, causing a glittery wave of lights in the dance arena. Many of us in the audience stand out of respect for the sacredness of these outfits and the sacrifice that these women make to dance for our people.

Lisa in her white dress appears confident, proud. Her cones move with each beat, her moccasins bounce upon the earth. She lifts her eagle feather fan for the honor beats. I watch her and all of the ladies in the arena with her. Cones crash together. It sounds like a healthy rain, a rain for cleansing and healing—it is the sound that I miss most.

I happen to look down at my feet. Unconsciously, my toes are tapping—specifically, the toes on my right foot. I don't feel the tear under my big toe. I pick my right foot up and check on the tape anyway. *Still holding—but not nearly as white as earlier in the morning.* I set my foot back down and secretly wish one of the dancers is praying for my injured ankle.

August 2010

Summer and I sit in her basement. Fabric pieces, ribbon pieces, and bits of hairy threads seem to be growing out of the busy tables where we work. The buzz of the sewing machine zips along smoothly as Summer guides pieces of dark green and beige fabric. The two bits of fabric magically became one piece of art: a future arm of a new dress.

My fingers are not nearly as certain as hers as I work on her second sewing machine. This dress matches the colors of my rose dress. She is forest green and maroon with a beige material that contains a slight sheen. We cut out numerous black designs, each one requiring a skilled hand to sew them on the fabric. A hint of copper thread is sewn throughout.

After several sessions of sewing in her basement, Summer has sewn together my fourth jingle dress. Summer's craft is breathtaking.

September 2010. Sunday morning.

This dress is amazing; she fills a slight hole that has resided within my heart. I stand alone when I roll the cones. Lines of sweet grass smoke circle the lids and I hold the braid of medicine like a conductor holds and moves a baton.

My fingers then stumble as I begin to work the needle-nose pliers around the first lid. It has been years since I rolled lids. *Do I feel arthritis?* I cannot think of my own pain.

My prayers are for the women who are fighting breast cancer, the grandmothers who can no longer dance, the mothers who are fighting loneliness, their daughters who are fighting with their mothers . . . or those daughters fighting the silence—where their mother once spoke wise advice.

Even though I am not supposed to think this way about this dress, I believe it is as much for me as the women out there that I love.

AMIRA

Jeanne's Northwest flight was scheduled to leave Detroit at 5:05 p.m. for JFK in New York. Much of the East Coast was undergoing bad weather in the aftermath of a tornado, but Jeanne was unaware of conditions when she boarded her plane in Marquette. All flights to JFK, LaGuardia, and Newark, even flights to Boston and Hartford, were cancelled.

Jeanne rescheduled. A 6:40 a.m. flight to LaGuardia. She got herself a TCBY yogurt—boysenberry and white chocolate swirl—and sat at one of those orange Burger King tables, just across from the yogurt counter. She would relax a little and then book a room for the night.

The yogurt soothed her. She threw the empty cup into a waste bin and headed for the airport hospitality counter. No rooms available within a fifty-mile radius of the airport. That meant no discount room rates and high cab fares. The woman behind the counter, smiling, not frazzled, handed Jeanne a synthetic white pillow without a case, a navy blanket, and an overnight pack. COMPLIMENTS OF WAYNE COUNTY DETROIT METROPOLITAN AIRPORT, it said, in large white letters. The faux leather kit was soft in Jeanne's hand. She made her way to the nearest women's room.

In a little alcove, two large leather couches the color of caramel faced each other. A small, dark-faced girl sat in the couch across from Jeanne. This is more like it, she said, smiling at the young woman, who smiled back. They're for nursing mothers, the girl said. That's what the woman who came to clean told me.

Are you going to New York? Jeanne asked. Yes, she said, this is my second night at the airport. I'm sorry, Jeanne said, surveying the other couch. This one taken? No, she said. Then it's mine, Jeanne said. She wheeled her small carry-on to the other side of the couch, took off her shoes, and dropped into plush leather folds.

I'm Jeanne Gaudet, she said, facing the young woman. My name is Amira Baro, the girl replied in elegant English. Jeanne couldn't quite place her accent, despite a dozen years of living in Berkeley, where she had become accustomed to most linguistic sounds of the world. What are you doing in New York? Jeanne asked. I'm staying there with friends until the twenty-second. Then I'm flying to Angola to visit my father. He's a diplomat.

Cool, Jeanne said. Where were you born? New Delhi, Amira answered. But I'm quite different from most in Delhi. I grew up speaking Bodo, a tribal language, passed on by word of mouth. The language is dying. The schools are encouraging parents not to speak it with their children. Sort of like me, Jeanne said. I grew up speaking Cajun French, also passed on by word of mouth, on the endangered list of linguistic species as well. My parents have stopped speaking it with us, too, sure that a solid grounding in English would guarantee our economic success.

Amira explained how, to accommodate her father's career, her family had moved about every three or four years. They'd lived in Rio de Janeiro, Jamaica, Costa Rica, Paris, and now her father was in Angola.

Wow how exciting, Jeanne gasped. To live in all those countries, learn all those languages: Portuguese, Spanish, French . . . Not really, Amira said. Everywhere we went, my classmates made fun of me because I was different. Even in India, I'm different. My relatives say that I speak our tribal language with an accent. To tell you the truth, I'm forgetting it.

Are you in college? asked Jeanne. Yes, I'm a student at Wayne State, Amira said. What in the world brought you to Wayne State? Jeanne asked, thinking a diplomat could send his daughter to one of the Ivies. I'm studying metallurgy and graphic art, but I have no idea what I will do when I graduate in December.

Do you live in New York? Amira asked Jeanne. No, I live in the Upper Peninsula, in Marquette. I teach there. What do you teach? Writing, I said. I took the job twenty years ago, and it's my last stop. Who would want to leave the Upper Peninsula of Michigan? Lake Superior so blue, so huge you see no end of it? Growing up along the Muddy Mississippi in New Orleans, I had never seen waters like these. In the U.P., in Munising, along rugged shoreline, the water is so clear you see rock bottom. You can tour shipwrecks, see everything, through huge glass panes on the boat's floor. Sandstone cliffs streaked with minerals, ochre, jade, dun rise high as two hundred feet!

I've heard about the U.P., said Amira, sounds beautiful. Many students at WSU come from there and can't wait to get back home whenever their schedule allows or even when it doesn't. Some go back for a long weekend during hunting season, while school is still in session. They say there's nothing like being at camp. And, despite leaving home for college, they stay close to their family, closer than I am to mine. I envy that. They seem quite connected to the physical place they come from—forests, beaches, water. I don't have any of that. I'm as uprooted as most Americans.

My people, the Cajuns, are very much like the people of the U.P., despite the huge difference in weather between Michigan and Louisiana. Like Yoopers, Cajuns have stayed on the same land for generations and their identity is shaped by it. Family, too, is sacred.

What takes you to New York? Amira asked. I'm going to read at an international poetry festival at the United Nations, to celebrate the millennium. That's impressive, Amira said. Not really, Jeanne said, I'm not the star of the show. I'm reading with a former US poet laureate, a Pulitzer Prize winner, a National Book Award winner, and a bunch of others. That is, if I get there.

They were both booked on the 6:40 for LaGuardia. A long night lay ahead, but neither was upset. They settled into the couches. Jeanne dug for her stash of Golden Delicious at the bottom of her backpack and handed one to Amira. Thanks, she said. They washed the apples in the lavatory. I'm hungry, Amira said, biting into the fruit, but I've been afraid to leave this couch, so I haven't tried to find anything to eat. Look here, Jeanne said, I've got these protein bars I bought at the Marquette Food Co-op before I left. Coconut Delight and Almond Supreme, and I've got more in my suitcase. Here, take your pick. I wouldn't normally, Amira said. Go ahead, Jeanne urged. Amira chose the Coconut Delight.

They tore open the cellophane wrappers. Are you a published author? Amira asked. Yes, Jeanne said, and unzipped the pocket of her backpack. Here's one of my books, in free verse. I'm going to read from it tomorrow night. May I, Amira said, reaching for the book. Oh, you don't have to, Jeanne said. I'd like to, Amira said. Jeanne thought she'd thumb through the pages, read a few stanzas, close the book, and hand it back, but Amira started with the first poem and read to the end. She handed the thin volume back to Jeanne. They're morbid, she said.

Well, there had been all those deaths in the family, Jeanne said: my brother in a car accident, my other brother from cancer. My dad. The poems helped me to deal with loss, I guess. I know, Amira said. My mother died of cancer last year. Oh! Jeanne exclaimed. I would never . . . had I known. It's OK, Amira said. What can you do? Life goes on. It's my father I'm worried about. He lives alone. That's why I am going to see him.

Jeanne remembered when her dad and brothers had died. How she had to tell their stories over and over again in her poems. Tell them to strangers, to her boyfriends. Anyone who would listen. Jeanne liked Amira and could tell that she needed to talk. Were you at your mother's bedside when she died? No, she died in India, Amira explained. I was here in Detroit. My brother Raj was in Silicon Valley, in San Jose. He's a software engineer, she said. Mm-hmm, Jeanne said. My other brother, Fareed, is a surgeon in Denver.

I was glad to be home, back at the old house. Yes, Jeanne said. The one good thing about funerals is how families get together. But I had little to do with the funeral, Amira explained. According to our family custom, the eldest son performs the rituals, so all the work fell on my brother Raj. He cut reeds from the back yard, covered them with cleared butter, and built mother's pyre. He placed her on the bier and covered her with cinnamon and other spices. That controls the smell of burning flesh, Amira explained. Then he covered her with a second layer of reeds. What's the purpose of the butter? Jeanne asked, It keeps the fire going, Amira said. Of course, said Jeanne.

Each day, for twelve days, my brother brought our mother her favorite dishes. That's the custom. Bananas and guava, green beans with coconut, fish cooked in dates, and yogurt sauce. Mmm . . . sounds delicious, Jeanne said. On banana leaves, Amira added. Raj brought her everything on banana leaves, sometimes steamed in banana leaves. We eat everything with banana leaves, she explained. Exotic, Jeanne said. I guess, said Amira.

Then Raj brought mother coins to give to the boatman when she arrived in the Underworld. The boatman? That blows my mind, Jeanne said. I know, Amira said. There must have been some sort of common root between the Greeks and my tribe. How fascinating, said Jeanne. It was my first funeral, Amira added. What a story! Jeanne said. What details! You need to write this story. Not now, Amira said. I couldn't do it. Maybe years from now. I understand, Jeanne said.

What was it like when your father died? Amira asked. Well, in our culture, we embalm the dead, said Jeanne. In New Orleans, people spend from fifteen thousand dollars on up for the most elaborate casket, the chicest dress or the tailored suit, that final outfit. Everyone wants to "look good" in the coffin, to look better dead than alive. I once knew a woman who joined TOPS at age seventy-five to lose weight so she would look good in her coffin. And even she, at her age, would be stunning. The mortician would erase her wrinkles with collagen, if she hadn't already had a face-lift, and apply a layer of wax onto her hairless face, to perfect its contours. A dye job and a youthful coiffure would subtract additional years. I plan to have my own body cremated, to save the trouble and expense, but my mother says that if I'm not interred with the rest of the family, I'll be lost to history.

Despite the commercialization and false show, our grief is real and deep. I remember the night my father died. By the time I finally arrived from Michigan, he had gone into a coma. I was the last of eleven children he was waiting for to say good-bye. He could no longer speak, and he could barely lift his hand, but he kept pointing to his watch, my mother said, his way of asking when I would finally arrive. I cried hard when he took his last breath, feel bad to this day that I arrived too late.

What about rituals? asked Amira. Well, younger folks favor funeral parlors, but elders do things the old way, especially if they're fairly well off, and their houses packed with antiques. See, we used to build into our beds a contraption that allows you to prop the mattress at an incline, the headboard up and the footboard down. Every bed was engineered with the ultimate in mind, the display of the corpse, either in the bedroom itself or in one of the parlors if the family expects lots of visitors. Because of the heat down there, we place huge tubs of ice under the bed to keep the body as fresh as possible. Gathered bed skirts, rather ornate, hide the metal tubs. I don't believe it, said Amira, today, in the United States? Well, tradition is king in Louisiana, said Jeanne. Funerals, like weddings, are carefully staged. Dramatic spectacle, and who can outdo whom, is the name of the game. Plus, depending on the weather, and how much you pay the embalmer, the battle against the inevitable is sometimes unsuccessful.

We stay up all night with the deceased, Jeanne added. This is an ancient Christian custom, practiced to assure that the body is not violated in any way. We sip black coffee from silver urns, reserved only for wakes, and we cover mirrors throughout the house with black crêpe, to make sure the soul doesn't fly through one of them and get lost before its ascension into Heaven.

We say the Rosary every hour or so, in Cajun French. Though our language is dying, like yours, it's alive and well in rituals like this and in folktales and jokes. The Rosary, I've heard of that, but I don't know what it means, said Amira. She yawned.

Jeanne looked at her watch: 3:00 a.m. Better get some sleep, she said. Or else we won't wake up in time for our flight. Jeanne closed her eyes.

Though the two women hastily exchanged e-mail addresses before they parted, Jeanne was sure she would never see or hear from the young woman again.

Five days later, when her plane touched down at K. I. Sawyer International Airport in Gwinn, Jeanne welcomed the fresh air, jack pine, and balsam atop rolling hills. She thought of Amira, stung by the memory of her lukewarm reception of her poems. Still, she liked the girl. She placed the boarding pass bearing her e-mail into a tiny drawer of the jewelry box atop her armoire.

Then Jeanne looked at herself in the mirror. She closed her eyes and took a deep breath. She imagined the aroma of banana leaves roasting in butter.

Janice Repka

TUG

As the needle pierced the vein on the inside of her right elbow, Nana counted Smurfs. There were hundreds of the little bastards all over the nurse's smock—Papa Smurf, Brainy Smurf, Clumsy Smurf—each with a blue body and white hat. She was at seven—Grouchy Smurf—when a tug on the needle told her the stopper was being pulled back to suck her blood into the vial. Wasn't it the damnedest thing? When she was ten and found the half-dead beagle under the International Bridge, she was the one who had carried it, blood dripping out its nose, all the way to her stepfather's house. And when she was twenty-three and Jimmy's Harley bit the dust, she was the one who had pulled the spoke, blood spurting everywhere, all the way out of his leg. Yet here she was, fifty-one years old, sitting on her couch in her own home with a home health nurse taking a simple hemoglobin sample and still unable to stand the sight of her own blood.

"All done," the nurse chirped. His nametag said Roger. Visiting nurses were a pain in the ass, and this new one was no exception. They all had that same look in their eyes, like you needed their pity. Like the fact that you had no legs made it okay for them to treat you like a four-year-old.

Roger slipped the vial in his bag and removed two cartoon-covered bandages. "I have Bugs Bunny and Daffy Duck. Which would you like?"

"Got any that look like this?" Nana pushed up the left sleeve of her sweatshirt to reveal her favorite tattoo. It was a Native American on a Harley—six inches tall, three colors, with flames shooting out of the headdress.

"Oh, you've got to be kidding," said Roger.

While he examined the tattoo, she told him about a rose trellis that went from her calf clear up her thigh, and about how, when they had to cut off her right leg the first time she got gangrene, they took the tattoo with the leg. All they left were some leaves. That hospital owed her one, Nana said. If not a whole new tattoo, then at least a touch-up of the one they butchered. Maybe add a couple daisies or rosebuds.

Roger ripped open the Daffy Duck bandage and let loose about how diabetics shouldn't get tattoos, and how it was especially dangerous, crazy really, for a double amputee with neuropathy to consider such a thing. He warned her to keep a better eye on her sugar level and to stay away from drinking and smoking. Nana counted Smurfs as he spoke. When he finally shut up, she told him it was time for him to go.

"Oh, I almost forgot. I found this on the sidewalk near the door." He pulled a notebook from his bag and set it on the pile of magazines on the coffee table. "Don't forget what we talked about earlier," he said, slipping on his windbreaker. "Choose complex starches over simple sugars, and get as many green leafy vegetables as you can."

"Have a smurfy day," she replied.

The second he was gone, Nana grabbed a stale Easter Peep from the bag she kept hidden under her couch cushion and bit off its sweet yellow head. Anybody who could endure half an hour with that one deserved a treat. She considered the next bite. The head had the best ratio of marshmallow to granulated sugar. After that it was a crapshoot. You could bite off the butt and get a nice taste of cane, but that would leave the final bite extra marshmallowy. You could bite the body in half, but the two sides still wouldn't have enough sugar on them to replicate that first perfect bite. What's a gal to do? She tossed the rest of the peep into her mouth and picked up the notebook.

"Private Journal! Keep Out! Do Not Read!"

Nana recognized her granddaughter's handwriting. The warning must have been intended for the kids at school. Jenny never kept anything from her. It was a one-subject, wide-ruled seventy-sheeter with the "SchoolRite Basic Brand" logo. Nana wondered why the kids nowadays didn't go for the real diaries they had when she was young.

Her first diary had cost seventy-nine cents, plus tax. Nana spent a whole day picking through trash cans for pop bottles that she could return for the deposits to raise the cash. It had been mid-October and already snowing in Sault Sainte Marie, and she could still remember the icy numbness from having to push off the thick layer of snow with her bare hands just to get to the trash. When she finally plunked down the cash at Arfstrom Pharmacy, Nana picked the red diary. It was made of imitation leather and had a flap for securing a tiny lock. The key was the size of her thumbnail. She held the diary close to her chest the whole way home, but once she got there, she couldn't think of anything elegant to write. So she wrote about buying a diary. The next few entries were about how boring her life was. She never wrote about anything she didn't want other people to know, like the time her stepfather had slapped her for talking back and she ran off and hitchhiked all the way down to Detroit where she smoked a whole pack of cigarettes with a black boy who asked if he could look down her shirt and she let him.

Even if she hadn't written anything important in her diary, Nana knew how pissed off she would have been if her mother had found it and read it. So, out of a sort of respect for her own past, she set her granddaughter's notebook on the lopsided pile of magazines and tried to interest herself in an old *National Geographic*. There was an article on the overharvesting of Alaskan salmon, but Nana couldn't get into it because she kept thinking about Jenny's notebook instead. She picked it up and fanned it from back to front, amazed at all the black-inked pages. Nana glanced at the brown plastic wall clock and fluffed her couch cushion. Maybe it wasn't even Jenny's. How would she know if she didn't at least take a peek?

She read about how Jenny hated her acne and limp waist-length hair. How her best friend, Marcie Bolinski, seemed different now that they had both turned fourteen and they didn't have so many classes together. She read about how Jenny loved the Nike sneakers that they'd found in almost-new condition at the Goodwill, but hated how the laces never stayed tied.

In one entry, Jenny described her walk home from school. How when the bus door opened it was like stepping out of a giant yawn. How the cars waited for her to cross no matter how slow she walked, as if the stop sign jutting out from the side of the bus had some magic power. Jenny said she tried not to look at the sad things along the way as she walked home, like the skeleton of a broken baby stroller, or the boarded-up house where one of her friends used to live. Instead, she tried to stare out at St. Marys River as she walked, watching the freighters heading in and out of the locks.

Nana agreed that the neighborhood had gone to hell over the

years. It was one of those make-the-best-of-it places, but they could do worse. The rent was cheap and the landlord left them alone. Their two-bedroom salt box reminded Nana of the house she grew up in, just a few blocks down the same street, with the same view of St. Marys River that allowed you to watch the gale winds whip the water into frosty peaks.

Nana skipped around in Jenny's notebook, skimming random entries about clothes and geometry that made Nana wonder why she was wasting her time, until she stumbled on an entry near the end about a party at Brianna Simon's house Friday night. *They say she has a big-screen television in her basement. Her Mom and Dad keep their beer down there. They don't even get mad if you drink one. But I don't care that I'm not going. I have better things to do.*

Who the hell was this Brianna girl and why hadn't Jenny ever mentioned her before? Then, Jenny started writing about some stupid television show and Nana had to read each entry carefully to try to find out more. *Parties are dumb. They're just bunches of people standing around or doing Dance Dance Revolution or whatever. Besides, everybody knows that the only reason Brianna Simon is popular is because she does it, which is gross. I don't care how cool her parents and her house are. And I totally couldn't be bothered about her lame party.*

Nana closed the notebook. So what if Jenny didn't tell her every little thing that happened at school. Jenny was still bright enough not to get mixed up with a crowd like that. Maybe Nana had screwed her life up, and maybe Nana's daughter, Karen, had done the same, but things were going to be different with Jenny.

The kitchen door groaned and Nana glanced at the clock. She stuffed the journal under a couch cushion, grabbed her magazine, and closed her eyes, pretending she had fallen asleep reading. After a while, the refrigerator door opened and closed and footsteps grew closer. Nana waited until she could feel Jenny's breath on hers. Then Nana popped her eyes open and watched Jenny recoil with a gasp.

"Gotcha," said Nana, smiling.

"Why do you do that?" Jenny asked, but Nana could tell she was more amused than angry. "You're going to kill me with that one of these days."

"How was school?"

"Same as always, except we had an assembly about dental hygiene. I'll get extra credit in civics class if you sign a sheet saying I flossed my teeth every day for a week."

"What moron thought that up?" asked Nana.

"That's what I said. But you still have to sign it."

"Did you eat all your lunch?"

"We were out of peanut butter. I just had jelly."

Nana frowned. "Skin and bones, that's what you are. Get me my cigarettes."

Jenny went to the top drawer of Nana's desk and fished out a pack of Marlboros. Nana knew that it made Jenny feel better thinking she only smoked when Jenny was there to make sure a hot ash on the sofa didn't catch fire. She didn't tell Jenny about all the times she had snitched a smoke when Jenny forgot to put them back.

Nana pulled a lighter from under a cushion. The first blast of nicotine was always like a breath of fresh air. She sucked hard and held the smoke in her lungs as long as she could, exhaling a long stream. Nana blew smoke rings and Jenny poked at them as they floated toward her.

"There's a girl at school who's having a party tonight," said Jenny.

"Don't take it to heart," Nana replied. "For every party you're not invited to today, there'll be two you will be invited to some other day."

"But, Nana, I *was* invited." Jenny moved to the window and cracked it to make sure the smoke alarm didn't go off. "Why wouldn't I be?"

Nana let smoke drift out of her mouth and inhaled it up her nostrils. "Isn't this a school night?"

"It's Friday."

"Don't you have homework?"

"Even if I had homework, I wouldn't do it on a Friday. So, can I go?"

Nana thought about the booze in Brianna's basement. "How would you get there?" she asked, while casually turning the pages of the *National Geographic*.

"I haven't got that worked out yet."

Nana took another deep drag on her cigarette, letting her words exhale with the smoke. "Well, let me know if you do."

"I hope my jean skirt is clean," Jenny replied. "I've got a million things that could go with that."

As soon as Jenny left the room, Nana looked in the full-length mirror hanging at an angle on the wall directly in front of her. A visiting nurse had hung the mirror there so Nana could see the reflection of the kitchen. It was supposed to make her feel less isolated. Nana watched Jenny in the mirror. When she heard her clomp upstairs, Nana pulled the journal from under the afghan.

I sat next to Brianna's brother, Eric, in study hall today. He hates his stepmother. She won't let his dad buy him a new car even though they can afford it. Plus, Eric says his stepmother is a drunk. I told Eric I knew what he was going through because sometimes my grandma gets spaced out on Vicodin.

Nana had to restrain herself from screaming for Jenny. She wanted to give her a piece of her mind for trash-talking like that, but Jenny wasn't talking, she was writing—in a private journal that Nana knew she shouldn't be reading. *I can't believe he even spoke to me because he's a junior and I'm only a freshman. Plus, he's Eric Simon. Then I saw him at his locker later and he said he's always pulling muscles during wrestling practice and coach won't give him anything for pain, which must suck. He asked if I could get him some Vicodin. Then, he asked me if I wanted to come to Brianna's party! Even though I said I didn't want to go, I really do.*

Nana dug for her bag of Peeps, yanked one out, and tossed it into her mouth. She was going for a second when she heard Jenny coming down the steps. She plunged the notebook under an afghan, grabbed the remote control, and clicked on the television. It was a *Law & Order* rerun. Nana stared blankly, her right hand clutching the journal below the covers as if it could float to the surface.

Later, Nana was still holding onto the notebook as the blended smell of macaroni and cheese and hot dogs wafted from the kitchen. Twice while Jenny was cooking, Nana saw her slip over to the kitchen phone to make sure it was working. Nana pulled the extension phone on the coffee table closer. By the time Jenny brought in the tray, the early news had come on and a cold breeze was slipping in through the inch of open window.

Nana wished the blinds were up so she could look out at St. Marys River. When she was little and her mother was upstairs with one of her boyfriends, Nana would watch the freighters so she didn't have to think about it. Once, when she was twelve, she saw a stout, white tugboat pull near a gray-and-red longboat that was easily ten times its size. The two boats just sat there, facing off, within thirty yards of each other. Nana knew that tugboats sometimes would help freighters by pushing or pulling them through the locks. Did the freighter need the tug's help? It looked so big and strong, Nana hoped that it could make it on its own. She watched for as long as possible, but her eyelids drooped. and when she woke a few hours later, both boats had disappeared. The next evening, Nana and her mother sat on the front stoop, as they often did, calling out the names of the ships they recognized as they headed down the St. Marys River toward Lake Huron. Nana wanted to say something about the freighter and tugboat she had seen the night before, but the image of the boats sitting there, which she had only to close her eyes to see again, had seemed too private somehow and she never spoke of it.

Jenny closed the window and slipped under the afghan on the brown and tan striped recliner next to the couch. She had already changed into her jean skirt and a button-down top that she had rolled up at the bottom and tied at the waist so that a tiny triangle of skin showed at her belly button. Nana watched her pick at her hot dog. Nana stared hard, head to toe, taking her all in: how Jenny nibbled at the edge of the bun, how she held her hair back as she ate, how she kept the afghan curled around her.

"What?" Jenny asked, staring back.

Nana shrugged and looked at her macaroni. What was she supposed to say?

When Jenny's mother, Karen, had suddenly gone to hell in a handbasket, Nana hadn't seen it coming. She was still full of piss and vinegar herself back then, with two healthy legs for jumping on and off hogs and dancing on car hoods. Karen's dad was never in the picture. Nana figured he was that boy she met at the Chippewa County Fair, but she couldn't be sure and she never really cared.

Karen was a good baby who hardly ever cried. When Nana had to waitress the night shift, she would bring Karen along and make a little bed for her with blankets in the broom closet until she got off. God knows she was a lousy excuse for a mom back then. Sneaking out to go drinking and bringing home men from bars. No wonder Karen found friends of her own, parties of her own, drugs, alcohol, boys of her own. It felt like it had happened overnight. One day she was giving Nana sweet, open-mouthed kisses and the next she was stealing Nana's rent money for meth. Nana fought like hell to get Karen back on track. Confronted her about the drugs. Screamed her lungs out about it. Threatened to throw her out, cut her off, if she didn't straighten up. Then one day, Karen disappeared.

She was gone for seventeen months. Every time someone asked where Karen was, Nana cussed and complained about thankless children, but every night, she would brush her finger against the bristles on Karen's toothbrush hoping it was wet. Hoping, against odds, to find Karen safe, back in her room, in her bed, sleeping under her mound of stuffed animals.

Then, as suddenly as she left, Karen walked back through Nana's door. She was hoping she could borrow some cash, hoping Nana could watch Jenny for a while because the kid cried so damn much she was afraid she might hurt her, hoping she could get a car so she could go somewhere to get her shit together. Karen got Nana's '89 Chevy Nova and Nana got Jenny. She was just six weeks old. Nana had carried the slumbering infant into her room and laid her on the bed. Then she had gently scooted her over and curled up alongside her, watching her, and thanking God for the second chance.

But the memory was of little comfort now. What made her think that a type 1 diabetic without a pot to pee in could raise a kid right and keep her safe in this rotten excuse for a world? What good was a second chance if you didn't know how to change the ending?

The phone rang. Nana was halfway through a humorless sitcom when she grabbed the receiver.

"Hey...um, yea," said the unmistakably male voice. "Is Jen around?"

Probably that Eric, Nana thought. She fought the urge to disconnect him. He would just call back. "Jenny, there's a boy on the phone for you," Nana yelled.

Jenny was elbow-deep in soapy dishwater. She wiped the bubbles off her hands and picked up the receiver. "I've got it," she yelled back.

Nana held her breath.

"You can hang up now," said Jenny into the receiver.

Nana saw Jenny approaching and reluctantly complied. Jenny turned her back and lowered her voice. Nana picked up the notebook, held the afghan over it like a hood, and read.

I was wearing my shirt with the butterfly print. Just because the top buttons weren't buttoned, Marcie said I looked like a slut. Wasn't that mean? Eric said the Vicodin worked great. He wants me to bring the rest of the bottle to the party so he'll be able to dance. I would drop dead if he asked me to dance!

Nana picked up her Marlboros, lit one, and sucked hard. When the red ash had crept to the filter, she used it to light another. After a third, the thickening smoke began to sting her eyes. She imagined Jenny knocking on a big door with beveled glass and a brass nameplate that read "Simon." She could almost smell the reefer on Eric as he put his sweaty arms around Jenny and led her into the basement.

Hot ash dropped from Nana's cigarette onto her stomach. She snapped forward and brushed the ash off. She leaned over the edge of the couch, found the ash on the carpet, and pressed a wet thumb to it for good measure. She snubbed the cigarette out and lit another one.

The smoke detector let out a piercing scream.

"My God!" Jenny yelled. She rushed to the window, flung it open, and fanned the smoke out. While the smoke drained, Jenny pulled off one of her sneakers, climbed onto the coffee table, and whacked the smoke detector. The defeated contraption dropped from the ceiling and plopped onto the floor.

"False alarm," said Nana, still stubbing out the cigarette in the ashtray. "No need to worry."

Jenny grabbed the pack of smokes, put them back in the drawer, and closed it. "No smoking while I'm gone, promise?"

"You found a ride?"

"Eric Simon is coming to get me around eight. You'll like him. He's very responsible."

Nana looked hard at Jenny: the way she tilted her head when she lied, the way she shifted from foot to foot, the tiny creases on her fore-head that betrayed her uneasiness.

"Nana, stop spacing like that. It's freaking me out."

But Nana was stuck in her thoughts. She could confront Jenny. Admit she read her notebook. Admit she didn't trust her. Forbid her to go to the party. Threaten to punish her. But how long would it take for Jenny to realize that Nana's threats were hollow? How long before her tough love felt like no love? How long before, after repeating that scene over and over, like with Karen, Jenny just disappeared?

She could call that Eric boy and confront him. That would be trick-ier, and would require a plan. First she would have to create a ruse to get Jenny out of the house.

"Do you have time to slip down to the corner drug store and get some lancets for my glucose monitor?" she would ask.

"Right now?" Jenny would probably respond. "You hardly ever use that thing."

"Don't you want me to keep a better eye on my blood sugar level?"

"Of course, but—"

"Hurry up so you won't be late for the party."

Then as soon as Jenny was out the door, Nana would pick up the phone and dial star sixty-nine. The phone would ring eight times be-fore being answered, and Nana would hear party music in the back-ground.

"Yea, this is Eric," a voice would reply. "Who's this?"

"I'm your worst nightmare," Nana would say. "Now listen and lis-ten good. I know all about your little scheme, and I don't give a crap about it except I'm not going to let you drag Jenny into it. So you've got a choice to make. You can call Jenny back and you can blow her off, or I can call the cops and tell them you stole my Vicodin."

"I didn't steal it. She gave it to me."

"My word against yours, kid," Nana would tell him. "People always believe the cripple."

Then Nana could fluff the cushion next to her and wait for Jenny to return. They could spend the evening watching television, and ev-erything would be the same as it was before Nana found the notebook. Except for when Monday came and Eric spread word around school about what happened and Jenny accused Nana of ruining her life.

Two blasts on a horn brought Nana back out of it.

"That's him," said Jenny, rushing to the mirror to check her hair. She used her fingers to part her hair on one side, and then the other, before returning to her usual part in the middle. She ran her hands down her skirt to smooth it, then untied the bottom of her shirt and tucked the ends into the skirt.

"It's over at eleven, so will eleven thirty be okay?"

Maybe I'm overreacting, Nana thought. Jenny isn't a little girl anymore. She's big and strong and knows how to take care of herself. Surely, Jenny will be all right.

Two more blasts.

They brought Nana's thoughts back to the tugboat and the long-boat on St. Marys River all those many years ago. The boats were next to each other, adrift and immobilized, while she waited to see if they could each make it through the locks alone or if the longboat needed the tugboat to help it navigate through. She remembered how she would sometimes play a game as a child and pick a boat she saw and pretend to be the boat. Nana wondered which she should pick, whether she was more like the tugboat or the longboat, and for a moment she thought about asking Jenny what she thought. But then she remembered that Jenny was waiting for an answer to a question of her own.

Tugboats, longboats—Jenny really would think she was spaced out on Vicodin if she didn't snap out of it. "Have a nice time," Nana replied.

She picked up her *National Geographic* and flipped to a double-page photo spread of salmon trying to throw themselves upstream. Nana disappeared into the article about fish harvesting in Alaska, and when she looked up, Jenny was gone, too.

Vincent Reusch

PLASTIC FANTASTIC

My wife was standing with our two girls, sifting through a table of books—twenty-five cents per paperback, a dollar per hardcover—when I saw the Han Solo and Princess Leia figures lying together in a cardboard box. Two thin plastic people, the original 1970s versions.

We had argued through dinner, the same argument as always, some small negligence—on this day, a forgotten loaf of bread—opening the door to a litany of past offenses, little injustices that fall like dominoes, trailing back nearly to the day we met. The evening was warm, the first summery day that early June, and we had taken our Sunday walk, despite the argument, and had stopped at this yard sale. The homeowners were closing down, the father and his sons carrying tables into the garage—lamps and dishes and small kitchen appliances balanced on their tops. I had been hoping to find some quirky yard-sale trinket that I could hold up to my wife, something we would laugh weakly about, a little talisman to ward off the fighting for another day. When I found the *Star Wars* figures, I had not, however, thought of them as charms for my wife and me, but for a boy I once knew, "a long time ago, in a galaxy far, far away." They were in perfect condition, as fresh and bright as when they were newly minted thirty years earlier, as fresh and bright as those Buffy held in his fists on a winter night in 1978, a night that I hadn't known I'd remembered, that I hadn't known I'd forgotten, one night among so many lost in the shadow of my parents' divorce.

I was ten years old. My brother, Eric, was thirteen, Buffy, seven. We were sitting on a yellow shag carpet in front of the woodstove at my father's house, an old farmhouse perched on a bluff above a lonely stretch of Lake Superior coastline. The wind blew day and night from the lake, the scattering of trees around the house beaten down from it, the sound of it forever in my ears.

My father and Buffy's mother, Joanie, had just gone to bed. Joanie didn't spend the night often, never before with her son. They'd been trapped on this night by a storm, the road drifted shut, snow sliding like waves across the field in front of our house. Eric had suggested a

210

slumber party, and our father had brought three army-issue sleeping bags, rolled and cinched with belts, down from an eaves closet. While Eric and I staked out our territory, Buffy looked uncertainly at his bag. His mother unbuckled the belt for him, the bag flopped open, and he crinkled his nose against the earthy scent of dry-rotting canvas. His mother unzipped the zipper partway and folded the fabric back so that it made a triangle. She went upstairs and returned with pillows, fluffed one, and laid it on the exposed lining of Buffy's sleeping bag. She kissed him on the lips, then on the forehead, and he watched her follow my father through the kitchen and into the bedroom. She blew him one last kiss, closed the door, and Buffy joined us at the woodstove.

The cast-iron doors of the stove were open, and a log smoldered in the fire, a few weak flames licking the circumference of charred bark, reflecting dully off our cheeks and throwing hollow shadows over our eyes. The storm rattled the double-hung windows, echoed down the metal stovepipe. Buffy flinched at every gust, looked at the windows, looked at us.

"Do you want to hear a ghost story?" Eric asked.

———

We had first met Buffy two months earlier, when our father had taken us to Joanie's house, a doublewide trailer that he called a modular home. It was newly delivered from the factory, and it sat alone in a mowed patch of field on the edge of town. We had gone there to build a toolshed in the backyard, a place for rakes and garden hoses and Joanie's push mower. We arrived just after sunup, and the field shone golden in the late-autumn sun, grasses as high as my chest walling the carved square of Joanie's yard. My father drove our Chevy Impala around the house and parked in back, the prefabricated parts of the toolshed in cardboard boxes tied to the car's roof.

We found Buffy sitting at a table in the kitchen. He wore a *Star Wars* T-shirt—Luke Skywalker with his light saber held in both hands over his head, the Death Star in the background. The shower was running, and my father ducked into the bathroom. He poked his head back out and said to Buffy, "Your mother says to show the boys your room." I said I was hungry, and my father said we'd have pancakes before we started on the shed. He stayed in the bathroom, and Eric and I followed Buffy down a narrow hallway to the back of the house. As we passed the closed bathroom door, I heard Joanie laugh. He must be tickling her, I thought.

The floor creaked as we walked down the hall. When I bumped Buffy's bedroom door with my shoulder, it swung into the wall with a hollow thud. I had never been inside a modular home, had never been in a home with floors that flexed beneath my feet, a home with doors light as cardboard, trim and doorknobs made of plastic. And I had never been in a bedroom like Buffy's.

His bed frame was shaped like a race car, his sheets printed with cartoon scenes from *Speed Racer*. His wallpaper was *Battlestar Galactica*. His carpet was bright red shag, his ceiling cornflower blue, pasted with planets and stars that I was sure glowed in the dark. And spanning one wall were half a dozen shelves filled with toys—toys made of plastic, toys that took batteries and came with accessories, toys that seemed a world away from our Lincoln Logs, board games, and books. He had the *League of Justice* superheroes and their Hall of Justice play set. He had the entire *Star Trek* crew and the Enterprise bridge. He had a dozen G.I. Joes, *Planet of the Apes*, Action Jackson, Evel Knievel and the Super Stunt Cycle. X-wings and Tie Fighters, and the Death Star, complete with trash compactor. He had Stretch Armstrong, Stretch Monster, and Stretch Spiderman and Hulk, which I hadn't even known existed. And in one corner, on his red-white-and-blue dresser, was an RCA color TV.

Buffy's action figures seemed a better fit for this house than did real flesh-and-blood people. They seemed a better fit for Joanie's car, too, which had amazed Eric and me when we first saw it. It was a Toyota Corolla, a new breed of automobile, with a plastic interior, plastic bumpers and grill. It squeaked when it hit bumps. Our car rattled over bumps, smelled of raw gas and mildewed floorboards. Eric called their car the Plastic Fantastic, and for years that's how I thought of this boy and his mother, as the Plastic Fantastics.

Buffy and Joanie. Ken and Barbie. Buffy was small and perfectly proportioned, without any outstanding feature, but with a beauty that came from his symmetry, from his flawless glowing skin, from his thick shiny hair, cut into the same perfect bowl that Eric and I saw on children's heads in the TV commercials for the toys that we saw in Buffy's bedroom. And Joanie looked the perfect TV mom, a short bob of sprayed hair, a beauty mark on her cheek in the exact same spot as Florence Henderson's.

If my brother and father and I had been on TV, our show would have been about survival, a bearded father whose eyes never seemed to rest, and two rail-thin boys, hair uncut since our mother left six months earlier, clothes half a size too small. Our show would be *Land of the Lost*, or *Swiss Family Robinson*, without the good looks and affable personalities. Without the dialogue. When I see our family photographs from that time, I think we look like the windblown trees on that hill, like the ancient fence posts scattered in haphazard lines between one forgotten field and the next.

———

A wash of snow and wind passed over the house, and the small flames flared in the fireplace. Buffy said he didn't want to hear a ghost story, and I suggested we put another log on the fire.

"We could turn on the lights," Buffy said. "I brought toys we could play with."

"We can't turn on the lights," Eric said. "Dad might come out."

Buffy looked at me. I looked at Eric. Then we all turned our heads toward the kitchen, to our father's bedroom door on the other side. A flickering orange glow reached out from beneath the closed door and spread across the black-and-white linoleum.

"He won't see," Buffy said. "The door's closed."

"That's candlelight," Eric said. "He can't take artificial lights after midnight. They burn his eyes."

Earlier that day, while my father and Joanie were attempting to dig out the driveway, Eric and I had taken Buffy into our father's bedroom, where Eric tried to convince him that our father was a werewolf. Our father was hairy enough, his body covered in an unbroken layer of fur, a mane of hair running up his spine. And on his new waterbed was the evidence of his barbaric feasts. Eric reached into one corner of the bed frame and lifted the free end of a leather strap. "This is where he ties up his victims," he said.

Our father had bought the waterbed while Eric and I were visiting our mother, who had moved back to her hometown, downstate in Kalamazoo. She was living with her sister and taking nursing classes at the community college. In two years, she told us as she put us on the Greyhound for the ten-hour ride back to our father's, she would have her license, would buy a house, and we could live with her. Eric told her we were fine where we were, and when she reached out to him he pulled away. Okay, honey, she told him. That's okay.

Our father hadn't only bought a waterbed while we'd been away, he had also bought himself a new wardrobe. When we returned from our mother's, he met us at the bus stop wearing flare-legged jeans and a polyester paisley shirt, unbuttoned to the bottom of his sternum, a gold chain nested in the thick mat of his chest hair. At home, he showed off the new yellow shag carpet in the living room. Then he brought us into his remodeled bedroom, a room in many ways similar to Buffy's. He had put in a thick burgundy carpet, several shades darker than Buffy's red. He had a color television, a Betamax videotape player beside it. Instead of a race-car bed, he had the new waterbed. Instead of *Speed Racer* sheets, he had burgundy satin sheets, covered with a faux bearskin bedspread. Instead of stars on his ceiling, he had mirrors. He smiled as I lay on the waterbed and looked at myself reflected in the ceiling, my skinny body in cut-off jeans and a Coca-Cola T-shirt. I waved my arms and legs, watching my knees and elbows move on the ceiling, and feeling some charge of excitement at the touch of the smooth satin on my skin.

My father had plastic toys in his new bedroom, too. I went often into his room to lay on those satin sheets and look into the mirrors, and I found the toys in one of the nightstand drawers, two oblong, colored objects—one hard and baby blue, the other soft and pink. I thought of them as rockets, though I knew they weren't rockets. The hard one had a knurled dial on its base, and when I twisted it, the rocket vibrated. I held it against my neck. "Hello, how are you?" I said, my voice quavering with the vibrations. "Take me to your leader. I come in peace."

Eric had been the one to find the leather straps tied to the four corners of our father's bed. "What are they for?" I asked, when he showed me.

"For tying people down," he said.

"Why?"

"Why do you think, dummy?"

I imagined myself strapped by my wrists and ankles, my father tickling me like he used to in the evenings on the living-room floor, when Eric would help to hold me down and our mother would warn that someone was going to get hurt. "I don't know," I said to Eric. "Tickle torture?"

"Yeah, tickle torture," he said. "Tickle torture with Joanie's plastic fantastic."

Buffy stood near the doorway, two steps into the bedroom, as Eric held up the leather strap. "See these red sheets?" Eric said. "They used to be white." Buffy said he didn't believe it, but I knew it was true. The sheets had been white as long as I could remember, and the bedspread beige, a wedding gift to our parents from our grandmother. Buffy asked me if it were true, and I looked at Eric and didn't answer. "You're such a fucking baby," Eric said to me. For the next hour, Buffy sat by the living-room window and watched the figures of our parents, the primary colors of their winter gear appearing and disappearing in the whitewash of snow, as they lost the battle with the storm.

———

Joanie appeared from her bathroom, from a door as narrow as any I had ever seen in a house, and she joined my father in the kitchen. He was just finishing up a stack of pancakes, our breakfast before we went to work on the shed. When he set the platter on the table, we saw that he had poured the batter into the shapes of animals—turtles, bears, Mickey Mouse. "I don't know why everybody thinks they have to be round," he said, as he forked a pancake onto his plate. He looked with comic intensity at his pancake, and added, "Oops, I think I gave the horse a hard-on." He laughed like Goofy, and Buffy laughed with him.

Buffy loved the animal pancakes. With the syrup, he made eyes and mouths and stripes. He bounced on his seat as he ate, and he chattered on about which animals Eric and I had on our plates, which parts we should eat first.

The morning was cold, and the thick field-stubble that was Joanie's yard was wet with dew. As we unpacked the aluminum strips that would frame the shed, my fingers grew red and stiff. Joanie brought me a pair of her gloves, flesh-colored and smelling of her rose perfume and the talcum scent of her makeup. They stretched over my fingers like thick nylons. Eric said he didn't need any gloves, and he and my father worked barehanded, bolting together the lengths of frame as I held them in place. Once the frame was finished, we stepped back to look at our work. The sun was high over the field now, warm on our faces, drying the yard. The frame glinted in the sunlight, an erector-set skeleton of a house.

"I bet this is the same stuff their house is built with," Eric said.

"Watch it, my man," our father said.

"Well, it's such a piece of crap," Eric said. "I'm waiting to step right through the floor."

My father wrapped his hand around the back of Eric's neck. "I might marry that lady someday," he said. "Don't piss in your own pool, son."

"This isn't my pool," Eric said, pulling himself away from our father's hand.

"You're damn right there," our father said. "So better yet, don't piss in my pool."

Joanie brought out coffee for Eric and my father. I'd never seen Eric drink coffee, and I watched his face sour as he took his first sip.

"What are you looking at?" he said.

My father laughed and swiped a hand over Eric's head. "Come on, let's get the sides up."

By noon, we had finished attaching the sides, Eric and I holding the plastic panels in place, while our father screwed them to the frame with sheet-metal screws. We broke for lunch, and Buffy joined us afterward. Joanie had put him in a white down vest and green mittens, and as he walked toward us, his vest blinding in the sunlight, I looked at my own jacket. It had been light blue when my mother had me try it on at the end-of-season sale at J.C. Penney that spring. But now the coat was more earth-toned than blue, the nylon fibers embedded with dirt from carrying firewood.

My father was inside the shed on a stepladder. He had taken off his shirt, despite the chill of coming winter that was in the air. "I never have a problem keeping warm," he liked to say, rubbing the hair that covered his chest and shoulders. Buffy stared at his hairy torso, displayed over the tops of the walls. Eric was outside the shed on another stepladder. I handed him the thin vinyl strips that would form the roof, and he and my father snapped them together, my father working the ridgepole, Eric working the eaves.

"Come here, Buff," my father said, motioning from over the top of the walls for Buffy to come inside the shed. "How about helping me with the roof."

Buffy looked up at the emerging roof and at my father's body, which might have been naked for all he could see from where he stood. He shook his head.

"Come on," my father said. "It's not going to bite you."

Buffy looked longingly back at the house, then stepped into the shed. He reappeared above the walls, standing near the top rung of the ladder, with my father on the ladder behind him. I handed a vinyl strip to Eric, and he swung it into place.

"See that hole there?" my father asked Buffy, pointing to the last strip they'd attached. Buffy nodded. "See this nipple?" my father said, and he pinched a round, flanged tab between his finger and thumb.

Buffy looked at my father's face when he heard the word *nipple*.

"When I get the piece in place, you line up that nipple with the hole, and push it until you feel it snap together."

"I want to get down now," Buffy said.

"You can do it. Just reach up there. I've got you."

"I want to get down," Buffy repeated.

"Oh, for Christ's sake," my father said. "Just do it." He held the piece in place and Buffy reached up and pushed.

When the pieces snapped together, they pinched the tip of Buffy's mitten between the slats. He shrieked and jerked his hand away, out of his mitten. My father lost his balance, and he and Buffy slid down the ladder and fell against the wall. I heard the pop of several screws as one of the vinyl panels tore away from the frame. Buffy jumped off the ground where he lay beside my father, and he ran out of the shed. In the middle of the yard he turned around, his white vest streaked with dirt, the corner of one pocket torn. My father stepped out of the shed, and Buffy ran into the house.

———

I didn't want a ghost story. I didn't want to talk about our father being a werewolf. I pulled the fire poker from the ash bin, prodded the smoldering log, and the fire flamed back to life.

"Once upon a time," Eric said, "There were two little boys, seven and nine, home for the night with the babysitter. It was getting cold, and they had only one log left for the fire."

Buffy and I looked at the paper-birch log that sat alone on the brick base surrounding the woodstove. I suggested we put it on the fire, and Eric said no, that it would spoil the mood.

I dropped the poker into the bin, and Eric told Three Knocks, a ghost story that he and I told each other often. He told an especially brutal version, dragging his knuckles on the end table each time he said, "knock . . . knock . . . knock." He fashioned the house in the story after our own, added a winter storm raging outside as it was that night. He gave the marauding murderer a beard and covered him in hair, like our father, gave the babysitter a mole on her cheek, "a mole so ugly that the two boys were afraid to look at it." At the end of the story, the babysitter stumbled into the house with an axe embedded in her skull, a bloody hole where her mole had been gouged out. Buffy pressed his body against my hip, and I pushed him away, told him to get off me.

When Eric's story was finished, Buffy listed his favorite cartoons and his favorite breakfast cereals, his favorite Disney characters, and his favorite rides at Disney World, where he had gone with his mother that summer. His lists were bright and colorful, confetti and silly string that he sprayed around that dark room, as if it might exorcise Eric's story. He listed the toys that he had brought to our house—D.C. and Marvel superheroes, Eagle-eye G.I. Joe, *Star Wars* characters and the Death Star—and he suggested again that we turn on a light and play.

Eric shrugged. "Okay," he said. "If you want to see a werewolf."

"There's not a full moon tonight," Buffy said.

"You just can't see it because of the storm," Eric said.

"Let's get your toys," I said to Buffy. "We can play with the light off."

The log had burned almost completely out, and the dim flame reflected in Eric's eyes. "Babies," he said. "Go ahead. Play with your little toys."

The toys were around the corner by the front door, and as Buffy and I stepped onto the enclosed porch, he slipped his hand into mine. We grabbed the backpack and duffel bag that held the toys, and we speed-walked back around the corner, the windows following us like eyes.

Buffy turned the backpack upside down in front of the fireplace, and toys spilled onto the carpet. I opened the Death Star, and he kneeled beside me. He dropped Princess Leia and Han Solo into the trash compactor and twisted the handle. The walls of the compactor slid together and squeezed the two figures out a hatch and onto the shag carpet. They lay side by side on their backs, their plastic hands touching. Buffy scooped them up and handed them to me. I dropped them into the compactor and twisted the handle.

While we played, Eric unzipped the duffel bag and pulled from it a plastic rifle with a parabolic dish at the end of the barrel. Buffy told us it was a microphone. "You can hear people whisper from across the room," he said. He held up a pair of stethoscope-style earphones that dangled from the stock. "You put these in your ears, and point at what you want to hear."

Eric tried it first. I went across the room and whispered, "Mary had a little lamb." Eric repeated it.

"Go around the corner," he said, and I stepped around the corner, onto the porch. "Whose fleece was white as snow," I whispered.

"White as snow," Eric said. "Cool." He pointed it through the kitchen toward our father's bedroom door, and for half a minute he sat listening. Then a smile worked across his face. He lowered the rifle and pulled the stethoscope tips from his ears. "Listen," he said, and he handed me the gun.

I put on the stethoscope and pointed the microphone at the bedroom door. Eric wasn't looking at me, but at Buffy, still with that smile on his face, a smile like a finger drawn across a throat. The first sound I heard was Joanie's voice, a quiet moan. Then I heard my father. I couldn't make out his words, but he sounded as if he were giving instructions, the same tone of voice he had used on me the day we built Joanie's shed. I heard Joanie's voice, a question, asking for clarification, then my father's again, this time a snippet of clear words "Oh, for god's sake, not like that. Let me get this tightened first." I heard another woman's voice, then, a surprised exclamation, "Oh, Mr. Hardwick!" the tinny voice coming from the television on my father's dresser. Joanie moaned again, then a man's voice from the TV moaned, then Joanie, then the other woman, then my father. Then they were all moaning, a rhythmic chorus, call and answer, the sloshing of the waterbed marking time.

"Give the gun to Buffy," Eric said.

I lowered the rifle and pulled the stethoscope ends from my ears. Buffy was on his knees, still playing with Han Solo and Princess Leia. He had them facing each other, and he was wiggling one, then the other, back and forth, as if they were carrying on a conversation. He didn't supply the words, and I had the feeling that he wasn't even thinking of words.

"Give Buffy the gun," Eric said.

Buffy didn't look up, though he must have heard my brother. I watched him wiggle those little people, watched them carry on some conversation that Buffy was content to let go over his head, that was comfort enough just in the fact that it was happening at all.

"We should put another log on the fire," I said. The log had not burned completely, but had finally sputtered out, and now there was no flame, just a trickle of smoke and patchy red coals shimmering over the log's surface.

"Just give it to him first," Eric said.

"It's going to burn out," I said.

"So what. Give him the gun."

"Just leave him alone," I said, looking into the dark woodstove.

"You're his protector now?" Eric asked.

"No," I said.

I took the poker and prodded the log that smoldered in the fireplace. A few orange sparks drifted up the chimney.

I could feel Eric behind me, staring at Buffy, then at me. "You're just going to screw it up," he said. He picked up the birch log from the bricks. "Pull that log forward, and I'll drop this one behind."

I hooked the smoldering log with the poker and pulled it to the lip of the stove. Eric dropped the birch, too far forward, and it landed on the tip of the poker. The smoldering log slipped free and rolled out of the fireplace. It bounced with a shower of sparks off the brick base and landed on the living room carpet. We all jumped away as black smoke rose up, the synthetic fibers of the new shag melting beneath the charred wood. Eric grabbed the poker from my hand and pulled the ash shovel from its bucket. He pinched the log between the poker and shovel, but as he lifted, the log twisted out and melted another line of carpet. He tried again, and more of the carpet bubbled and threw up black smoke. Then the fire alarm rang out.

Eric was standing on the back of the couch, pulling the battery from the alarm, when the bedroom door burst open, and our father ran naked into the living room. The curled bark of the paper birch caught fire and flared, spotlighting my father's naked body, his coat of hair glittering in the firelight. He stepped on a spot of melted carpet, and I heard a quick sizzle of flesh before he tossed back his head and howled. Buffy backed against the wall. My father hopped around, landed in more molten carpet, and howled again. Buffy still held his *Star Wars* figures, one gripped tightly in each fist. He was shaking, and though he seemed mentally to be somewhere else, I saw that his eyes were fixated on my father's penis, which jostled wildly as my father danced around the room on his burned feet.

I stared along with Buffy, and for a moment there seemed nothing in that room but my father's penis. It banged back and forth off his inner thighs, always one beat behind as he went first for the log, then for the fire poker, then to the kitchen for a towel, then finally for the welcome mat on the front porch. As he scooped up the log in the mat, I looked toward his open bedroom door. I could see one corner of his bed, and on it I saw Joanie's foot, a leather strap wrapped around her ankle. I looked again at Buffy and saw that his expression of shock had settled into something more complex, something helpless and quietly desperate, the first expression I had seen on his face that didn't look as if it had been sculpted by a doll maker. And I saw that he was no longer looking at my father, but at the open bedroom door where, just out of his sight, his mother lay beneath the mirrors, wrists and ankles tied with leather straps, spread-eagle on that slick red satin sheet. Before I could stop him, Buffy ran toward that open door.

We finished the shed just before sunset. Buffy and Joanie had come out to see the final step, the hanging of the sliding doors, and they stood with me as Eric and my father fit the doors into their tracks. My father pulled them aside, and they stuttered hesitantly open. He slid them shut, and he and Eric joined us, his hand gripping the back of Eric's neck. "Thanks for the help, son," he said.

The ground wasn't quite level, and the doors were out of square, an uneven gap between them. A dozen black spots showed on one side of the shed, where my father had used drywall screws to reattach the panel that he had stumbled against. "It looks wonderful," Joanie said. My father nodded. An autumn breeze blew through the back yard, fluttering the corrugated vinyl panels, lifting the bottoms of the sliding doors away from the shed and dropping them gently back against it. "Well," my father said. "At least it'll never rust."

I never saw the shed again. I imagine it today, standing exactly as it had that autumn, whatever may have become of Buffy and Joanie, whom I last saw on the morning following the snowstorm, Joanie carrying Buffy to her Toyota after the plow came through. I imagine the shed, unchanged, as winters pass and other women appear briefly in our lives. Unchanged as the hair on my father's body turns silver, as his back curves into a buffalo hump. Unchanged as he quietly drains the waterbed, takes the mirrors down from the ceiling, the wind on that bluff finally extinguishing the dim red ember of his remodeled bedroom. Unchanged just like those *Star Wars* figures—us, not them, inevitably sliding into the long ago and the far away.

I held Han and Leia on that early June day at the yard sale, as my wife stood framed by the garage door, pulling coins from her purse to pay for the picture books that our girls gripped tightly against their bodies. When she turned toward me, I held up Han and Leia and made them kiss. She smiled, a little sadly, and as our girls raced over with outstretched hands, she pulled out the billfold that she'd just put away. The *Star Wars* figures disappeared into the girls' fists, and I thought once more of Buffy, of his face as he looked at the open bedroom door, and I realized that I had seen in his eyes the plight of us all, desperate to find a home as bright and lasting as that fantastic plastic.

Ron Riekki

WE TRIED TO SACRIFICE
ED TO THE DEVIL

I'd discovered the book in the Lakeview Elementary School Library. You weren't supposed to be in the library during recess, but the students were a little too violent for me. I didn't like the yelling and name-calling and occasional fistfights that seemed to break out when I least expected them, mostly not involving me, but I didn't want to be around anyone fighting or yelling or name-calling. I liked the library, where it was quiet. And I also liked that I wasn't supposed to be there.

The library was in two parts: the main room—which often would have clubs, like The Philatelists, who would meet and talk about stamps for an entire hour, which I didn't think was possible, but it was—and then there was the back room, which was separated by a heavy black curtain. No one usually looked back there because it was so dark. I could have kept hidden every recess and have never gotten caught, but I liked to read, so I'd risk being discovered by inching close to where the light broke through the breaks in the curtain, reading with the help of its little slivers of brightness, moving the book across the sentence in order to read. There was a buzz to doing this, with people a few feet on the other side not realizing I was there. I also found the books to be intriguingly inappropriate for my age. I think they were high school books that got donated and the librarian simply didn't have time to read them, because there were books that seemed simply pornographic and others that had the strangest tales of zombies and superstitions and witches, except the odd part was the way the books were presenting it—not as stories, but as reality, that witches actually existed. I'd always considered them fantasy, but the books explained paganism and how there were clubs of witches, organizations, like the people on the other side of the curtain. I wondered if they were a collection of witches themselves, if the stamps were a front for what they were really doing. Then I got discovered. I remember the horror of it, one of them seeing a slight movement from something (me) behind the curtain, pulling it back, and revealing this kid sitting alone with a book in his lap. What was he doing back there? They called a teacher, like it was some sort of felony, and I was told I was banned from the library, surprised at how angry they were that I wanted to read. I remember the explanation of consequences if I was found again. They told me I needed to learn not to be so afraid of people; I needed to learn how to be social, to learn how to step out into the violence of play.

And I tried. But I hated having my ankles kicked during soccer, not being able to walk without pain for the rest of the day. And there was simply a pull to go back to the library, my banishment making it even more intriguing, tempting. And one thing in particular that stuck in my mind was a magic spell. I still remember it, all of these years later. I don't like even thinking of it, the rhythmic incantatory rhymes, the awful content. Why was that book there for children to read? It haunted me. I couldn't remember the steps that went along with the recital of the spell, so I had to sneak back to write it down. I waited until the library was open, after school, when it was OK to be there. I grabbed the book and wrote down the steps. Then I had to convince my cousin and Ed. Surprisingly, they agreed to do it.

We had to wait until midnight. We'd decided that Ed would be the one sacrificed. Mike, my cousin—we called him "Mice"—was a Lutheran and so he thought perhaps something might actually happen and, if it did, he didn't want to be the one standing in the circle, because what was supposed to happen, according to the book, was the ground would lower and that person standing in it would descend to Hell, the ground giving way like an elevator. Incredibly terrifying. But we had to find out if it would work. I wanted to know if the world was truly that insane, that horrible.

The first night, Ed backed out.

A night later, he backed out again.

Until finally, one night, a raging full-moon night, hardly a night he could refuse with its soft wind and the distant nearness of Halloween, he agreed.

We found a spot by my old fort, a really simple fort, a few boards carelessly nailed to a tree—our neighbor, an old, thin Air Force retiree not liking that, wanting us to respect those trees . . . He would really not like what we were doing now. We drew the circle, made the insignias on the ground with a stick, set up Ed precisely as it instructed, in the circle's center, and said the words in unison, which was not easy to do, simply because it gave you a chill to utter what we were required to chant. (I am not kidding, writing this now, even at my age, even with my lack of belief in ghosts, I still looked behind me into the dark of this room at 3:58 a.m. to make sure nothing was behind me.) But Ed was positioned in the moonlight. Ed, a thick future high-school football star for Negaunee, his simple kind demeanor. If there was ever somebody who should not have been sacrificed to the Devil, it was Ed.

We said the words and waited.

The dark hole of night. The sounds that came from the woods, so eerie, subtle, hints at things alive. You can say you're the type to not be afraid of things, but if you put yourself in specific environments, like a witchcraft circle on a breezy full-moon night, there are undeniable emotions that curdle up, horrors that run under and over the skin, and none of us liked what we were feeling. But Ed remained immobile. With a flashlight I looked at the instructions, wondering if I had copied something down wrong. I said we should start over, retrace the drawings, maybe say the chant louder, but they didn't want to, and that was probably good.

If we did do it correctly, if the ground did open up, what then? Would we be immediately damned ourselves? Were we already anyway?

I talked to Mice about this months later, and he said he didn't want to talk about it, that he had gone to church and confessed, that it was something he didn't want me to bring up.

I wonder sometimes, years later, if every failure I've ever had stems from that night, linked to it, a constant karma.

And Ed, what happened to him—fabled football success in high school, then getting a girl pregnant (someone who he'd later wish he'd never met), then getting another girl pregnant, and another. So many children, a complication of kids, a full family, so that visiting his house later always had a circus feel. What, in many ways, I've always wished for.

Me, still single. I have dated two perfect Christian girls. And those relationships collapsed, women who haunt me with their perfection. I don't know if you've ever dated someone you felt was perfect for you, who gave you real happiness, only to have that relationship fade in a way that frightens you, in a way that leaves you trembling from the loss. I'm talking about the terrors of loneliness that only magnify the older you get. And you wonder why it keeps happening, where it all started.

But maybe it was worth it, that tingling when we were waiting for the earth to collapse, so much potential in the horrors of our youth.

John Smolens

MEZZANOTTE

For Filiberto Bracalente, Angelica Bonilla, and Antonio Zampa

"Then the pernicious charm of Italy began to work on her, and,
instead of acquiring information, she began to be happy."
—*A Room with a View*, E. M. Forster

The third week of March the class went on a four-day excursion to Florence. Wednesday afternoon they boarded a bus for the ride north, and in the evening they checked into a hotel that looked across the piazza toward the green-and-white marble façade of Santa Maria Novella. The following morning Dr. d'Arpino sent word around to all the students that they were to meet in the center of the piazza at eight o'clock. Many of the students arrived early; everyone was on time. Something was up. They fell silent as Dr. d'Arpino strode toward them, overcoat billowing behind him, his cell phone pressed to his ear. He paused a ways from the group until he finished his call, continued across the grass, and waited for everyone to gather close.

"I must tell you that last night American military forces entered Iraq." There were a few gasps from the students. "Reports I have received," he continued, "are not certain. Some claim that Saddam Hussein has been killed, but I'm not sure that this is to be confirmed."

"Will we go home?" Janine asked. She was a tall blond girl from Illinois, and she was often the first to speak up on behalf of the other students.

"Home?" he said. "To the United States?"

After a moment, she said, "No, I meant to Montenero, to La Scuola."

He glanced at Laura Cast, the American professor who was teaching at La Scuola winter semester, and then offered Janine the faintest smile in appreciation. "No," he said. "We have just arrived in Firenze, the heart of the Renaissance, and we are to follow our itinerary." Clearly, there was relief among the students. "But—" he waited until they quieted down. "I must tell you that in response to this invasion a general strike has been called throughout Italy. There is going to be great protest here in the streets of Firenze, probably starting later today. Certainly during the days that we will be here. So, we must stick together. Do you understand?"

"*Si,*" they all said.

"*Va bene.*" He started walking toward Santa Maria Novella, saying, as he often did when they were on excursions, "*Andiamo.*"

And as the students followed, some said to the ones behind, "*Andiamo,*"—except for Ashleigh, who, adamant in her refusal to speak any Italian, said, "Let's go."

As always, Laura fell in behind the students, so she could urge stragglers to keep up—Dr. d'Arpino set a good pace.

———

La Scuola, a school for American university students in Italy, was housed on the third floor of Palazzo Bollini, which had been built in the fifteenth century in the walled hill town of Montenero in the central region of Le Marche. On a clear winter's day the Adriatic Sea was visible several kilometers to the east, and from the west side of town there was a view of the snow-covered Sibillini Mountains. Yet elderly Italian men and women, walking the narrow lanes amid the decrepit stone and stucco buildings, rarely looked up, as though the sight of the mountain range and the sea were too oppressive to bear, or perhaps too beautiful, and therefore, sinful, to gaze upon with human eyes.

Each semester one American university professor was invited to teach at La Scuola, taking up residence in an apartment within the palazzo, across the courtyard from the wing that housed the school. The classrooms and offices had twenty-foot ceilings painted with murals that were centuries old and in need of restoration. The ceilings created an echo so that a spoken word seemed destined to reverberate for eternity. Even silence in these rooms had a symphonic effect, as though it were a moment's pause in the song of angels.

Laura Cast taught poetry at Deaver College, a small liberal arts school in Michigan. After the Consortium for Study and Exchange

Abroad (CSEA, commonly referred to as "C. C.") selected her for the position at La Scuola, she was invited to Chicago in the spring of 2002 to have dinner with the director, Dr. Giancarlo d'Arpino, during his annual visit to the States. He was perhaps fifty, Old World formal, yet avuncular, and he drank two bottles of Chianti with his Black Angus steak. He told her that C. C. ordinarily offered the visiting faculty position at La Scuola to professors whose field of concentration was some aspect of Italian history or art, but in her case he wanted to try something different, a writing workshop. Sometime during her second glass of wine she noted that she spoke no Italian, had not a drop of Italian blood in her Yankee veins (she was born and raised in Maine), and her international travel experience was limited to visits to Canada and Baja California.

He waved this off, saying, *"Non e' necessario."*

She nodded.

Smiling, he added, "See? Already you are beginning to understand."

She arrived in Italy the first week of January. There were twenty-two students, eighteen girls and four boys from Midwestern colleges and universities. They were placed in various apartments around Montenero, usually in groups of four, and some shared apartments with Italian students, who were attending the art institute that was behind the church of San Stefano (the town was at first an incomprehensible maze, and directions were often given in relation to churches, of which there were at least a dozen). The first week most of the students were ecstatically disoriented: they were actually in Italy. A few became homesick, and there were some roommate "issues" that had to be ironed out. When a girl from Indiana named Ashleigh learned that there was no McDonald's in Montenero, she cried (over her plate of *gnocchi*), saying she would simply die of starvation before the semester ended in May. But most of the students happily "went Italian"; they bought Italian–style clothes and some were remarkably quick at picking up the language.

Laura's class was the last of the day, from three to five; it followed studio art, so that the students entered the room smelling of clay and oil paint. Several times a week she would plan some occasion in the evening with a few students: sometimes it would be cheese and wine at her apartment, or sometimes she would walk with a group to a café. It was not like at home, where there are the classroom and office hours. Here, she lived among them. They took her aside to tell her about each other. They cried sometimes, but even that seemed different. You were supposed to feel like crying in Italy, and then the next moment you laugh. And they asked about her. Was she married? (No.) Had she ever been married? (Yes.) Does she have children? (Yes, a son, in college now.) But such personal information didn't seem necessary in Montenero. (*Non e' necessario.*) Who you were back home didn't seem important; it tended to get in the way. Much of the time Laura felt at a complete loss. Outside herself. The predictable routine of her days in Michigan seemed to be the life of someone else. In Montenero, she couldn't stop walking. In the course of a day she walked several miles. Mornings she'd walk until she found a place to read and write. In the evening, after dinner, she'd go to a café, where they served a local liqueur called *mistra*, which had a strong taste of licorice. She kept a notebook with her at all times. She wasn't writing poems; hadn't even tried. The poems would come later. Now it was better to just walk and fill her notebook up with whatever came to mind.

———

One afternoon in class, a tall, lanky student from Ohio named Jared Thomas was reading his poem, "Before Montenero" ("I didn't know my ass from my apse / My navel from my nave" brought laughter which seemed to descend from the murals overhead) when Ashleigh opened one of the gigantic double doors. Laura was about to tell her that she was late and to wait out in the hall until Jared completed his reading, when she realized the girl was weeping. A day didn't pass when Ashleigh didn't cry or complain, and the other students were beginning to cut her out of the herd.

"Ashleigh," Laura asked. "What is it?"

"It broke up!" she shouted. "The Columbia space shuttle—it just came apart. They're *all* dead!"

In the days that followed the students tended to huddle together in the cold around the courtyard below Laura's apartment. They smoked cigarettes, they embraced each other. It was as though they had suddenly realized that America didn't encompass the entire world. Computer service was erratic and getting news in English was difficult.

The shuttle disaster soon morphed into Iraq. News stories from back home described Americans laying in provisions and taping their windows as though preparing for a siege. There was a run on gas masks. Some parents called to ask when the students would be sent home. The Italian press speculated that if the United States invaded Iraq, Saddam Hussein might fire his WMDs at Europe. Or he may use nerve gas. Or possibly (and perhaps most devastating), millions of Muslim refugees would flood the Continent to escape the devastation of war in the Middle East.

Dr. d'Arpino called a special meeting with the students, to assure them that in the event of an international crisis there were evacuation plans already in place that would get them home as soon as possible. But really, he explained, they were much safer here in central Italy than they would be in New York's Central Park. He explained that whenever they went on an excursion the police were notified in advance, and indeed when they visited Loreto one cold, drizzling Friday, Laura realized that there was an inordinate number of *polizia* positioned all around the piazza in front of the cathedral. Jared was a few years older than the other students, and he was more solitary and independent. He approached two police officers, standing by their car, and tried to say something in Italian. He was much taller than either of the officers and his boldness clearly disturbed them. Dr. d'Arpino steered Jared toward Laura as though he were her personal responsibility. After an animated discussion with the two policemen, Dr. d'Arpino gathered the students together in the center of the piazza and said, yes, the police were there specifically at his request, and that in the future there was to be no interaction whatsoever with them.

"I swear they have Uzis," Jared said. "I could see them in the back seat of the car."

Dr. d'Arpino raised his hands in exasperation, and then he walked away, toward the entrance to the basilica. The students followed, Laura acting as the shepherd. Jared, as he often did, tried to fall behind, but she took him by the arm and continued on toward the cathedral.

"Do you really think there will be terrorists here?" he asked.

"That's not Dr. d'Arpino's point."

"What is?" When she didn't answer, he said, "Their peace of mind? Half these kids can't find Iraq on a map."

"What's your point? Geography?" Now he didn't answer. "You don't even know what an Uzi looks like. You're a little older, Jared. You could be more—"

"More what? A leader? You want me to set an example?"

"The idea frightens you?"

He laughed as they climbed, arm in arm, the basilica steps. "I have a little secret I should, you know, confess—since we're about to enter a cathedral. I have Googled you." He paused, as though he expected to be reprimanded. "You have published two collections of poems, *Full Light* and *Toys*, and a collection of essays, *Hard Water*. You're forty-one, a New Englander who lives in Michigan. You write about ice and snow, and long winter nights. A review said you were Robert Frost on a menstrual cycle."

"You think it was intended to be a compliment?"

Inside the basilica at Loreto there was the house where the Virgin Mary was purported to have been born, a tiny dwelling that the angels were said to have dismantled stone by stone and flown to this hill overlooking the Adriatic. People stood in line to get inside the house, and while they waited Dr. d'Arpino discussed the statues, friezes, and high reliefs that embraced the outer walls and had been designed by Bramante, who had been commissioned by Pope Julius II. At the base of the walls of the house there was a marble curb, perhaps two-feet wide, which had two parallel, wavering grooves worn into the top.

"Over the centuries," Dr. d'Arpino said sotto voce, "millions have made pilgrimages to Loreto. This holy place is second only to the Vatican, and when the pilgrims reach the base of the hill a few kilometers below, they no longer walk, but proceed in this manner, as a form of worship." To demonstrate, he drew back his overcoat, knelt on the curb, pressed his hands together in prayer, and then crawled forward along the grooves. Some of the students' eyes welled up when they understood, and Dr. d'Arpino seemed to have forgotten his outburst in the piazza, as he continued to explain certain features of the cathedral.

Only a handful of people were allowed inside the little house at one time. There was an altar, crudely but lavishly decorated. The centerpiece was the Black Madonna, a statue of Mary carved out of ebony (it was a copy; Napoleon's army had taken the original Black Madonna, along with a great deal of other artwork, back to France). The air smelled of stone and it seemed fitting that such an enormous cathedral had been built up around this tiny dwelling. Upon leaving the house, Dr. d'Arpino said that the house wasn't really transported by angels, but by a wealthy family named De Angelis, who centuries ago had had the house dismantled and brought to Loreto where it was reconstructed, as a wedding gift for their daughter.

"So it wasn't really a miracle," Janine said.

"But it's a good story," Jared said. "And a good story's better than a miracle."

"*E' vero,*" Dr. d'Arpino said. "True."

When they left the cathedral it was nearly dark. As their bus wound down the hill, Jared's roommate, Eric, a boy with hair to his shoulders who drank a lot of beer, spoke up from the back of the bus. "These pilgrims, did they really *crawl* all this way on their *knees*?"

The bus was very comfortable and equipped with a microphone, which Dr. d'Arpino used often during their travels. He held the microphone to his mouth and said, "Not just up, but back down, *si*, on their knees." And then he pointed toward the valley ahead; in the distance the lights of the hill towns were just coming on, jewels suspended in the dusk. "And down there in that valley, during the Second World War, a terrible battle. Thousands killed, many of them Polish soldiers. After John Paul was elected pope, the first trip he made from the Vatican was to the cemetery here. In a few miles we will pass Roman ruins, where gladiators were trained to fight in the coliseum. You see? Everywhere, layer upon layer of history. Like a nice lasagna—pain and beauty, pain and beauty, always together. One needs the other. Otherwise, how can we explain the Renaissance?"

———

The four days in Florence were difficult. It wasn't any one event, but the accumulation of small occurrences. There were reports that hundreds of thousands of people were coming into the city to march against the war. Dr. d'Arpino was clearly nervous. Yet it was all so remarkable. They visited churches, Il Duomo, San Lorenzo, Santa Croce, Santa Maria Novella, and the beauty of the city was palpable in a way that Laura hadn't experienced before—Stendhal had been so overwhelmed by the art and architecture of Florence that he became ill, a medical condition which has since been called Stendhal's Syndrome.

The second day, as they were herded through the corridors of Uffizi, gazing at statues and paintings, protest marchers could be heard outside. When the group left the museum, the arcade in front of the main entrance was jammed with people, marching from Piazza della Signoria toward the Arno River. Some of the students wanted to join, and Laura and Dr. d'Arpino hurriedly clutched and grabbed at coat sleeves, keeping them from getting caught in the flow of marchers. "Bread and wine!" Dr. d'Arpino said to Laura. Then turning toward the students he pointed toward the piazza and shouted, "If you're hungry, follow me!"

The students were always hungry, and they marched behind him against the stream of protesters, until they entered the open space of Piazza della Signoria, with its statues and fountain, and the looming presence of Palazzo Vecchio. Thankfully, the discussion moved from the present to the past; Dr. d'Arpino showed the students the spot where Savonarola had been burned at the stake, and Laura reminded them that it was also here, by the Loggia dei Lanza, that E. M. Forster's Lucy Honeychurch witnesses the murder of the Italian man over a five-lire note.

Soon they found a restaurant looking out on the piazza, and once they were all seated Dr. d'Arpino said to Laura, "Dictators, communists, anarchists, fascists—*Italiani* are a very old people and we have been living with terrorism for thousands of years. In the early seventies I was a student here when Aldo Moro was kidnapped and murdered by the Red Brigade. There was a general strike, riots in these streets. What we are seeing here in this moment, it's very peaceful really. But you don't know if it will remain so."

"I doubt any of them have ever seen a protest march before." Laura nodded toward the students, who sat at several tables that had been pushed together. "It's like a parade to them."

The last morning in Florence the students again gathered in the piazza in front of Santa Maria Novella. The air was chilly and they hopped in place, trying to keep warm. As always, Laura counted heads and she came up with twenty-one. It took only a moment to determine who was missing. Eric was sent back to the hotel to see what was keeping Jared, and a few minutes later he returned holding his hands out. "The last I saw of Jared," he said, "he was going into the bathroom to take a shower. I keep calling him but he doesn't answer."

The students all looked at Dr. d'Arpino, who was getting out his cell phone. "I will talk to the hotel clerk, asking him to tell Jared to meet us at Gallerie dell'Academia. We have reservations to see David and we must not be late. *Andiamo.*" He began walking, tapping the numbers on his phone.

Later that afternoon, when they boarded the bus, there was still no sign of Jared.

"We're just going to leave him here?" Ashleigh called from the back of the bus.

Dr. d'Arpino did not use the microphone; instead, he and Laura worked their way down the narrow aisle to the middle of the bus. "The hotel manager informed me that Jared removed his belongings from his room this morning," he said. "The authorities have been notified." Ashleigh began to speak but he raised his hand. "The best thing for us to do is to follow our itinerary. He will find us where we all belong, back in Montenero. You must understand that in more than twenty years I have had this happen several times. A lost sheep always finds the flock—not the other way around. But then Jared is not lost, is he? He is in Italia."

Again, Ashleigh began to speak, but Janine said, "Oh, grow up. Jared knows how to buy a train ticket. *Vorrei un biglietto per Montenero.* He's probably on his way back there now."

Ashleigh put on her iPod earphones, pulled the hood of her sweatshirt up over her head, and buried her face against the window. The students called it Going Under.

Laura wasn't surprised that it was Jared who had gone missing. The previous weekend Dr. d'Arpino had called her before eight o'clock Saturday. He was at the police station, where Jared had spent the early morning hours in a cell. The night before he and Eric had thrown a party, until the *polizia* arrived about 3 a.m. The landlord wanted both American boys evicted.

Laura met Dr. d'Arpino and Jared at the apartment. The place had been trashed. Dr. d'Arpino was so angry he could barely speak. He walked around the apartment, toeing broken furniture with his shoe, ripping pictures of naked women off the bathroom wall. Jared, contrite, hungover, didn't know where Eric was—only that he had fled before the *polizia* arrived. The Italian roommates, according to Jared, had nothing to do with this; he seemed too willing to take full responsibility, and Laura suspected there was more to it. When the landlord arrived—he wouldn't even climb the three flights of stairs to the apartment—Dr. d'Arpino went down to talk to him in the lobby.

"You want to get sent home?" Laura said to Jared. He had a mass of dark hair spilling out from under the large wool cap, which he wore all the time, indoors and out. Just shaking his head looked like a painful balancing act. "Don't be surprised if Dr. d'Arpino puts you on a plane tonight."

"I can't go home."

"First, your parents will have to pay dearly for your plane fare, and—"

"I don't have a home. I don't have parents." He looked toward the windows. It was a cruelly brilliant day, the distant hills rolling away to the horizon beneath a cloudless sky.

"Jared, you didn't do this alone."

"I can't say, so please don't ask. I didn't know most of the people here last night."

"What about Eric?"

"He saw where things were headed and he took off earlier."

"Well, if you get sent back to the States, you'll flunk your courses—you haven't been keeping up with my assignments."

"Whatever," he said. "I'm not going back to school anyway."

Dr. d'Arpino's weary footsteps echoed out on the stairs, and when he came into the apartment, his hands were stuffed deep in the pockets of his overcoat. "You are to go around and clean up all these cans and bottles." He didn't wait for an answer. "Then you pack your things and you come to my office. When you leave, don't lock the door, but put your key on the kitchen table. The landlord will come up later to assess the damage." He left the apartment and Laura followed.

They spent most of the afternoon in Dr. d'Arpino's office with Jared, and later Eric, whom they had located by cell phone. It was like a police interrogation: they talked to the boys together; then separately; then together again. By mid-afternoon it was clear that the boys would not be sent home.

"To put you on a plane, this is the easy thing to do," Dr. d'Arpino said. "There would be much regret, but no opportunity for redemption. You understand what I am saying, about redemption?" Sitting across the desk from him, both boys nodded, without raising their eyes. "Do you? What is redemption?"

Eric's hair hung down both sides of his face, and he only shook his head.

"It's what you do to return to the flock," Jared said finally.

"Correct," Dr. d'Arpino said. "I have rented apartments for my students from that landlord for years, but now a sense of trust has been lost. It may make it difficult for me to rent from other landlords as well—this is a small town and people talk. They like having American students here, but this can change very quickly." At this point tears began to drip off of Eric's nose. "Now, both of you go, and come back this evening. In the meantime, I will try to find another place for you to live."

After they left, Laura sat in one of the chairs in front of his desk.

"The ones with the free spirits, they often bring the troubles with them." Dr. d'Arpino touched his forehead. "Sometimes here." He then tapped his chest. "And sometimes here."

"Jared," she said, "he told me he has no home—"

Dr. d'Arpino nodded. "No parents. *E' vero.* His father disappeared when he was small and his mother died a few years ago. He has some aunt and uncle who raised him, but I gather they pretty much dumped him at his school and don't really want him around. To ship him home would be to give up. Besides, if we were going to do that, it should have been done weeks ago—when it would have made a statement to all the students."

"Send them back now," she said, "and there will be a lot of explaining to do with C. C." He was gazing down at the ink blotter, nodding agreement. "But tell me," she said. "There's something else?"

"The Italian students. They were in on this just as much—I'm sure of it—but they're not being evicted and they didn't spend the night at the police station. Eric, he is, we agree, a nice boy who drinks too much beer and has not much what you call 'structure.' His first instinct is to run and hide." He smiled. "Jared is a little older. He leads and, of course, Eric follows."

She nodded. "Jared is very smart, but he's a poor student."

Dr. d'Arpino put his elbows on the desk, placing his head in both hands. "Jared believes he's doing the right thing, protecting the other boys. I must respect this." He rubbed his forehead and eyes, and for a moment she thought he was about to cry. "If we send them home, the other students will mention it to their parents—it only takes one or two. And then they'll all want their children sent home, thinking they can keep them safe from this war thing. So we keep Jared and Eric here. *D'accordo?*"

"I agree. Everyone stays."

———

Jared didn't return to Montenero. Three days later, Dr. d'Arpino held another meeting with the students, informing them of the steps he had taken. Along with the police, the American embassy had been notified, as well as Jared's relatives and his university. "The authorities are certain that he has not boarded a plane," Dr. d'Arpino said. "Nor do we think he has crossed a border by train or bus. So I believe he is still in Italia, unless he is crossing the Alps on the back of an elephant."

The students weren't sure whether they should laugh or not, though a few snickered. He gestured toward Laura, who was seated beside him at the desk. She gazed out at the students, who were motionless, somber, and she suddenly realized that they often found Dr. d'Arpino unfathomable—and they expected her to provide a translation.

"I know you are all deeply concerned," she said. "We have spoken to a number of you individually, but no one has any idea where he has gone." She paused a moment; but that wasn't enough. "Listen. Even if you have promised him to remain silent, you should tell us."

Now they seemed to understand. Several glanced around, but no one spoke.

"He said nothing," Eric said finally, his voice pleading. "I had no idea about this—honest."

"Of course," Dr. d'Arpino said. "We take you at your word."

"He could be in a hospital," Ashleigh said.

"In that case," Dr. d'Arpino said, "we would be notified."

"He could be somewhere, dead," Ashleigh said.

Eric shifted in his chair. "No, they'd find his body."

"What do we *do*?" Ashleigh's voice broke.

There was silence from the other students as her sobs echoed off the high ceiling.

"Nothing," Janine said finally. She sat up a little straighter as the other students looked at her. "We do nothing. We have work to do for classes tomorrow. We wait."

———

Jared never returned to La Scuola. The last few weeks of the semester the students seemed overwhelmed. Papers, exams, art projects were due. Most of them seemed so busy that they forgot Jared. When he was mentioned now, his name only brought silence, as though he were a distant relative who had died years ago.

"All empires end," Dr. d'Arpino said the evening before Laura was going to fly back to Michigan. "And now time is up for this little semester-long empire. Some of these students you will never hear from again, while others will write you regularly for years. I will never want for Christmas cards from America."

The café bar was lined with bowls of nuts and potato chips, plates of *bruschetta*, and a good glass of Le Marche wine was two euro. Later in the evening there would be a final dinner with the students—which everyone called *L'ultima Cena.*

"I've never lost one," he said. "One of my sheep. I worry what C. C. will do. It is always political, you understand. Some of them would like to close La Scuola, or at least see me go."

"You are La Scuola."

"My parents lived in Milano during the war," he said. "They loved Americans because of what the GIs did to push the Germans out. Much sacrifice. We appreciate sacrifice. It seems that George Bush is determined to destroy all that good will."

"I cannot explain George Bush," she said. "It isn't sufficient to say that this is all sad."

"Triste." He would often give her a word or phrase that might be useful. "Sad, very sad. With a prime minister such as Berlusconi, we understand there's a difference between a government and its people. But the news, it is frightening. I have never had a group of students with such concern as this."

"For most of them this is the first time they've really left home," she said. "They are discovering that the world is a big, unfamiliar place. And then one of them goes missing. But at that meeting Janine said the right thing."

"You see, Laura, what this adversity does for them?"

"Some of them get stronger."

Dr. d'Arpino put his empty wine glass down, nodding solemnly.

At the dinner there were presents, and hugs, and tears; there were photographs; and there was a great deal of laughter and wine. When it was over Laura was exhausted. She walked outside the restaurant, where there were still more goodbyes. Finally, groups of students wandered off in different directions, their voices echoing off the ancient buildings. Standing by his car, Dr. d'Arpino, flushed with wine, took Laura in his arms, kissed her on both cheeks, and then he held her tightly for a long moment—she wanted it to pass quickly and waited for him to let go, but then when he did, she gathered his tweed coat in her fists and crushed his bulk against her.

And then he was in his car, waving as he pulled out into the street.

Laura was wide-awake. She began to walk.

———————

Mezzanotte. Midnight.

Laura left the café called *da Simone,* and as she crossed Piazza Cavour she heard footsteps echoing behind her. She turned once and looked back toward the lights of the café, but a dense fog hovered over the cobblestones and she saw no one. When she continued on, the footsteps resumed, and the second time she turned around she saw a shadow move behind the columns in front of Teatro Giacomo Leopardi.

"Jared?" she said.

There was no response.

Laura began walking toward the theater, but hesitated when she reached the steps. Then she climbed the steps and entered the cortile that fronted the theater. After a moment, he appeared, leaning against one of the columns, his hands stuffed in the front pockets of his hooded sweatshirt. Somehow she was afraid to approach him, as though he were a cat that would flee if she made any sudden move.

"I went by your apartment earlier," he said. "To say good-bye."

"We had a dinner. You should have come."

He only shook his head. "When do you leave?"

"Tomorrow." She looked toward the small café at the corner of the piazza. It was a place she'd been in only once, when she'd first arrived, a haven for old men, and she had not felt welcomed at all. "Come with me," she said as she began walking toward the café.

Jared caught up to her, pushing open the glass door. Just as before, there were only a few old men, playing cards at a table. The walls were decorated with framed photographs of popes (Pius XII, John XXII), a commemorative plate bearing the bearded face of Padre Pio, and above the bar was a black-and-white Juventus banner. The men stared briefly at Laura, and then returned to their cards and glasses. No resentment this time: she was escorted.

The bartender put down his cards and came around the end of the bar, which had a white marble top, very old. Laura ordered *mistra* for both of them. The bartender, a stout man with a gray moustache, poured their drinks and then returned to the card game.

Jared was staring at the walls. "First time I was in here I tried to ask why no picture of John Paul the Second and they couldn't understand me. I know why now." The light was dim. He seemed different; tired but somehow more assured. "Because he's not Italian, some won't accept that he's really the pope."

"Where have you been, Jared?"

"Rome, mostly. I've only returned to collect the rest of my stuff."

"You'll have to talk to Dr. d'Arpino—"

"No, I'll be taking the first train back tomorrow."

"Back?" she said. "To Rome?"

"I'm not going home. Yes, back to Rome—I have a job."

Laura picked up her glass, which was filled to the brim, and a little *mistra* ran down over her fingers. She took a sip and then put the glass back on the marble top. The sound of glass on marble was something she would take from here. It wouldn't be an entry in her notebook; it wouldn't be information. It would be more than that, and it would be there when she needed it. She licked her fingers and for a moment she felt elated. "Doing what?"

He smiled, and said, "Being a tour guide, what else? I walk English-speaking tourists all over, showing them the ruins, the Vatican, the Pantheon, Spanish Steps, whatever. At night I read the history of these places. It's helped me appreciate Dr. d'Arpino—he talks about the thirteenth century as though it were last week, and Pope Julius the Second as though they were personal friends. I try to give my tour groups a little history, but most of them just want to stay in any one place long enough to shoot everything on their camcorders."

Laura had a habit of imagining what kind of adults her students would become, and over the years she'd gotten fairly good at it; some wrote to her years after taking her class, telling her about their marriages, their children, their careers, and in many instances she seemed to have been right, as though unwittingly they had gone out into the world determined to fulfill her predictions. But then it was usually only the ones who had suffered significant disappointments who bothered to get in touch with her.

"Perhaps," she said as she gathered up some peanuts from the bowl and rattled them in her hand like dice. "Perhaps you should stay."

"Eric wants to go home and enlist in the marines. I tried but I can't talk him out of it."

"There will be a lot of that, I gather," she said. "Is that why you're staying, the war?"

"It's not like I'm dodging the draft. I just wouldn't know who I'd be, you know, back there."

She tossed the peanuts into her mouth and chewed. "I think this will be difficult for Dr. d'Arpino to explain."

"I already wrote him," Jared said. "He should receive the letter in a day or two. I apologized. He was right, you were right—I've been so much trouble. But I'm getting a work visa and I'm staying, and I've let my family know back home. I've explained everything. No one will blame La Scuola." He drank down his *mistra*, and for a moment she thought he was through. He had come to say only this, and now she expected him to turn and walk out the door. But he didn't, and he leaned down until his face was close to hers, and she took a step back, but he gently placed a hand on her arm. "No," he said. "I understand that you purposefully kept your distance from students as much as possible. You think of it as being 'professional.' But, you see, I'm no longer your student." He held her arm, leaned closer, and when he was certain that she wasn't going to back away he let go. Now she was the cat.

"What are you doing?" she asked.

He hadn't shaved in days. "I'm talking to you, Laura. Is it all right, that I call you Laura?"

After a moment, she said, "It's fine."

"I have to tell you that we were all so curious about you at first. You talked about poets and poetry, but we learned nothing about you. Any attempt to find out—you fended off. As though it wasn't important. The other students, they didn't understand. How could these things be unimportant? You know, the details: marriage, kids, where the hell you're from, whether you vote Republican or Democrat, blah, blah, blah. To them, that's who you are. But then, after I left the group in Florence, I just hung out for several days. First there, and then I took the train down to Rome. And I began to understand, or I thought so." He looked around at the walls for a moment, as though he were admiring some majestic sight, but there were only the old photographs and a dusty football banner—and then, smiling, he leaned closer. "I lost myself," he said. "And I realized that that was behind much of what you were saying in class—saying and not saying. It was *implied*, which is one of your favorite words." He straightened up a bit so he could have a better look at her face. "Tell me I'm right."

"I can't." Laura finished what was in her glass and put it down, listening for the click on the marble. "You're an adult. It's your decision." She began to open her purse.

"No," he said, pulling a wad of euro bills from his pocket. Looking over his shoulder, he said something in Italian, something rapid and, to Laura's ear, incomprehensible, and yet the bartender merely glanced up from his cards and waved as he said, "*Buona notte.*"

As they left the café, she said, "I think you will get along fine here."

Outside they walked through the fog and he took her by the arm. "You know, a lot of us, we thought that there was something going on between you and Dr. d'Arpino." He said this as though he were sharing a joke. "Sometimes we talked about the two of you, what you'd be like in bed. I said he was a widower and you'd have to be extremely quiet because his old mother would be lying in the next room."

Laura placed her free hand over her mouth, attempting to suppress her laugh. "It's true, he does live with his mother, but—"

"I never thought you and he were, you know, like that. I never thought you—"

He stopped and she felt his hand begin to release her upper arm, but she held it tighter to her side as they walked on down the narrow street.

"I have an admission, too," she said. "I envy you. I don't look forward to flying back home tomorrow."

"But you have obligations. You aren't free to just stay."

"True," she said. "*E' vero.*"

"It feels like the world is about to change," he said. "And we'll never be able to go back to the way it was. It seems like I've given something up, but I've never been happier. That's the way it is with you and poetry, right? You give yourself up to it. It's like that for me, but with this place. You abandon yourself to it, and only then do you find yourself in it. It's completely random, arbitrary, but somehow secure. You feel like you belong. You don't write the poem, it finds you. You wait until it comes."

"Yes, sometimes," Laura said. "You learn to wait."

They turned the last corner and stopped at the gates outside the palazzo courtyard. The town was no longer an incomprehensible maze; she had a bird's-eye view of it from above, every street, alley, and piazza, they all wound about each other, all eventually leading back to here, outside the gates of Palazzo Bollini. In the courtyard there was a water fountain—a perpetual stream arcing from the mouth of a marble lion.

Jared released her arm and stepped in front of her. He was going to kiss both cheeks, she knew, and when he leaned down to her she turned her head for him, left, then right, feeling his warm, unshaven skin. He began to straighten up, but hesitated, and she realized he was afraid.

"I'd like to stay here," she said, "and at a different point in my life I might have. I'm happy for you, Jared." She raised her arms and put them around his neck, and drew him to her again. He held her tightly, and for a moment she felt a shudder run up through his back and shoulders. When he let go of her and stood up straight his eyes were glistening with tears, but he was smiling.

"*Grazie*," he whispered stepping back from her. "*Buona notte.*"

She felt chilled suddenly and folded her arms. He nodded, as though she had said something, the right thing, whatever it was; but there wasn't anything else to say—*Non e' necessario*—and then he walked down the street, and after he turned the corner she was left with only the sound of water streaming from the lion's mouth into the basin, a light, trickling music that reminded her of distant voices—generations of voices that said *You can't stay, and you'll never forget.*

ACKNOWLEDGMENTS

I'D LIKE TO THANK ANNIE MARTIN AND WAYNE STATE UNIVERSITY Press for believing in this book and for believing in U.P. writers. It's been fun to watch this emergence of talent over the years, and it feels like that level of talent is growing exponentially.

Extra thanks to Russell Thorburn, Jonathan Johnson, my parents, and my sister (and my parents' dog for cuddling on my lap while I was typing).

I researched the poorest and richest cities using census statistics and was surprised to learn that of the top 175 wealthiest towns in Michigan, none of them are in the mainland Upper Peninsula. Mackinac Island is the sole exception, but, again, not mainland. Of the top eight poorest towns in the state, though, we have two. So it's helpful—maybe even arguably necessary—to have backing from a publisher as prestigious as WSU Press, to have those lower Michigan cities with average per capita incomes of over one hundred thousand dollars to help those economically struggling U.P. towns, e.g. Daggett's per capita income has been listed as less than ten thousand dollars and Baraga has had the highest unemployment rate in the entire country, let alone the state. So thank you Wayne State for giving these voices a louder voice.

And thank you U.P. writers for the working-class fiction and poetry that comes out of the area, a writing of struggle and *sisu*.

Thank you to Lindsey Alexander for her wonderful editing skills.

Thank you to *Verse Wisconsin* for their consistent support of my writing.

I'd also like to thank the Michigan Humanities Council, Pam Christensen and Lynette Suckow and the others at Peter White Public Library, and all of the other libraries and bookstores who have been so embracing of the U.P. Book Tour to bring these writers to the community. Thank you, thank you, and thank you.

(The writing in this anthology is previously unpublished with the sole exception of Ellen Airgood's "The Wanderer," which was published in Grand Marais's local newspaper.)

AUTHOR BIOGRAPHIES

Marty Achatz lives in Ishpeming, Michigan, with his wife and two children. He has taught writing, literature, and composition at Northern Michigan University since 1998. He holds a Master's Degree in Fiction and an MFA in Poetry. His poems have appeared in magazines such as *Paterson Literary Review* and *Kennesaw Review*. Mayapple Press published his book of poems, *The Mysteries of the Rosary*, in 2004. His most recent work can be read on his blog *Saint Marty* at saintmartymarty.blogspot.com. Writer Jack Driscoll said of Achatz, "I found the quiet ferocity of this new voice to be graceful and powerful, and absolutely convincing in its ambition and in its honesty."

Ellen Airgood runs a small diner with her husband in Grand Marais, Michigan, on the edge of Lake Superior. She learned most of what she knows about story, as well as about charity and compassion, from waiting tables there for the past twenty-one years, and from listening and watching the lives of her customers. Her first novel, *South of Superior*, was published by Riverhead Books in June 2011. Her second, *Prairie Evers*, will be released by Nancy Paulsen Books in August 2012. She is currently at work on a third in a small cabin near Grand Marais that she shares with her husband, dog, two cats, and eight cactuses.

Robert Alexander grew up in Massachusetts and attended the University of Wisconsin. One summer, while driving around the top of Lake Michigan, Alexander discovered the Upper Peninsula, and he has returned there ever since whenever he gets a chance. Alexander has published two books of poetry (*White Pine Sucker River* and *What the Raven Said*) and a book of creative nonfiction about the American Civil War (*Five Forks: Waterloo of the Confederacy*). He has edited several anthologies of prose poetry and is currently co-editor, with Nickole Brown, of the Marie Alexander Poetry Series at White Pine Press. For more information, see his website: www.robertalexander.info.

Julie Brooks Barbour's chapbook, *Come to Me and Drink*, was published by Finishing Line Press in 2012. Her poems have appeared in *Kestrel, Waccamaw, UCity Review, Migrations: Poetry and Prose for Life's Transitions*, and *Bigger Than They Appear: Anthology of Very Short Poems*. She teaches at Lake Superior State University where she is co-editor of the journal *Border Crossing*.

Sally R. Brunk (Lac du Flambeau/Ojibwa) is Bear Clan and the youngest of eight children. She was born and raised on the Keweenaw Bay Indian Reservation. She credits Northern Michigan University and Michigan Technological University in her educational journey. She enjoys writing short stories and poetry, centering on the bond of family and the Anishinabe way of life. Her work has appeared in *SAIL, C-Literary Magazine, Sinister Wisdom, Moccasin Telegraph*, and *Quiet Mountain Essays*. She was recently published in the anthologies *Sharing Our Stories of Survival: Native Women Surviving Violence,* and *Voice on the Water: Great Lakes Native America Now*. She has her own book of poetry titled *The Cliffs—Summer Soundings* with paintings by Jim Denomie.

Jennifer Burd has had poetry published in numerous journals, most recently in *Beloit Poetry Journal* and *Modern Haiku*. Her full-length book of poems, *Body and Echo*, was published by Plain View Press in 2010. She is also the author of a book of creative nonfiction, *Daily Bread: A Portrait of Homeless Men & Women of Lenawee County, Michigan* (Bottom Dog Press, Inc., 2009, with photographs by Lad Strayer), based on her experiences reporting on local homelessness for the Adrian, Michigan, *Daily Telegram* newspaper. A visit to Marquette and Negaunee, Michigan, as an author-participant for the U.P. Book Tour in 2011, inspired Burd's poem that appears in this volume. Burd received her BA in English and her MFA in Creative Writing from the University of Washington. She currently works as an editor and writer for HighScope Educational Research Foundation in Ypsilanti, Michigan.

Lisa Fay Coutley is the author of *In the Carnival of Breathing*, winner of the Black River Chapbook Competition (Black Lawrence Press, 2011), and *Back-Talk*, winner of the ROOMS Chapbook Contest (Articles Press, 2010). She earned her MFA at Northern Michigan University, where she was poetry editor for *Passages North*, and is currently a doctoral fellow and poetry editor for *Quarterly West* at the University of Utah. Her work has appeared most recently or is forthcoming in *Seneca Review*, *Third Coast*, *The Journal*, *American Literary Review*, *Best New Poets 2010*, and on *Verse Daily*.

Sharon Dilworth is the author of two collections of short stories—*The Long White* and *Women Drinking Benedictine*—and a novel, *Year of the Gingko*. The winner of the Iowa Award in Short Fiction and a Pushcart Prize, she lives in Pittsburgh, Pennsylvania, where she is a professor at Carnegie Mellon University and the fiction editor at Autumn House Press. Much of her fiction was inspired by the years she spent living in Marquette while an undergraduate at Northern Michigan University. She is also a proud graduate of the Masters Program in English at Wayne State University.

Amber Edmondson is a poet and book artist living in Marquette, Michigan. She studied English at Northwestern Michigan College and Northern Michigan University and continues to draw inspiration from the natural setting of the Upper Peninsula and its rich history.

Chad Faries is the author of two poetry collections, *The Border Will Be Soon* (Emergency Press, 2006) and *The Book of Knowledge* (Vulgar Marsala Press, 2010). His memoir, *Drive Me Out of My Mind: 24 Houses in 10 Years* (Emergency Press, 2011), chronicles five unhinged women in 1970s Upper Peninsula. He can also be seen raconteuring with the Unchained Tour. He has a PhD in Creative Writing from the University of Wisconsin–Milwaukee and was a Fulbright Fellow in Budapest. He has lived extensively and taught in Central Europe. Currently he is an Associate Professor at Savannah State University where he also hosts a theme-based storytelling and music program on WHCJ 90.3. He now owns a house in Thunderbolt, Georgia, but lives abroad and gets lost on his motorcycle whenever he can, especially in Iron County, Michigan.

Matthew Gavin Frank is the author of *Pot Farm* (University of Nebraska Press/Bison Books), *Barolo* (University of Nebraska Press), *Warranty in Zulu* (Barrow Street Press), *The Morrow Plots* (forthcoming from Black Lawrence Press/Dzanc Books), *Sagittarius Agitprop* (Black Lawrence Press/Dzanc Books), and the chapbooks *Four Hours to Mpumalanga* (Pudding House Publications) and *Aardvark* (West Town Press). Recent work appears in *The New Republic*, *The Huffington Post*, *Field*, *Epoch*, *AGNI*, *The Iowa Review*, *Seneca Review*, *Crazyhorse*, *Indiana Review*, *North American Review*, *Pleiades*, *Crab Orchard Review*, *The Best Food Writing*, *The Best Travel Writing*, *Creative Nonfiction*, *Prairie Schooner*, *Hotel Amerika*, *Gastronomica*, and others. He was born and raised in Illinois, and currently teaches Creative Writing in the MFA Program at Northern Michigan University, where he is the Nonfiction Editor of *Passages North*. This winter, he prepared his first batch of whitefish-thimbleberry ice cream.

Manda Frederick holds an MFA in Nonfiction and an MA in Literary Studies. Though she is now an Asst. Professor of Writing in New Jersey, she spent five years in Marquette, Michigan. There, she came to know poetry with the help of Jonathan Johnson and Russ Thorburn, who generously invited her to join their summer writing circle when she was barely twenty. She spent her summers jogging along Lower Harbor, suffering in the swarms of black biting flies. At night, though afraid of the enormous spiders' nests that draped from everything, she'd make her way, on foot, to Vango's to sing along with Jim and Ray. But, mostly, she did what everyone in the U.P. does: she spent summer waiting for winter, for snowstorms to build layers in varying shades of white, slowing the city, giving a poet the space she needed to focus on every word of every poem.

Randall R. Freisinger has lived in Houghton, Michigan, since 1977. From then until he retired in 2009 as Emeritus Professor, he taught undergraduate and graduate classes in writing and literature at Michigan Technological University. He has been a frequent participant in poet-in-the-schools programs, writing workshops, and poetry readings across the Upper Peninsula. His poems have been included in nationally recognized U.P.-based magazines such as *Passages North*, *PANK*, and *The MacGuffin*, as well as in many other literary journals and anthologies. His four published collections include *Running Patterns* (1985 Flume Press National Chapbook Prize), *Hand Shadows* (Green Tower Press, 1988), *Plato's Breath* (1996 May Swenson Poetry Prize, Utah State University Press), and *Nostalgia's Thread: Ten Poems on Norman Rockwell Paintings* (Hol Art Books, 2009).

Eric Gadzinski has lived in the U.P. for nearly twenty years, having blown there in a balloon from Philadelphia, where he got his Doctorate from Temple U. He teaches all manner of English at Lake Superior State University, and otherwise likes to explore the woods in all seasons, with a compass for survival and a shotgun for a prop. Originally from Vermont, Gadzinski finds the U.P. congenial and refreshingly free of a certain kind of affectation. Of course, the U.P. has its own charms, including Mossy Oak ball caps and large pickup trucks, which Gadzinski finds preferable to L.L. Bean. Gadzinski's poems have appeared in a wide variety of small journals.

Steve Hamilton is the two-time Edgar Award-winning, *New York Times* bestselling author of the Alex McKnight series, featuring an ex-Detroit police officer relocated to the Upper Peninsula town of Paradise. (*Let It Burn*, the newest book in the series, will be out in the summer of 2013.) He's either won or been nominated for every other major crime fiction award in America and the UK, and his books are now translated into fifteen languages. In 2006, he received the Michigan Author Award from the Michigan Library Association and the Michigan Center for the Book, in recognition of his overall body of work. He attended the University of Michigan, where he won the prestigious Hopwood Award for writing. He currently lives in upstate New York with his wife and their two children.

Sue Harrison was raised in Michigan's Eastern Upper Peninsula and graduated summa cum laude from Lake Superior State University. Harrison's first novel, *Mother Earth Father Sky*, was a national and international bestseller and was named by the American Library Association as one of 1991's Best Books for Young Adults as a crossover from the adult market. Her other novels include *My Sister the Moon*, *Brother Wind*, *Song of the River*, *Cry of the Wind*, *Call Down the Stars*, and *SISU*. Harrison's novels have been published in thirteen languages in more than twenty-five countries around the world.

Joseph Daniel Haske was born in Sault Sainte Marie, Michigan, and grew up in the nearby Les Cheneaux area, where he graduated from Cedarville High School. Haske's fiction, poetry, and essays have appeared in publications such as *Boulevard*, *Fiction International*, *The Texas Review*, *Southwestern American Literature*, *Alecart*, *Dark Sky*, and *American Book Review*. His work has also been featured in several anthologies and he was recently named a finalist for the *Boulevard* Emerging Writers competition. In December 2011, he was interviewed, along with several other American writers, for a feature in the French magazine *Transfuge* and he has been published in various international venues in countries such as France, Romania, Canada, and Mexico. Most of Haske's work is inspired and informed by his experiences growing up in the Upper Peninsula of Michigan, and he is nearing completion of his first novel, set primarily in the Eastern U.P., as well as a collection of poetry.

Barbara Henning is a poet and fiction writer. She teaches for the Jack Kerouac School of Disembodied Poetics at Naropa University and Long Island University in Brooklyn, where she is Professor Emerita. She is the author of three novels and seven books of poetry. Her most recent books are a collection of poetry and prose, *Cities & Memory* (Chax Press); a novel, *Thirty Miles from Rosebud* (BlazeVox); a collection of object-sonnets, *My Autobiography* (United Artists); and a book of interviews, *Looking Up Harryette Mullen* (Belladonna). Henning grew up in Detroit and has lived in New York City since 1983. As a child she spent many of her summers camping in the Upper Peninsula. After her sister moved to Marquette in 1969, she started spending months at a time in the Marquette area.

Jennifer A. Howard grew up a first-generation Yooper in Escanaba, in the U.P.'s Banana Belt, and after some time below the bridge found her way back up north to Marquette, where it takes much more snow to justify a snow day. She teaches English at Northern Michigan University and serves as the editor of *Passages North*.

Austin Hummell has lived in the Upper Peninsula since 2000. His books are *Poppy* (Del Sol Press) and *The Fugitive Kind* (University of Georgia Press). He teaches at Northern Michigan University.

Jonathan Johnson is a 1986 graduate of Marquette Senior High School. He is the author of two books of poems, *Mastodon, 80% Complete* (2001) and *In the Land We Imagined Ourselves* (2010), both from Carnegie Mellon University Press, and the nonfiction book *Hannah and the Mountain: Notes toward a Wilderness Fatherhood*, from the University of Nebraska Press (2005). His work has appeared in *Best American Poetry* and numerous other anthologies, as well as *Southern Review*, *Missouri Review*, *Ploughshares*, *North American Review*, and *Prairie Schooner*. He migrates between Marquette, where he spends every summer and Christmas; northern Idaho, where he and his wife built a secluded log cabin; Scotland, where his maternal relatives still farm the ancestral croft on the Highland coast; and eastern Washington, where he has won a number of awards for his teaching as a professor in the Master of Fine Arts in Creative Writing program at Eastern Washington University. Johnson is married to the social worker and photographer Amy Howko, a 1987 graduate of Marquette High whose solo exhibition *Year of Shadow and Light* showed at the Oasis Gallery in Marquette in 2010, and the couple has one daughter, Anya.

Born in Vienna, **Linda Johnson** has deep ties to the U.P., where she has made her home-base for over forty years: she has lived in Marquette with her husband for five years, and before that, she lived in the Brimley area where her three children and eight grandchildren are members of the Bay Mills Indian Community. A nonfiction piece, *Sitting in the Rain: A Memoir*, was published in *Briar Cliff Review*, her poetry in *Voices of Michigan* and *Toronto Native Times*, and other essays in *Woods-Runner*. She is a winner of the LSSU Short Story Contest. Linda holds an MA in English from Northern Michigan University and a BA in English Language and Literature and also in Sociology from Lake Superior State University. She has worked in the U.P. as camp counselor, social worker/protective services, fin-clipper, and in the late 1960s in Whistle Stop, her family's restaurant in Eckerman.

Ron Johnson, author of *Silver Thaw and Selected Stories* (2005) and the novel *The Last Rodeo* (2012), is Professor of English at Northern Michigan University, where he teaches writing and literature. He has published short fiction in the United States and New Zealand, and his creative nonfiction has won prizes from *Grain* (Saskatchewan Writers Guild, Canada) and the *Missouri Review* First Place Editors Award. Chapters from his book *Anton Chekhov: A Study of the Short Fiction* (Twayne Press) have been reprinted in volumes of *Short Story Criticism* in sections on Chekhov (2011, 2008, 2006) and Russian Realist Short Fiction (2004). He holds an MFA in creative writing from the University of California, Irvine, and a PhD in English from the University of Utah. He has lived in Marquette since 1984 and as often as possible walks at Presque Isle City Park, where he talks with the squirrels and the deer and an occasional moose.

L. E. Kimball's stories have appeared in top literary journals including the *Alaska Quarterly Review*, *The Massachusetts Review*, *Lynx Eye*, *Orchid*, and *Washington Square*. Her first novel, *A Good High Place*, was published June 2010 by Northern Illinois University. Her essays have been published in dozens of venues such as *ByLine*, *Heartland Boating*, *Country Almanac*, *Exceptional Parent*, and *The Detroit News* op ed section. Her latest fiction piece, set in the Upper Peninsula, appeared in the March/April issue of *Gray's Sporting Journal*. She is working on her MFA in Creative Writing at Northern Michigan University and working on her second novel, which is a novel of linked stories all set in Michigan's Upper Peninsula. She lives with her son and dog part of the year in Marquette, Michigan, and the rest of the year near Tahquamenon Falls, where she lives off the grid on a trout stream.

April Lindala (Grand River Six Nations) obtained a Master of Fine Arts degree from Northern Michigan University (NMU), where she is currently the director of the Center for Native American Studies. Lindala has had several poems published in various anthologies and publications. Most recently, she was the project director and assistant editor for the anthology *Voice on the Water: Great Lakes Native America Now,* published by NMU Press. The book also features two of her poems. Lindala enjoys doing beadwork, watching films, listening to blues music and relaxing with her husband, Walt, and their cat, Merlin.

Raymond Luczak, originally from Ironwood and Houghton, Michigan, is the author and editor of fifteen books, including *How to Kill Poetry* (Sibling Rivalry Press, 2013) and *Among the Leaves: Queer Male Poets on the Midwestern Experience* (Squares & Rebels, 2012). His other poetry collections include *Road Work Ahead* (Sibling Rivalry Press, 2011), *Mute* (A Midsummer Night's Press, 2010), and *This Way to the Acorns: The Tenth Anniversary Edition* (Handtype Press, 2012). His novel, *Men with Their Hands* (Queer Mojo, 2009), won first place in the Project: QueerLit 2006 Contest. He resides in Minneapolis, Minnesota. He can be found online at raymondluczak.com.

Matt Maki lives in Marquette, Michigan, where he teaches workshops in writing, collage, yoga/dance, and creativity and coordinates the Marquette Poetry Circle and local National Poetry Month activities. He has studied and taught creative writing and literature at Northern Michigan University and the University of Alabama. He has served on the editorial staff of *Passages North*, as Poetry Editor of *Greatest Lakes Review*, and as Fiction Editor of *Black Warrior Review* and *Flywheel Magazine*. Although he was raised in Michigan's lower peninsula, his move to the U.P. while in high school sparked an interest in his Finnish heritage, which led to his study of Finnish and Finnish-American literary connections, myth and archetypal criticism, and borderlands, including between-genre work, such as the *Kalevala* and Juhani Aho's *Shavings*, and writing prose poetry, flash fiction, and creative criticism.

Seth Marlin is the current Web Editor of *Willow Springs*. Growing up in Michigan, Marlin made his home for six years in the Upper Peninsula, where he resided on three of the five Great Lakes, hunted bear in the Keweenaw, and eventually married a girl from Newberry. His fiction and poetry have appeared in *M-Brane*, *Short Story America*, and *Greatest Lakes Review*, and his nonfiction appears in the newly revised Fourth Edition of *Curious Writer*, now available from Longman Press. He resides in Spokane, Washington, and still dreams of the shores of Lake Superior.

Beverly Matherne arrived in the U.P. twenty years ago and so fell in love with it that she plans to finish out her career as poet and professor of English at the NMU campus. Former director of its Master of Fine Arts program in creative writing, she is now poetry editor of *Passages North* literary magazine and director of the Visiting Writers Program.

She is the author of six books of bilingual poetry: the latest, *La-mothe-Cadillac: Sa jeunesse en France* (*Lamothe-Cadillac: His Early Life in France*), from Les Éditions Tintamarre. The winner of seven first-place poetry awards, including the Hackney Literary Award for Poetry, her work appears in anthologies from houses such as Beacon Press and Louisiana State University Press as well as in publications such as *Interdisciplinary Humanities* and *Metamorphoses*. Her bilingual writing process is documented in a doctoral dissertation from the University of Paris III.

Mary McMyne teaches writing at Lake Superior State University, where she co-edits *Border Crossing*, a journal of literature and art featuring international writers and Upper Peninsula visual artists. Her work has appeared or is forthcoming in *Phantom Drift: A Journal of New Fabulism*, *New Delta Review*, *Exquisite Corpse*, *Double Dealer*, *Prime Number Magazine*, and other journals. She won the Faulkner Prize for a Novel-in-Progress for her project reimagining the Odysseus myth from the perspective of an American soldier's wife during the Vietnam War. She is currently at work on a novel reimagining the Red Riding Hood fairy tale from the perspective of an institutionalized woman. The poem published here is one of hundreds recovered from the character's room after her death in 1961. McMyne lives in Sault Sainte Marie with her husband and daughter. Her fiction is represented by Kathleen Anderson of Anderson Literary Management. Visit her online at www.marymcmyne.com.

Jane Piirto is a Finnish-American native of Ishpeming, Michigan, and spends summers there in her childhood home in Cleveland Location. Northern Michigan University awarded her a BA and an honorary Doctorate of Humane Letters. She is Trustees' Distinguished Professor at Ashland University. Her literary books are *A Location in the Upper Peninsula* (collected works), *The Three-Week Trance Diet* (award-winning novel), *Saunas* (poetry), *The Arrest* (novel), *Labyrinth* (novella), as well as eight chapbooks. Her scholarship is in the area of the psychology of creativity and in the study of gifted children. Many of these works are available as e-books on Kindle and Nook. She received Individual Artist Fellowships in poetry and fiction from the Ohio Arts Council. Garrison Keillor read her work on *The Writer's Almanac*. She is one of fourteen hundred American writers listed in the *Directory of American Poets and Writers* as both a poet and a writer.

Saara Myrene Raappana was born in Marquette General Hospital and was raised all around the Upper Peninsula of Michigan, including in Palmer, Sault Ste. Marie, Suomi Location, Rudyard, and Menominee. She's currently a Peace Corps Volunteer serving in Guizhou, China, where she teaches English to future English teachers. She's an editor for *Cellpoems*, a text-message-based poetry journal. Her poetry appears or is forthcoming in such publications as *Blackbird, Harvard Review Online, The Cincinnati Review, The Gettysburg Review, Subtropics*, and *Verse Daily*; her criticism can be found in *American Book Review* and *The Rumpus*. She misses sauna, juustoa, and pasties.

Janeen Rastall lives by Lake Superior in Gordon, Michigan. She is a member of the Marquette Poetry Circle. Her poems have recently appeared in *Raleigh Review*, *Blue Lake Review*, and *apparatus magazine*.

Janice Repka's short stories and poetry have appeared in journals such as *Potomac Review*, *The Louisiana Review*, *Writers' Journal*, and *Antietam Review*. She is also the author of two novels, *The Stupendous Dodgeball Fiasco*, a Junior Library Selection and 2008 Nebraska Golden Sower Award Honor Book, and *The Clueless Girl's Guide to Being a Genius*, both published by Dutton Children's Books. She has a MFA in Creative Writing from McNeese State University and a law degree from the University of Pennsylvania. Born in Pennsylvania, she taught college English in Louisiana before moving to and settling in Sault Sainte Marie, Michigan, where she is an Assistant Professor of English and Creative Writing at Lake Superior State University. While at Lake State she has helped create the LSSU Visiting Writer Reading Series to bring literary authors and poets to the Eastern Upper Peninsula.

Vincent Reusch attended Western Michigan University's PhD program in Creative Writing, where he studied with fiction writers Jaimy Gordon and Stuart Dybek. His recent work has been published in *Madison Review*, *Alaska Quarterly Review*, *Big Fiction*, and elsewhere. He was the winner of *Roanoke Review*'s 2006 fiction prize, runner-up in the DANA Awards Portfolio Contest, and runner-up and finalist in a number of other national fiction contests. He has just finished a collection of stories and is at work on a novel set in northern Michigan. Research for this novel has been aided by a grant from the Lakes Region Arts Council. He teaches English at Concordia College, in Moorhead, Minnesota.

Ron Riekki has published *U.P.: A Novel* (Ghost Road Press), *Leave Me Alone, I'm Bleeding, I Want to Date a Girl Who's a Rage Against the Machine Fan: Poems about Love, Death and Heavy Metal*, and *She Took God: A Memoir in 34 Poems* (Gypsy Daughter Poetry Chapbooks and Literary Publishing), *Dandelion Cottage, A Play* (produced by Lake Superior Theatre) and *Your Map is Wrong: A Collection of Plays Set in*

Michigan's Upper Peninsula (the Center for U.P. Studies), *Carol* (Smith & Kraus, *The Best Ten-Minute Plays 2012*, produced by Stageworks/Hudson), and *How to Kill Yourself with a Gun and a Bottle of Pills* (upcoming, Original Works Publishing, produced by Ann Arbor Civic Theater). Ruckus Theater also produced *All Saints' Day: 44 Poems about Jeffrey Jones.*

Catie Rosemurgy is the author of two collections of poetry, *My Favorite Apocalypse* and *The Stranger Manual,* both published by Graywolf Press. Her work has appeared in such places as *American Poetry Review, The Gettysburg Review,* and *Ploughshares.* She is the recipient of a Rona Jaffe Foundation Writers' Award and a National Endowment for the Arts fellowship. She grew up in Escanaba, Michigan, and spends time there every year. She currently lives in Philadelphia and teaches at The College of New Jersey.

Andrea Scarpino is the author of the chapbook *The Grove Behind* (Finishing Line Press) and a forthcoming full-length poetry collection from Red Hen Press. She received an MFA in Creative Writing from The Ohio State University, has been nominated for a Pushcart Prize, and teaches with Union Institute and University's Cohort PhD program in Interdisciplinary Studies. She moved from Los Angeles—where her poems often contained fire—to the Upper Peninsula in 2010. Now, most of her writing involves snow or Lake Superior. She is a weekly contributor for the blog Planet of the Blind, and can be found online at www.andreascarpino.com

John Smolens has published eight novels and one collection of short fiction, including *Quarantine, The Schoolmaster's Daughter, The Anarchist, Fire Point, The Invisible World, Cold, My One and Only Bomb Shelter* (short stories), *Angel's Head,* and *Winter by Degrees.* His work has appeared in publications such as *Columbia: A Journal of Literature and Art, The Massachusetts Review, The Virginia Quarterly Review, The William and Mary Review, Turkish Book Review, Boston College Magazine, Redbook, Yankee, Writer's Digest, Writer's Market, Los Angeles Times,* and *The Boston Globe.* He was the recipient of the Michigan

Author of the Year Award for 2010 from the Michigan Library Association. He is a professor of English at Northern Michigan University.

Keith Taylor has published collections of poetry, short fiction, edited volumes, and translations. Two of his most recent books were published by Wayne State University Press.

Emily Van Kley was raised in Ishpeming and Wakefield, Michigan, but currently lives in Olympia, Washington, where she writes, works at a cooperative grocery, and dreams of snow. Her poems have won the *Florida Review* and *Iowa Review* prizes, and have also been published in *Cutthroat* and *Oberon* Magazines. Her fiction was a finalist for *Narrative Magazine*'s Below 30 Award, and has also appeared in *Faultline* and *Salamander*.

Cameron Witbeck is twenty-four years old and has spent over a quarter of that time living in Marquette, Michigan. He is currently an MFA candidate in poetry at Northern Michigan University, where he also works as an associate poetry editor for *Passages North* literary magazine. When he's not teaching, reading, or writing, Witbeck enjoys hunting and woodworking. His work has appeared, or is forthcoming, in *Rosebud, Cream City Review, Controlled Burn*, and other publications.

Jim Zukowski has lived in Sault Sainte Marie, Michigan, for twelve years, where he's an Associate Professor of English at Lake Superior State University. He holds an MA and PhD from the University of Pittsburgh and an MFA in Creative Writing from Warren Wilson College. His work has appeared in *Nimrod, Northwest Review, Provincetown Arts*, and other journals. He has recently completed work on his first manuscript, *The Vanisher*.